THE AMERICAN DREAMS OF JOHN B. PRENTIS, SLAVE TRADER

RACE IN THE ATLANTIC WORLD, 1700–1900

THE AMERICAN DREAMS OF JOHN B. PRENTIS, SLAVE TRADER

KARI J. WINTER

THE UNIVERSITY OF GEORGIA PRESS

ATHENS AND LONDON

© 2011 by the University of Georgia Press
Athens, Georgia 30602
www.ugapress.org
All rights reserved
Set in New Caledonia by Bookcomp, Inc.

Printed digitally in the United States of America

Library of Congress Cataloging-in-Publication Data

Winter, Kari J.
  The American dreams of John B. Prentis, slave trader /
Kari J. Winter.
      p. cm. — (Race in the Atlantic world, 1700–1900)
  Includes bibliographical references and index.
  ISBN-13: 978-0-8203-3838-5 (hardcover : alk. paper)
  ISBN-10: 0-8203-3838-9 (hardcover : alk. paper)
  ISBN-13: 978-0-8203-3837-8 (pbk. : alk. paper)
  ISBN-10: 0-8203-3837-0 (pbk. : alk. paper)
  1. Prentis, John B. (John Brooke), 1788–1848. 2. Prentis,
John B. (John Brooke), 1788–1848—Family. 3. Prentis,
John B. (John Brooke), 1788–1848—Political and social
views. 4. Slaveholders—Virginia—Biography. 5. Slave
traders—Virginia—Biography. 6. Slavery—Social
aspects—Virginia—History. 7. Virginia—Race relations.
8. Virginia—Social conditions. 9. Williamsburg (Va.)—
Biography. 10. Richmond (Va.)—Biography. I. Title.
  F230.P8W46 2011
  975.5'03—dc22

                                  2010047425

British Library Cataloging-in-Publication Data available

For Zane

The past is infinite . . .

—TONI MORRISON

And I asked myself about the present: how wide it was, how deep it was, how much was mine to keep.

—KURT VONNEGUT, *Slaughterhouse Five*

CONTENTS

ILLUSTRATIONS

ACKNOWLEDGMENTS

Writing requires solitude, but it is also, in my experience, a profoundly social, collaborative process. Many people enabled this book. First and foremost, it would not have come into existence without the inspiration of my writing partner, David R. Castillo. Several of the book's central concepts emerged from our conversations. David commented extravagantly on countless drafts and helped me believe that writing about a slave trader was worthwhile. I am grateful indeed for his generous friendship.

SUNY at Buffalo's Humanities Institute offered crucial support at every phase of the writing process. Our intellectual community has been enormously enhanced by the dynamic leadership of founding executive director Martha Malamud, founding director Ewa Polonowska Ziarek, and current director Tim Dean. Their generous support and friendship have inspired me personally as well as professionally. Rachel Ablow helped launch this book by inviting me to present my earliest findings at an HI-sponsored workshop, where I received helpful feedback from many colleagues. Ewa Ziarek and David Castillo were a pleasure to work with when we co-organized a Humanities Institute international conference on the topic of human trafficking, where I presented a portion of this book. I am grateful to the other participants, especially Julia O'Connell Davidson, Michele Goodwin, Dominick LaCapra, and Laurie Anne Whitt, for their inspiring comments. An HI Faculty Research Fellowship enabled me to devote the fall of 2009 to research and writing and to present a portion of the book to a marvelous cohort of colleagues. I also am indebted to SUNY at Buffalo's Baldy Center for Law and Social Policy, the Gender Institute, and the Canadian-American Studies Committee. In the Department of American Studies, Swati Bandi, Alison Blaszak, and Betsy Thornton helped transcribe some of the Prentis documents.

Amani Whitfield invited me to present a section of this book at the University of Vermont. I am grateful to him and to many other dear friends in Vermont, especially Philip Baruth, Emily Bernard, Alan Broughton, Tina Escaja, Leslie Fry, Huck Gutman, Major Jackson, Mary Lou Kete,

Dennis Mahoney, Elaine McCrate, Molly Moore, and Nancy Welch. Conversations with Betty L. Moss about this book and everything else in the universe were an immeasurable benefit. Terry Rowden was one of the first people to whom I showed John Prentis's peculiar last will and testament. Terry's intelligent, probing questions and warm friendship are much appreciated. I am more grateful than words can convey to Rhonda Brace, James Brace, Jeffrey S. Brace, Ronald Brace, and sixty other descendants of Jeffrey and Susannah Dublin Brace for their inspiring presence in my life. Thanks to Karen Bravo, Moíses Castillo, Stephen Fuchs, and Carmen Moreno-Nuño for helpful suggestions. I might not have been able to continue writing were it not for the expert chiropractic care of Dr. Stephen Grande and Dr. Jonathan Danner.

I am grateful, as always, to William L. Andrews for generous and meticulous comments. Likewise, Richard Newman's suggestions were enormously helpful; I am grateful for his insights and his broad knowledge. My research was aided by countless staff at various libraries and historical societies, especially Heather Beattie, Sarah Bouchey, Jamison Davis, and Lauranett Lee at the Virginia Historical Society; Marianne Martin at the John D. Rockefeller Jr. Library; and Bobbe Redding, who gave me a private tour of the St. George Tucker House in Colonial Williamsburg. It has been a delight to work again with Nancy Grayson at the University of Georgia Press. I am grateful to Jon Davies, Ellen Goldlust-Gingrich, Mindy Basinger Hill, John McLeod, and Beth Snead at the press for their careful work.

Finally, I am grateful to my husband, Donald A. Grinde Jr., and my mother, Dorothy Winter, for their comments on the manuscript and countless other forms of support. My sister, Kris, and her husband, Rich; my brother John, and his wife, Amélia; my nephews and nieces, Alexander, Jonathan, Selma, Hugo, and Ava; and my Aunt Joan and Uncle Emil provided love, encouragement, and wonderful vacations from work. My son, Zane, is an endless source of delight, and I dedicate this book to him with love and gratitude.

NOTE ON THE TEXT

The documents transcribed in this book present many difficulties of interpretation as a consequence of their sometimes fragile condition, poor penmanship, meager punctuation, and random capitalization. John B. Prentis rarely used periods to mark the end of sentences; he sometimes used commas, colons, or dashes but usually simply ran sentences and phrases together. He also sometimes inserted periods at random points in the middle of sentences. I have attempted to reproduce excerpts from correspondence and other documents as exactly as possible in regard to diction and spelling. However, for the ease of the reader, I have sometimes inserted punctuation and standardized capitalization.

I have used the following abbreviations when citing archival sources:

PFP   Prentis Family Papers, Rockefeller Library
WPFP Webb-Prentis Family Papers

THE AMERICAN DREAMS OF JOHN B. PRENTIS, SLAVE TRADER

INTRODUCTION

In a world that was largely unfree, the Enlightenment visions of liberty, equality, and brotherhood simultaneously inspired alarm and hope. At the heart of conflicting ideologies of governance lay the question of who had the right to control material resources and to profit from human labor. Most men were ready to embrace the notion that they were as entitled to the fruits of their labor as were their social "betters," but few were prepared to accept the notion that their social "inferiors" possessed similar inalienable rights. The dream of human equality simultaneously enlivened and threatened the dream of personal wealth. *The American Dreams of John B. Prentis, Slave Trader* examines the development of and clash between the dream of equality and the dream of wealth as they shaped three generations of a prominent Virginia family from 1715 to 1872. Just as major players on the world stage such as Benjamin Franklin and Thomas Jefferson articulated and embodied paradoxes at the heart of America, so too less famous white men made choices that were infused by and helped to perpetuate social dreams and nightmares. *American Dreams* analyzes the economic, racial, and sexual dynamics of family systems, multiracial households, and class networks by exploring the social origins, public careers, and emotional investments of the Prentis family of Williamsburg and Richmond. The clan's founder, William Prentis, was an English indentured servant who rose from rags to riches by clerking in, then managing, and finally becoming the major shareholder in the colony of Virginia's most successful store, which is still standing in Colonial Williamsburg. His son, Joseph Prentis Sr., became an influential Revolutionary-era judge and politician, exhibiting both the radical and the reactionary potentialities inherent in a movement for human freedom led by slaveholders. The sons of the third Prentis generation, Joseph and John, embarked on divergent paths, colluding and conflicting with one another during the first half of the nineteenth century, when the radical promise of the Revolutionary age was betrayed as the United States expanded its dedication to slavery and empire.

A close analysis of the development of John B. Prentis's life and ideas forms the book's center. As a youth, John expressed distaste for Virginia's peculiar institution. In 1805, he went to Philadelphia as an indentured apprentice to study architecture with a Quaker builder. His letters home were filled with righteous indignation about the ways slavery corrupted Virginia's young gentlemen and destroyed "the poor slaves." He identified with hardworking tradesmen and prided himself on his physical strength and manual skills. Determined to make his way by the sweat of his brow in Richmond after his apprenticeship ended, John abruptly accommodated himself to slavery and soon grew besotted with it. After inheriting a slave woman from his father, he quickly acquired several more slaves, ran a jail in which slaves were imprisoned, and began to speculate and trade in slaves. By the end of his life, he had transported thousands of slaves from Virginia for sale in the Deep South. In short, his ascent in American society involved abandoning his innate sense of justice and equality in favor of a frenzied investment in violence, exploitation, and dehumanization. This book pays close attention to the reasons that although he became wealthy, John Prentis repudiated the ideological gentility of his birth family to embrace a working-class identity. His letters and other documents illuminate why and how many working-class white men rejected class solidarity with blacks and indeed behaved in viciously racist ways. John's evolution provides a powerful case study of how the ideological crisis caused by the dissonance between the two American dreams—the dream of possessing wealth and the dream of social equality—was resolved, in a restless and unsustainable fashion, through an aggressive cult of violent white masculinity that married "democracy" to white male supremacy.

Slave traders are typecast in both pro- and antislavery literature as execrable wretches around whom genteel folks held their noses. Proslavery literature romanticized the image of aristocratic plantation patriarchs surrounded by contented subordinates, while antislavery literature represented the subjection and violation of victims who would be or ought to be rescued by "the heroic actor[s] of the romance of resistance," to use Saidiya Hartman's apt phrase (*Scenes* 54). Both camps excoriated slave traders as the source of everything that was most odious about the peculiar institution. Adam Rothman observes that the ideological line between slave trading and slaveholding "originated as a useful fiction written by planters in the upper South during the revolutionary era. They contrasted the vicious commercial world of the Atlantic slave trade, which was dominated by British merchants, with the more virtuous agrarian world of the American plantation" (20). Walter Johnson incisively notes, "In the figure of the slave trader were condensed the anxieties of slaveholding society in the age of capitalist transformation: paternalism overthrown by commodification, honor corrupted by interest, and dominance infected with disorder" (25). Hyperbolic caricatures of slave traders disguised the reality that a "lively commerce in slaves, both local and interstate, sustained the economic efficiency and profitability of the slave system. During the period 1790 to 1860, some 3 million slaves changed ownership by sale, many of them several times. Almost all slaveowners bought or sold slaves at some point in their lives" (Howe 56).

In the figure of Dan Haley, Harriet Beecher Stowe penned the most famous and influential portrait of a slave trader in American literature, but she pointedly rejected the fiction that a moral line could be drawn between the slave trader and the slave owner or even between the slave trader and readers of her novel. After describing Haley's stone-hearted, self-pitying response to the suicide of an enslaved mother whose baby he had just sold, Stowe imagined a conversation between two of her readers only to scold both with a direct address:

> "He's a shocking creature, isn't he,—this trader? so unfeeling! It's dreadful, really!"
>
> "O, but nobody thinks anything of these traders! They are universally despised,—never received into any decent society."
>
> But who, sir, makes the trader? Who is most to blame? The enlightened, cultivated, intelligent man who supports the system of which the trader is the inevitable result, or the poor trader himself? You make the public statement that calls for his trade, that debauches and depraves him, till he feels no shame in it; and in what are you better than he?
>
> Are you educated and he ignorant, you high and he low, you refined and he coarse, you talented and he simple? (112–13)

Stowe accurately emphasized that virtually all slaveholders were engaged in slave trading, and all slave traders were slaveholders, at least temporarily.

Over the past thirty years, research on virtually all aspects of modern slavery—on the transatlantic slave trade, on slave revolts, on abolition—has grown exponentially. Innumerable discoveries in African American, feminist, and working-class research have transformed our collective understanding of Atlantic world history. Electronic resources such as the *Trans-Atlantic Slave Trade: A Database*, compiled by David Eltis, Stephen D. Behrendt, David Richardson, and Herbert S. Klein, and *North American Slave Narratives, Beginnings to 1920*, a University of North Carolina Web site funded by the National Endowment for the Humanities, have enabled new levels of knowledge acquisition. We can now readily access not only the writings of abolitionists and former slaves but also hundreds of thousands of documents produced by people and institutions directly involved in the slave trade, such as shipping and customs records, advertisements for runaways, court testimony, and logbooks, letters, diaries, and memoirs written by captains, surgeons, and sailors who worked on slave ships. Members of all classes and professions, including royalty, aristocrats, legislators, bankers, merchants, lawyers, insurance agents, clergymen, policemen, soldiers, newspapermen, teachers, widows, society belles, laborers, adventurers, sailors, pimps, madams, and even some freed slaves, participated in the slave trade. Indeed, "it is scarcely an exaggeration to say that every person in the Europeanized world who put sugar in their tea or coffee, spread jam on their bread, who ate sweets, cakes, or ice cream, who smoked or chewed tobacco, took snuff, drank rum or corn brandy, or wore colored cotton clothes, also benefitted from, and participated in, a globalized economy of tropical plantations worked by slaves forcibly brought from Africa" (St. Clair 4). Recent prodigiously researched studies of the domestic slave trade such as Walter Johnson's *Soul by Soul: Life inside the Antebellum Slave Market* and Steven Deyle's *Carry Me Back: The Domestic Slave Trade in American Life* have provided rich insights into how the trade functioned regionally in the South and how it contributed to both the development and the fracturing of the United States.[1] Yet, as far as I know, no recent historical book has focused on the life story of a slave trader who failed to repent and become an abolitionist. John B. Prentis offers an unusual opportunity for in-depth investigation because he wrote dozens of letters and other documents that are still extant. Scholars and curators previously have referenced small portions of Prentis family archive, mostly in relation to John's father and brother, both of whom were prominent lawyers and judges. The Prentis family saga has never before been pieced together, however, and John's activities as a slave trader have not been examined. Building on current scholarship and mining untapped archives, then, *American Dreams* reveals a complex set of relationships that tell an unprecedented story about slavery's intimate dynamics.

In the 1820s and 1830s, Joseph and John Prentis lamented that they knew almost nothing about their family's origins. They particularly longed to learn more about their grandfather, William Prentis, who had died long before they were born but whose brilliance at business and dedication to education had enabled the genteel luxury of their childhood. Joseph asked relatives and friends for information, but no one appeared to know much. A cousin, David Meade, told Joseph that lack of familial knowledge was a cultural phenomenon.

> I find all the young men of my acquaintance nearly in the same predicament with You—they know nothing of the genealogy of Their Families— I am not qualified to answer your querie to Your satisfaction it was well know[n] that Your Grandfather Prentis was a native of England & there is some reason I think to presume that He was Born in London—Your Grandmothers maiden name was Brooks—thus far & no further does my information go relative to your paternal ancestry. (November 7, 1825, WPFP)

If the Prentis brothers had been historians or genealogists, they could have pieced together a story from archives; if they had remained committed to exploring the truths of their history, their lives no doubt would have taken an altogether different course. Although John often expressed dislike for writing and his letters tended to be grammatically clumsy, his prose sometimes sparkles with an artist's fire and passion for truth. His decades of letters to his brother bespeak a primal desire for openhearted, intimate dialogue.

John B. Prentis and the members of his extended family were not entirely masters of their destinies, but they made significant daily choices within the options that society made available to them. Their choices had enormous consequences for themselves, their kin, and thousands of other people. Like all human beings, the Prentises possessed both admirable and monstrous capacities. They struggled to make a living while dealing with vexed individual, familial, and societal needs, desires, hopes, and disappointments. The antebellum South, as William Freehling demonstrates in his magisterial *Road to Disunion*, was a "chaotic kaleidoscope" of people and places in which "change was omnipresent, varieties abounded, visions multiplied" (vii). Rather than present thick compilations of data, I analyze and contextualize primary documents to flesh out a narrative history. Sharing Freehling's view that "the narrative literary form . . . remains invaluable to humanize how a collision of abstractions helped produce the crisis of a people" (ix), I tease out complexities, vexations, and nuances in the Prentis family saga in the belief that our understanding of history is enriched when instead of isolating data from its context, we attend carefully to the particularities of characters who, in specific times and places, simultaneously negotiated multiple aspects of life. Such components of human identity as gender, race, class, health, and age take their meanings in relation to and interaction with each other. They do not exist independently.

If John Prentis preserved any of the letters that he received from family and friends, they are no longer extant. His brother, Joseph Jr., in contrast, was the gatekeeper and guardian of the family archive. A prolific, elegant, conventional writer whose prose showed little imagination or openness to uncomfortable truths, Joseph assumed, as a birthright, that the Prentises were personages in whom posterity would be interested. Cherishing personal correspondence, he carefully organized and filed his ancestors', siblings', children's, and friends' letters, an enormous portfolio of which passed to descendants from one generation to the next until boxes and boxes of it ended up in collections at the University of Virginia, the College of William and Mary, and the Colonial Williamsburg Foundation. My rendering of the Prentis history emerges primarily from careful readings of texts authored by various members of the clan. Most of them survive because Joseph Prentis Jr., in collaboration with his ancestors and heirs, willed it so. I reproduce long excerpts from original documents for three reasons. First, I want the Prentises to speak in their own voices, revealing their quirky truths in their distinctive ways. Second, I believe that rich knowledge can be gleaned from archival documents when they are read as literary texts that reveal more than their authors intended. Third, I hope that readers will bring their own critical methodologies and bodies of knowledge to bear on the material and will discover truths that I have overlooked or misread. In short, this book aspires to create a truly interdisciplinary and open-ended space for contemplating the cultural work of American dreams.

While foregrounding John B. Prentis's interior life and public career, this book also calls attention to lives that are forced to the background by the nature of historical archives. The closing chapter, "Relic(t)s," meditates on the after-effects of the Prentis lives, paying particular attention to the final years of John B. Prentis's widow, Catharine Dabney Prentis, amid the catastrophe of the Civil War. The chapter illuminates ways in which cultural memory is haunted by historical ghosts—invisible men and women whose absences signify the meanings of history as deeply as the presences of the elite whose lives we can see. Historical documents illuminate the successes and failures of antebellum Americans primarily in terms of the acquisition of possessions: wives, children, slaves, horses, cattle, land, money, and other items deemed sufficiently valuable to be certified, baptized, taxed, and/or hunted down if lost, stolen, or runaway. As Hartman observes, "The archive dictates what can be said about the past and the kinds of stories that can be told about the persons catalogued, embalmed, and sealed away in box files and folios. To read the archive is to enter a mortuary" (*Lose*, 17). The archival mortuary primarily documents the elite whose possessions counted and were counted and who had the inclination, leisure, and means to express themselves in letters, diaries, or other forms of writing. In short, those people most empowered to master possessions continue to dominate the way we imagine the world after their deaths almost as forcibly as they dominated their worlds during their lifetimes. I invite readers to meditate on possibilities and foreclosures as well as on documents and facts. Understanding the past requires imagination and speculation as well as research and detection.

Rather than focusing on how John B. Prentis and his social system constructed racial others, this book searches through documents related to kinship and notions of possession in hopes of registering the significance of relics that haunt our mundane spaces as well as our dreams and nightmares because we have not yet found an adequate way to recognize our investments in them and their claims on us. "Trauma," according to Cathy Caruth, "does not simply serve as record of the past but precisely registers the force of an experience that is not yet fully owned" (417). Sifting through the fragmented wreckage of historical archives, I strive to understand how people shape themselves and are shaped through their possessive relations with other people, objects, places, and time itself. I investigate how various members of the Prentis clan formulated their identities and bound themselves affectively to family, friends, and home. For William Prentis's charter generation, happiness was largely connected to public life, but in Revolutionary and early nineteenth-century Virginia, "the family became the focus of men's and women's deepest longings.

The family signified, and it sanctified as well" (Lewis xiv). The enormous violence of slavery was directed first against the unfamiliar, the foreign, the other, but its damage reverberated throughout family systems. *American Dreams* focuses on how a society predicated on slavery functioned in relation to kin—the familiar, the domestic, the intimate core.

CHAPTER 1 Possessive Relations

March 23, 1707

To the Right Honourable, Right Worshipful, and Worshipful, the
Governours of Christ's-Hospital, LONDON.

The humble Petition of John Prentis Citizen & Embroderer of
London Humbly sheweth: That the Petitioner hath formerly lived in
very good repute but by great losses in his Trade of a Baker is fallen to
decay and hath the charge of five motherless children the which he is
not able to maintain by his imploy of a Porter without the help of charity

Therefore he humbly beseeches your Worships, in your usual Pity
and Charity to distressed Men, poor Widows, and Fatherless Children,
to grant the Admission of one of his Children into Christ's-Hospital,
named William Prentis of the age of 8 years, ½ there to be educated and
brought up amongst other poor children.

And He shall ever Pray, etc.

John Prentis

This is to certify to whom it may concern that William Prentis son of
John Prentis by Sarah his wife was born on the 10 Day of October 1699
in St. James Dukes Place London.

Christ's Hospital in London offered terror, excitement, confusion, education, opportunity, and loneliness to the twelve hundred pupils who lived
there at the dawn of the eighteenth century. They were called the Blue
Coat Boys after the school's uniform: long blue gowns, knee breeches,
and yellow stockings. The widowed, impoverished father, John Prentis,
succeeded in his 1707 petition to gain his son, William, admission to the
school, which had been founded by King Edward VI to educate orphans
and sons of poor free men in commerce (Gill 15–18). At eight years of
age, William Prentis was the median age of boys entering the school.

On holidays, the Blue Coat Boys could stroll down Warwick Lane, opposite Christ's Hospital, to Ludgate Hill and the grand entrance of the

Joseph Prentis son of William Prentis and Mary
Prentis was born at Williamsburg on the 21th of
January in the year 1754. —

Margaret Bowdoin daughter of John and Grace
Bowdoin was born on the 27th day of November
in the year 1758.

Joseph Prentis
Margaret Bowdoin were married on the 16th
of December 1778. " — " — " —
1st William Bowdoin Prentis born on the 17th of April 1780.
— Died on the 15th day of October 1783. " — " — "
2d Joseph Prentis was born on the 21th of January in
the year 1783. " — " — " —
3. William Prentis was born on the 13th of January
1785.
— Died 9th of August 1790. " — " — "
4th John Bowdoin Prentis was born on the 15 of Febru-
=ary 1787. " — " —
— Died on the 13th of February 1789. " —
5th John Brookes Prentis was born on the 1st of February
1789. — Died Richmond Va
6th Elizabeth Prentis was born on the 14th of April 1791.
7th Robert Waters Prentis was born on the 6th of November
1794. Died the 19th 1796
8th Mary Anne Prentis was born on the 19th of March
1796. " — " — " —

Margaret Prentis Died the 27th of August
1807. " — " — " —

Joseph Prentis died on 18th of June at 9 OClock
Tuesday morning in the year 1809. . . in his
56th year:

Genealogy from the Prentis family Bible. Courtesy of the Colonial Williamsburg
Foundation.

towering St. Paul's Cathedral, which had opened for services in 1697 but was still being built under the watchful eye of architect Sir Christopher Wren. Dashing in the opposite direction, the boys would come to New-gate Street, a pungent thoroughfare of shoppers, butchers, bakers, bas-ket makers, brewers, drapers, herb women, street urchins, maids, slaves, prostitutes, thieves, cattle, poultry, dogs, cats, and rats. At the end of Newgate Street, on the corner of Old Bailey, was the infamous Newgate Prison, where Daniel Defoe had been confined in 1703 after spending three days in the pillory at Charing Cross for his bold political protests and pamphlets, which included satirizing English notions of racial purity and High Church Tories' violence against religious dissenters. Passersby tossed him flowers instead of bombarding him with the customary rotten fruit and vegetables that bruised, wounded, and attracted pests to the hapless prisoners.

When hungry for adventure, the Blue Coat Boys might sneak out to the Bear Garden of Hockley-in-the-Hole, famous for its parades and bait-ings of bulls and bears on Mondays and Thursdays. In 1710, while snack-ing on beer, fermenty (boiled wheat and milk sweetened with sugar and spices), or hasty pudding when they could buy or steal it, the boys might have seen four "Indian kings" from America who came to observe bloody sparring matches between combatants with backswords, daggers, and quarterstaffs. Promiscuous crowds ate, drank, gambled, whored, played cards, cheered, and spat at cockfights and dogfights. Baited with fire-works, bears, bulls, and dogs died bloody, fiery deaths. This was the Lon-don of Defoe's *Moll Flanders*, in which children as well as adults could be imprisoned for debt or hanged for stealing a dress or a loaf of bread. The title character of Defoe's story was born in Newgate Prison and after a colorful career as a prostitute, wife, con artist, and thief was transported as a felon to the colony of Virginia, where she grew rich enough to find religion, repent from sin, live honestly, and return to London for a pros-perous old age.

William Prentis's way to wealth was less circuitous than Moll's, but he shared her creator's proclivity for counting things: objects, children, busi-ness transactions. The English novel, birthed by Defoe as well as Aphra Behn, wrestled with the major cultural traumas at the dawn of moder-nity—slavery, colonialism, class oppression, and gender violence—by fo-cusing on resourceful individuals fighting to survive amid nearly ubiqui-tous violence, exploitation, and deprivation. Defoe's Moll had to exercise enormous creativity and courage to make her way in the world. Since criminality offered her the only available avenue to an adequate livelihood, the novel endorses her sense of pride in becoming "the greatest artist (i.e., thief) of my time" (Defoe 208). Defoe imagined human subjectivity primarily in terms of social relations and material acquisition, not in terms of interiority. Morality, his novel implied, was a luxury that only the wealthy and aged could afford. Like *Robinson Crusoe*, *Moll Flanders* helped to shape the ways that ordinary English citizens and colonial subjects imagined their possibilities of self-advancement in the world.

Like Moll, William Prentis was determined to make a living through the means available to him. Fortunately for him, he had access to legal paths to wealth. To his descendants, he would pass on an abundance of tangible commodities—slaves, horses, land, buildings, furniture, dishes, clothes—but he left few clues about his inner life. Sensitivity to the predicaments of other people—or even to one's own psychological state—might have made life unbearable in an age when the tragedies of hunger, disease, exploitation, and violence saturated the streets of London and the byways of empire. The class that controlled most of the land and other material resources had an acute sensitivity to property rights but virtually no notion of human rights. In a society where a mother could be hanged for stealing a loaf of bread to feed a hungry child, it might have been safer to imagine that bread was worth more than a human life than to imagine that all was not right with the world. The social order, undergirded by state-sanctioned terror, was impressed on people in virtually every aspect of daily life, including architecture, religion, family structures, clothes, and diet.

Like most pupils at Christ's Hospital, William Prentis completed his education around the age of fifteen. He headed for Virginia not as a felon, like the thousands of wretches exported to work in the colony as an alternative to imprisonment or hanging, but as an indentured servant for whom America represented a dream of open-ended possibility despite its violent inequities. He arrived in 1715, about a century after the first English settlers had arrived in Jamestown with their white indentured servants and had purchased African slaves from a passing Dutch ship, thus inaugurating the presence of African slavery in the British colonies. As in Britain, wealth and power in the colony of Virginia were based on how the land was organized and controlled. The English settlers' first goal in the so-called New World was to take possession of the land. Indian

nations imagined relationships between people, animals, and land in reciprocal and communal ways that differed markedly from the European
notion of private property. As Rhys Isaac notes, "The most decisive act
of the invaders in reshaping the configuration of the Chesapeake landscape was the imposition of the lines of exclusive property rights" (19).
English colonists attached "sacred importance" to landownership (Isaac
19). The men to whom the Crown granted the largest tracts of land became Virginia's ruling patriarchs. According to Isaac, "In the formative
years of the colony, entitlement to land was assigned on the basis of 'head
rights.' Fifty acres of land were allowed for each man, woman, or child,
servant or slave, whom the claimant was considered to have imported,
bearing the cost of transportation across the ocean. Extensive tracts of
land thus went to those rich and influential men who stood at the center
of large clusters of dependents bound to work at their bidding. The workers were not employees on wages, but bond servants who lived under
their master's roof (or an annex of it) and ate his 'meat.' He was deemed
a father-king over them, and they were liable to fearful legal penalties for
petit treason should they strike him down" (20).

Despite its feudal social order, Virginia's need for labor and midlevel
managers offered many opportunities for perspicacious white men. William Prentis put his commercial training to good use during his seven-
year apprenticeship to Archibald Blair, a wealthy Scottish merchant and
physician who had immigrated to Williamsburg, Virginia's capital city, in
1690. Blair's family held significant cultural influence; his brother, the
Reverend James Blair, founded and became the first president of Williamsburg's College of William and Mary. William worked as a clerk in
Dr. Blair's small wood-frame store on the Duke of Gloucester Street.
The store had prospered since its opening around 1702, and within three
years of William's arrival, Governor Alexander Spotswood called it "one
of the most considerable Trading Stores in this Country" (qtd. in Riley
36). In addition to offering one of the largest stocks of goods in the British colonies, the store served as a vibrant social center, offering patrons
gossip, debate, and transatlantic news.

A decade after his arrival, William had the good fortune of courting
and winning the teenaged Mary Brooke, daughter of Anne and John
Brooke, owners of a prosperous Williamsburg tavern and many slaves.
On August 16, 1725, John sold William a small (twenty-five feet by six-
teen feet) house on Nicholson Street along with a shed and an old stable

William Prentis (1699–1765). Prentis arrived in Williamsburg from London around 1715 to work as an indentured apprentice in Archibald Blair's store. Brilliant at business, Prentis rose from rags to riches, becoming store manager, major shareholder, and wealthy citizen. This portrait, attributed to Charles Bridges (1670–1747), hangs in the foyer of the Rockefeller Library in Williamsburg. Courtesy of the Colonial Williamsburg Foundation.

Mary Brooke Prentis (ca. 1700–1768). Daughter of wealthy Williamsburg tavern owners, John and Anne Brooke, Mary married William Prentis in the 1720s. Oil painting by unidentified artist, ca. 1720. Courtesy of the Colonial Williamsburg Foundation.

for the horses that William and Mary enjoyed riding (March 18, 1724/25, York County Records). The Brookes' house, which faced the Duke of Gloucester Street, was unusually well furnished for an early eighteenth-century Virginian home, featuring tables, chairs, a corner cupboard, curtained beds, pictures, a large amount of silver, and a well-stocked kitchen (M. Stephenson, *Prentis* 4).

When John Brooke died in 1729, his will revealed a strong respect for his female kin, including his wife, daughters, a sister, and a niece, to whom he left significant legacies. He also left tokens for a nephew and grandson. His wife received his land and houses for use during her lifetime, along with "all my Negroes and personal Estate of what Nature or kind soever." He appointed her executor with "full power to sell otherwise dispose of same or any part thereof as she shall think most conducive to her advantage and welfare." He left his daughter, Mary, one slave and a silver tankard and placed her and her husband, William Prentis, in line to inherit most of the estate after Anne Brooke's death. He mentioned his slaves casually, en masse, without names (Will of John Brooke, November 17, 1729, PFP).

Between 1729 and 1754, Mary Brooke Prentis gave birth to six children who survived to adulthood: John (b. 1729), Daniel and William (b. 1730s), Sarah (b. 1749), Elizabeth (b. 1752), and Joseph, born on January 24, 1754, when Mary was fifty-four. The couple also offered a home to an orphan, David Long, and to William's nephew, Robert (1741–1809), who followed in his uncle's footsteps by immigrating from England and working in the store under William's tutelage. The Prentis children were nursed and cared for by slaves who slept wherever they were ordered to: in the nursery, at the foot of a bed, or in slave quarters in the yard near the other outbuildings. As Isaac notes, the family home was not idealized as "a center of private domesticity [for] Anglo-Virginians in the mid–eighteenth century. They lived or aspired to live in the constant presence of servants [slaves] and guests" (70–71). Like most elite families, the Prentises prided themselves on their ability to offer hospitality and to take in orphans and other dependents. They gradually expanded their estate on the lot between Nicholson and Duke of Gloucester Streets, adding bedrooms for each child, a dining room, a hallway, and little rooms and chambers, along with outbuildings such as a kitchen, a washhouse, a meat house, a cellar, a storeroom, and an outhouse.

In 1733, William acquired some shares in Blair's store and became its manager. Running a retail store in colonial Virginia presented many challenges, as the colony had no banks, no stable credit system, and multiple transnational currencies with no authoritative exchange rates. Communication with trade partners in Europe, in Africa, and along the eastern seaboard from Nova Scotia to the Caribbean was slow and often disrupted by war, piracy, and shipwreck. Catering to the gentry, William Prentis proved brilliant at evaluating merchandise and managing money while Virginia underwent a transformation from a rough imperial outpost with an immigrant population of 60,000 in 1700 to a mature colony of 230,000 Euro-Virginian and Afro-Virginian inhabitants in 1750 (Isaac 12). As an import-export merchant, he played a key role in a culture that "was dependent for its prosperity on the export of a staple to the parent society and on returns received in manufactured articles. Material reliance entailed also cultural and psychological dependence. With goods came tastes, standards, and a whole set of assumptions about the proper ways of ordering life" (Isaac 16).

The store grew vigorously under Prentis's management, and the partners soon agreed to change its name to William Prentis and Company. In 1738, the city of Williamsburg agreed to lease the partners an additional lot on Main Street, on which they built a large brick storehouse adjacent to the old one on Duke of Gloucester Street. This store is still standing in the living museum of Colonial Williamsburg. Prentis's annual compensation of between £113 and £162 in the 1730s was equivalent to the income that Virginia's largest planters, such as Robert Carter of Nomini Hall, derived from their annual tobacco crops. As his stock in William Prentis and Company also continued to rise in value, Prentis became one of Williamsburg's wealthiest men. He conducted trade with and extended credit to some of the most powerful families in the British empire. Garnering sufficient respect and wealth to overcome, to a large extent, the colony's class biases, Prentis often was addressed by the title *Gentleman* (Richter 8–19). By building his fortune through commerce and money, unlike the traditional gentry, whose wealth and power were based primarily in their landholdings, he became, like his Philadelphia contemporary Benjamin Franklin, a pioneer in an economic reorganization of power relations based on shifting definitions of property rights and the status of labor. In Isaac's words, "In its purest form the wealth of the patriarch consists

The Prentis store on Duke of Gloucester Street. Photograph by Kari J. Winter.

primarily of the accumulated obligations of dependents to show submission, render service, and supply needs. Money, by contrast, is a form of wealth that operates very differently. It is impersonal, being designed to establish a universal scale of values that transcends the particular ties of persons; and, unlike the personal obligations contributing to patriarchy, it is in essence composed of discrete units. Money not only expresses obligation in precise amounts but also instills the idea of obligations as calculable debt rather than as forms of service and submission" (21). Future generations would wrestle with vexed feelings about how to understand the relations among morality, wealth, labor, and power. William's son, Joseph, would cringe with shame at the imagined taint of wealth gained through commerce and money. He would aspire to become an agrarian patriarch whose power was based on a hierarchy of personal relationships. He would serve and submit to God and would expect his wife, children, slaves, and social inferiors to serve and submit to him, all in the name of goodness and love. William's grandsons, Joseph Jr. and John, would diverge sharply in their styles and philosophies of moneymaking.

In 1754, the same year that Mary Brooke Prentis gave birth to Joseph, the Virginia General Assembly published forty-six pages of laws (Acts of Assembly) formulated during two years of meetings at the College of William and Mary. These laws supported two goals that were foundational to the social order: to promote the possession of land taken from Indians and to enhance control of slaves. After a two-paragraph "Act for further encouraging Persons to settle on the Waters of the Mississippi" to "cultivate a better Correspondence with the neighboring *Indians*"—by which the Assembly meant to promote the further acquisition of Indian lands—eight of the pages were devoted to "An Act for the better Government of Servants and Slaves." Land and slavery were the sine qua non of the social order.

Through his success as a merchant, William Prentis achieved sufficient status to be appointed paymaster of the colony of Virginia and justice of the court in Williamsburg, James City County, and York County. Most justices at the time were untrained in law, capricious in their judgments, and powerful in their ability to disburse offices and contracts. A case over which Prentis was one of the presiding justices in March 1754 reveals the ruling class's investment in imposing order in ways that would keep slaves and white workingmen in their places and safely segregate the two classes from each other. John Holt, an ambitious merchant who soon would become mayor of Williamsburg, accused a business rival, George Fisher, of selling rum to Negroes. It was illegal to sell or serve alcohol to blacks, whether free or enslaved. According to his memoir, Fisher defended his innocence by declaring that "no Negro had ever been served with Rum by my family" (148). He contended that a third merchant, John Greenhow, a friend of Holt's, was "infamously remarkable for trafficking with Negroes in wine, or any other commodity, Sunday not excepted" (149). The court called Fisher to order, and Prentis told him to be quiet. As part of a conspiracy to ruin him, Fisher alleged, Holt and other city leaders had burned down Fisher's store and destroyed all of his merchandise. He decided to leave Virginia.

Having prospered as an Enlightenment man, Prentis expressed gratitude for his education at Christ's Hospital by opening a school to make a classical education available to local children, including his own. He personally taught the pupils the classics of Latin and Greek literature. He also assembled an impressive family library, hundreds of volumes of which still survive in collections at the Colonial Williamsburg Foundation, the University of Virginia, and the College of William and Mary, which pays tribute to his memory by bestowing the annual Prentis Award on individuals who exemplify "strong civic involvement and support of the College" (College of William and Mary).

Raised in one of the most important British cities in the Americas, William Prentis's children imbibed an atmosphere of violent contradictions. The elite increasingly embraced Enlightenment ideals of liberty, equality, and reason at the same time that every imaginable form of violence and vice abounded, from genocide to slavery to public and private forms of torture and sexual degradation. Warfare against Indians and theft of Indian lands were part and parcel of daily life, as were slave ships arriving from the West Indies and Africa. Children were bombarded by and in many cases acquired a taste for the gory sights and mournful sounds of violence: slave coffles in chains, auctions of slaves and servants at Raleigh's Tavern and elsewhere, and public whippings and hangings. Colonial Virginia society was obsessed with appearances and spectacles. Many people assumed that everything they needed to know about others was revealed by their skin, hair, and clothes. Farmers and slaves in muddy buckskins drove wagons and cartloads of merchandise to and fro, while gentlemen in powdered wigs wearing velvet breeches and shiny boots rode horseback; and ladies with ornate, pearl-draped hairdos, silk or satin gowns, and high-heeled slippers were transported to social events in coaches and gigs. During the 1760s, Governor Francis Fauquier, a bon vivant whose tastes included art, music, and gambling, hosted elegant dinners and balls at his palace at the top of the Duke of Gloucester Street. An ornate coach drawn by six white horses carried him to meetings of the House of Burgesses, which met in a stately capitol with a tall portico (Axelrad 42).

Black workers were omnipresent, dressed in clothes that testified to their masters' social aspirations, wealth, and whims. Some wore the elegant garb of aristocratic servants, others covered themselves in their rough annual allotments, and a few were shackled, naked, or in rags. Black men and women worked as barbers, tailors, shoemakers, cooks, waiters, maids, carpenters, blacksmiths, seamstresses, gardeners, musicians, wagoners, and sailors. Children deprived of clothes, food, and parental care were a common sight to which the elite accustomed themselves, their senses dulled by vinegar, herbs, and perfume as well as wine, rum, and smoke. Wealthy men gambled late into the night, playing cards, rolling dice, and racing horses. Prostitution and sexual violence were rampant. Many contemporary Virginians were horrified by the state of their society, though they disagreed vehemently about the sources of vice and decadence. Religious dissenters, inspired by the antiestablishment beliefs of the New Light faction of the Great Awakening, fomented rebellion against Virginia's established Church of England as well as against the colony's corruption and profligacy.

The Seven Years' War, also known as the French and Indian War, intensified the chaos, excitement, and anxiety of life throughout the British colonies. William Prentis served on a wartime committee charged with overseeing military expenses, and his oldest son, John, served as an officer. Although Virginia's economy prospered during the war—merchandise was plentiful and prices high—the uncertainty of war heightened William's awareness of mortality. As 1761 came to an end, he turned his thoughts to his will.

> December 31, 1761
> IN THE NAME OF GOD AMEN
> I, William Prentis, of the City of Williamsburg Virginia Merchant [illegible]
> I devise to my beloved Wife Mary Prentis, that part of the Lott whereon I now Live which was Conveyed to me by my Father in Law Mr Brookes to her and the heirs of her body . . . for ever.
> ITEM. I give and Devise to my said Wife all my Lands and Slaves except those hereafter particularly mentioned . . . Stocks . . . Hogs . . .
> ITEM. I give to my Said Wife the use of my Chariott and Harness during her Natural Life and after her decease I give the same to my Daughter Sarah Waters.
> ITEM. It is my Will and Desire that all my Slaves and Personal Estate of what Nature or kind soever except my Stock in Trade should be inventoried and Appraised, and as I have already given to my daughter Sarah Waters a Negroe Woman Nanny, Daughter of Venus whom I value at forty Pounds I also give and Bequeath to my Sons John, William, Daniel, and Joseph each the Sum of forty Pounds Current Money exclusive of what I shall here [torn]. ITEM. I give to my Daughter Elizabeth [torn] Negro Woman Judith with her Daughter Increase.

He estimated his share in the store to be worth "seven thousand one hundred and fourteen Pounds," which he divided among his family members.

> To my beloved Wife One thousand Pounds part of said Stock, to my
> Son John one thousand four hundred and forty four Pounds other Part
> thereof, to Mr. William Waters the Sum of Six hundred and seventy
> Pounds other Part thereof, to my Son William one thousand Pounds other
> part thereof, to my Son Daniel One thousand Pounds other part thereof,
> to my Son Joseph one thousand Pounds other part thereof, and to my
> daughter Elizabeth One thousand Pounds the residue thereof, but it is
> farther my Will and desire that such parts of the said Stock as I have given
> to my Children who are under Age may during their Minorities be contin-
> ued in Trade under the Management of my Son John.

Finally, he turned to the matter of guardianship for his younger children.

> ITEM. I do appoint Mr. Robert Carter Nicholas Guardian of my son
> Joseph. ITEM. I do constitute and appoint my Son John Prentis and my
> Friends Mr. Benjamin Waller, and Robert Carter Nicholas Executors of
> this my Will and Guardians of my other Children. . . . And Lastly I do
> revoke all other Wills by me heretofore made. . . .
> IN WITNESS whereof I have hereunto set my hand and affixed my Seal
> this thirty first Day of December 1761
> Wil Prentis
> (York County Records)

In a codicil, only fragments of which survive, Prentis distributed his slaves
and the stock in his store to his heirs.

William Prentis died four years later. The timing was momentous. Wartime prosperity had collapsed into postwar depression. Unemployment
and bankruptcy were rising, prices of merchandise falling. The British
Crown, struggling to pay for the war amid tumbling revenues, imposed
strident new taxes on its colonies in the form of the 1764 Stamp Act,
thus setting the stage for the American Revolution. In May 1765, Patrick Henry, a budding backwoods lawyer, electrified Virginia's House of
Burgesses, into which he had just been sworn, by declaiming eloquently
against the Stamp Act, a taxation scheme by which the British monarchy
intended to dump its debts on the backs of colonial taxpayers. His audi-
ence included prominent planters—George Washington, Thomas Jefferson, Peyton Randolph, Richard Henry Lee—as well as such members
of Williamsburg's elite as George Wythe. The planters' tone toward the
Crown was cautious and conciliatory until Henry began speaking. Amid

fierce denunciations and shouts of "Treason! Treason!" he proclaimed the
Stamp Act tyrannical and lawless. Jefferson declared that Henry spoke
"as Homer wrote, with torrents of sublime eloquence" (qtd. in Axelrad
42). Newspapers carried Henry's resolutions throughout the colonies, in-
flaming the sentiments that soon would result in war.

On the same day that Henry delivered his incendiary call for rebellion,
three black men were hanged from public gallows down the street for a
minor infraction against implacable oppression. They were accused of
stealing three hundred pence (Levy 20). Such executions had long been
a feature of Virginian life. Courts routinely tried, without jury, slaves accused of theft. If the value of the stolen goods exceeded five shillings
(sixty pence), the perpetrator could be hanged (Isaac 92).

The colonists' grievances pale in light of the inventory of William Prentis's estate and what it reveals about the economic brutality practiced by
the colonists against those people on whose backs they built—or strove to
build—their fortunes. "Old Nanny," an elderly woman who had spent her
life in service to William and Mary Prentis and had earned their affection
with her diligent nursing and tending of their children, lived in a ram-
shackle outbuilding. The worldly goods allotted for her use amounted
to no more than "a frying pan, a pot, a grindstone, and a few tools . . . no
furniture at all" (Tate 62). She could not claim to own even these meager
items, since she too was legally defined as a piece of property. Slaves
were rarely provided with furniture; at best they received discarded beds
or cots. The names William Prentis imposed on the four slaves whom
he identifies individually in his will—"Nanny, Daughter of Venus whom
I value at forty Pounds" and "Judith with her Daughter Increase"—lay
bare the libidinal fantasies that slaveholders commonly invested in their
ability to fix the value of other human beings, to possess and enjoy them,
and to imagine relations of violence, conquest, and rape as account book
abstractions.

Mary Brooke Prentis survived for three years after her husband's death.
On April 14, 1768, the Virginia Gazette noted, "Last Saturday morning
died in the 58th year of her age, Mrs. Mary Prentis, relict of the late William Prentis, a Lady of exemplary piety, and most affable disposition."
Aside from a share of stock in Prentis and Company, Mary personally
owned very little—clothes, a cabinet, an easy chair, and a sidesaddle—
but William's estate, which Mary had held in trust for the duration of her
life, was lavish. Her will favored her sons at the expense of her daughters:

Sarah received "all my Cloaths," while Elizabeth got nothing but "my Cabinet." To Ann Walker, Mary Prentis's companion, who lived in her house and presumably helped to care for her, she gave twenty pounds, and to her nephew, Robert, thirty pounds. She divided the rest of the estate equally between her four sons, appointing the elder two, John and William, as executors (Will of Mary Prentis, PFP). They sold the estate at a public auction in Williamsburg on August 8, 1768, summarizing the inventory in an advertisement published in the *Virginia Gazette*:

> *To be* SOLD *at* PUBLIC AUCTION, *to the* HIGHEST BIDDER . . .
>   EIGHT valuable house SLAVES,
> and sundry kinds of household and kitchen furniture, such as plate, china, tables, chairs, pictures, looking-glasses, beds, quilts, blankets, table and bed linen, a couch, clock, dumb waiter, chest of drawers, bureau, cooler, two suits of fine bed curtains and bedsteads, a large quantity of pewter, & c. A single chair, a cart, and several horses, a pipe of fine old Madeira wine, and several dozen of bottled wine; also two tracts of land in the county of *York*, each containing 150 acres, more or less . . . also a water grist mill in the same county. . . . The above estate is to be sold for the benefit of all Mr. PRENTIS's children; and the sale is to continue till every thing is disposed of.
>   The sale is to begin at 11 o'clock.

John Prentis retained his parents' house and purchased £560.2.11 worth of slaves, stock, and goods. According to the settlement filed in York County on June 15, 1772, the estate sale generated £1736.10.4.

Two years later, eighteen-year-old Elizabeth Prentis died. Her siblings idealized her in an obituary filled with piety and affection. John managed the store, while William Jr. moved to Richmond, where he flourished as a printer, publishing books, almanacs, plays, and speeches by Virginia's leading lights. In the 1780s, he won the contract to publish the documents of Virginia's General Assembly. While maintaining his Richmond printing business, he eventually moved to Petersburg, where he published a newspaper, the *Virginia Chronicle*, and was elected to four terms as mayor. He married and had several children with Mary "Polly" Geddy.

William and Mary's youngest child, Joseph, who had lost his father at the age of nine, his mother at thirteen, and his sister at fifteen, moved to the estate of his guardian, Robert Carter Nicholas, on South England Street. Like his ward, Nicholas had been orphaned at a young age, and like his ward's father, Nicholas was a money man. Grandson of Robert "King" Carter and cousin of Robert Carter III, Nicholas was a graduate of the College of William and Mary, a prominent lawyer, and a member of the House of Burgesses who was appointed treasurer of the colony in 1766. As part of Virginia's wealthiest clan, which competed with the Randolphs for top rank in terms of power and influence, Nicholas had ambivalent feelings about the revolutionary fervor building among his peers. He opposed both the Stamp Act and Henry's resolutions against it. In Nicholas's household, Joseph Prentis was buffeted by personal, political, economic, and racial turbulence. During the summer of 1768, while he was adjusting to his new residence, slave catchers showed up to search for a runaway slave, Gaby. Gaby's master, James Burwell, suspected that his slave was hiding with one of Nicholas's slaves, a woman whom Gaby considered to be his wife. Beginning on September 15, 1768, Burwell ran runaway ads for five weeks in the *Virginia Gazette*, describing Gaby as "about 40 years of age, round shouldr'd, bends in one of his knees (in which I have forgot) is very subject to sore legs, has a very long foot; and had on when he left me the usual winter clothing of corn field Negroes." Burwell preferred to have Gaby returned dead rather than alive, offering "a reward of ten pounds . . . for his head, or twenty shillings if safely delivered to James Burwell." A sentimental teenager wrestling with loss and grief, Joseph may have sympathized with Gaby's plight, but his sense of identification with a propertied class that prized its possessions trumped other claims of morality and sensibility.

Under Nicholas's tutelage, Joseph interacted on a daily basis with Virginia's leading families. Edmund Randolph married Nicholas's daughter, Elizabeth, and became mayor of Williamsburg in the 1770s. Randolph served as an aide-de-camp to General George Washington during the Revolution and as governor of Virginia from 1786 to 1788 before becoming U.S. attorney general under President Washington. In 1794, Randolph succeeded Jefferson as U.S. secretary of state. Although William Prentis's wealth had not wholly cleansed the charter generation of Prentises from the stigma of lowly birth and indentured servitude, Nicholas's status enabled Joseph to aspire to the highest level of gentility. With his guardian's approval, he began reading law at the College of William and Mary. Like William Prentis, Nicholas was a staunch advocate of education. He served on the college's governing board and from 1761 to 1774 held the position of trustee for the Bray School, a charity school for Williamsburg's black children. His belief in education did not spring from a vision of social equality; rather, he viewed education as a forum for promoting social order and ideological conformity.

Religious devotion was not customary among Virginia's eighteenth-century elite—indeed, most of the gentry reacted to it with hostility and suspicion because, as Isaac shows, "churchgoing in colonial Virginia had more to do with expressing the dominance of the gentry than with inculcating piety or forming devout personalities" (120). Nicholas ran against the grain of the age by cherishing a deep devotion to the reassuring rituals of the rigorously hierarchical Church of England, known in Virginia as the Protestant Episcopal Church. Until the state of Virginia, guided by Jefferson and James Madison, passed laws mandating the separation of church and state, the Protestant Episcopal Church was Virginia's established church, meaning that it was supported by taxes and was entitled to enforce mandatory attendance. A vestryman, Nicholas regularly brought his family and dependents to services at the Bruton Parish Church, which was also attended, at least intermittently, by the families of Jefferson, Washington, Henry, St. George Tucker, Madison, Richard Henry Lee, Wythe, and George Mason as well as the Randolphs and other Carters. The church underscored order and authority through its architecture, its liturgy, and its doctrinal emphasis on obedience to earthly and heavenly powers. A brick building with large arched windows, a towering steeple, a high pulpit, and an impressive organ, the Bruton Parish Church was situated near the center of the Duke of Gloucester Street, alongside the Palace Green. Elite parishioners sat in boxed pews that displayed their occupants' rank while offering a modicum of privacy and protection from winter drafts.

Nicholas chaired the House of Burgesses' Committee for Religion and worked arduously to enforce orthodoxy. Alarmed by the rising popularity of evangelicalism, which appealed strongly to poor whites and slaves and was even making inroads among the gentry, he wanted to prescribe how dissenters could establish churches and to "guard against the Corruption of our Slaves" (qtd. in Isaac 220). When a new rector from England, the Reverend Samuel Henley, began preaching in 1773 against bigotry and persecution and in favor of toleration and religious freedom, Nicholas was scandalized. "Suppose . . . every Man was allowed . . . *Freedom of Judgment*," he sputtered in the *Virginia Gazette*, "let all Men, think and speak and preach as they will, or rather, as they *can*; instead of

William Prentis II. (ca. 1740–1824). William Jr. imitates his father's pose in the portrait by Charles Bridges, holding a copy of the *Virginia Gazette and Petersburg Intelligencer*, which William edited. Having grown up in Williamsburg and worked for several years as a printer in Richmond, William Jr. settled in Petersburg, where he became that city's first printer, editor, and publisher and served four terms as mayor. Oil painting by Robert Fulton, 1786. Courtesy of the Virginia Historical Society.

Mary "Polly" Geddy Prentis. Oil painting by William Lovett, 1792. Courtesy of the Virginia Historical Society.

the Uniformity of Doctrine which our Church has formerly been blessed with, what a Babel of Religions should we have amongst us?" He insisted that "the necessity of Rules and Articles must also be allowed; a Society without these is an Existence to me unintelligible" (qtd. in Isaac 238). His young ward, Joseph Prentis, deeply internalized Nicholas's passion for propriety, decorum, and order. In the 1780s and 1790s, Joseph would join Patrick Henry in an active campaign to promote Anglican notions of virtue and religious devotion.

The Virginia elite's difficulties in negotiating among conflicting emotions—rage at exploitative taxes warred against cultural as well as personal loyalty to the Crown—are dramatically illustrated in the predicament of William Prentis's oldest son, John. During the Seven Years' War, he had served the British empire as both a military colonel and mayor of Williamsburg, a post to which he was appointed by the royal governor in 1759. After his father's death, John took over management of the Prentis store, and after his mother's death, he acquired the family estate, where he lived a life that was simultaneously luxurious, thanks largely to the service of fifteen slaves, and intimately painful. He and his wife, Elizabeth Pierce Prentis, had no children, and her behavior diverged so markedly from the norms of genteel womanhood that she was suspected of insanity. He found himself trapped in a web of unfortunate personal, economic, and political alignments. In 1771, most wealthy Virginians reacted negatively to the Crown's appointment of a coarse, ill-mannered, iron-fisted Tory, John Murray, Earl of Dunmore, as governor of Virginia. John Prentis, however, attached himself to the new governor. He tottered, like his friend Nicholas, between loyalty to the Crown, whose favor enabled his wealth, status, and mercantile business, and solidarity with rebellious Virginians, whose rage against oppressive taxes he shared. The pious Nicholas responded to the crisis caused by the British embargo against Boston by introducing a resolution, which was adopted by the House of Burgesses, to set aside June 1, 1774, as a day of "Fasting, Humiliation, and Prayer, devoutly to implore" God to inspire "the Minds of His Majesty and his Parliament . . . with Wisdom, Moderation, and Justice" (*Virginia Gazette*, June 2, 1774). Desperately hoping for a peaceful resolution of differences, John Prentis and Robert Nicholas firmly opposed Henry's efforts to raise an army. Disappointed by the outbreak of war, both Prentis and Nicholas in the end had little choice but to support the rebellion.

In 1774, Prentis ill-advisedly ordered two half chests of tea from London, thereby betraying his fellow Virginians' agreement to bar British imports. On November 7, when the tea arrived in port at York, enraged Virginians held a protest modeled after the Boston Tea Party, hurling all of the tea into the river. Publicizing the controversy, the *Virginia Gazette* ran three November 24 articles that included a narrative of the events and official condemnations issued by the Gloucester County Committee and the York County Committee against Prentis, his London merchant, and the ship captain. Prentis was mortified. The *Virginia Gazette* concluded its series of articles by publishing his abject apology: "It gives me much Concern to find that I have incurred the Displeasure of the York and Gloucester Committees, and thereby of the Publick in general, for my Omission in not countermanding the Order which I sent to Mr. Norton for two Half Chests of Tea; and do with Truth declare, that I had not the least Intention to give Offence, nor did I mean an Opposition to any Measure for the publick Good. My Countrymen, therefore, it is earnestly hoped, will readily forgive me for an Act which may be interpreted so much to my Discredit; and I again make this publick Declaration, that I had not the least Design to act contrary to those Principles which ought to govern every Individual who has a just Regard for the Rights and Liberties of America. John Prentis."[1]

In December, the James City County Committee thanked Prentis and his partner "for their Candour in giving the above information" and advertised a public auction of the other goods they had imported (*Virginia Gazette*, December 22, 1774). During the same month, Nicholas's political and religious enemies charged him with violating the nonimportation agreement, and a series of heated newspaper exchanges on the matter continued for several months. John Prentis's death garnered just a tiny notice in the November 2, 1775, *Virginia Gazette*: "Died, after a lingering illness JOHN PRENTIS, of this city, Merchant." Nicholas surmounted the criticism and retained enough influence among Revolutionary leaders to be appointed to Virginia's new Court of Chancery in 1778. He died in 1780.

Joseph Prentis thus found the uncertainty of war intensified by the deaths of his oldest brother and his guardian, but he could comfort himself with a significant inheritance. John Prentis bequeathed to his brother a great deal of land; an enslaved waiting boy, Alexander; and several other unnamed slaves. One line in John's will suggests that he may have felt an occasional twinge of discomfort with slavery. Virginia barred masters from freeing their slaves outright, but John requested that "my Man Squire may Chuse his Master."[2] Allowing Squire a choice in such an important matter expressed a degree of respect and affection. Many slaveholders in eighteenth-century Virginia made similar provisions for their most valued slaves, enabling the masters to salve their consciences without challenging the social order. In 1782, Virginia lawmakers would ease restrictions on manumissions, but they would continue to hotly contest the matter until the Civil War, in part as a consequence of white anxieties about the presence of free blacks (see Wolf).

Elizabeth Prentis appeared completely undone by the public scandal and death of her husband. Doubting her mental competence, the court debated whether to permit her to assume control of John's estate. In 1775, the court declared that she was "of unsound Mind and incapable of Managing her Estate" and appointed a committee to take care of her. She was awarded dower rights in the lands and slaves of her husband's estate on the condition that her brother-in-law, Joseph, and her husband's cousin, Robert, would rent her land and houses.[3] William, Joseph, and the other partners in Prentis and Company debated whether to keep the store open. The boycott of British goods and the turbulent politics of the early 1770s made obtaining stock and collecting from debtors difficult. The partners tentatively decided to keep the store open under Robert's management, but business did not go well. A loyalist dismayed by Virginia's revolutionary turn, Robert relocated to Trinidad.[4] In 1807, Joseph and William Prentis Jr. would sell the store, which their enterprising father had gradually built into the most important store in colonial Virginia, for a mere five hundred dollars.

The 1770s were saturated with anxiety and exhilaration. Although Joseph's personal fortunes were destabilized by the war, the newly constituted state of Virginia and United States of America had a bottomless need for capable city, county, state, and federal legislators. This need helped Joseph's career to flourish. More fortunate in his political alignments than his brother, John, had been, Joseph was well positioned to assume a prominent role in constructing the new nation. By the mid-1770s, he was serving as a member of the Virginia Convention, as a representative to Virginia's House of Delegates, and as a judge of admiralty. He developed vital friendships and political alliances with Patrick Henry, who had become the most popular politician in Virginia and soon would be elected governor, and with a fellow judge and neighbor, St. George Tucker, who would become one of the most influential legal scholars of the era.

In October 1776, Joseph and his uncle, Robert Prentis, whose money-management skills were widely recognized as a result of his management of the Prentis store and of his service as an agent for Robert Carter III, were appointed to a committee charged with overseeing the accounts of Virginia's treasury. Financial oversight was extraordinarily difficult. Neither the Commonwealth of Virginia nor the fragile, newly consti-tuted United States had an official currency, and both were struggling to find a way to finance the war. Nine foreign currencies, including En-glish pounds, French livres, and Spanish dollars, were widely accepted, but their values were in constant flux and were often assigned haphaz-ardly. The new country lacked even rudimentary laws and regulations that would assign fiscal responsibilities and constitute relations between state and federal governments, commerce and credit, and the private and public sectors. Many daily transactions, large and small, depended on the reputations of individual planters, politicians, and businessmen. Joseph Prentis embraced Revolutionary ideals, but like Jefferson and other Vir-ginia aristocrats, Prentis expressed distaste for the hurly-burly world of commerce, credit, and market relations. Preferring the romantic pater-nalism of agrarian gentility to the crass commercialism of modern capital-ism, these elites downplayed their interest in acquiring money.

Spending it, however, was an entirely different matter. Joseph never ceased to indulge in a lifestyle that exceeded his means. Less than a year after graduating from the College of William and Mary, Judge Joseph Prentis, aged twenty-four, used his inherited wealth to purchase a large estate on Henry Street in the heart of Williamsburg, just a block from the Governor's Palace. In December 1778, Prentis married twenty-year-old Margaret Bowdoin of Northampton County and brought her to the estate, which he named Green Hill. Although they enjoyed the stylish figures they could cut by riding horses or taking carriages around town, a fifteen-minute walk would take Joseph and Margaret virtually every-where they needed to go in daily life. Duke of Gloucester Street, one block from their house, stretched from the college to the Capitol and fea-tured the Prentis store along with other shops, businesses, taverns, and the Bruton Parish Church, where they regularly attended services. They followed Nicholas's example by remaining among the most religiously devout and politically conservative members of their social circle. Joseph served on several church committees and participated actively in church conventions in Richmond. The contradictions between his antimaterialist piety and his extravagant behavior left his children a legacy of moral vexations (see Oakes 96–122).

Joseph's legal practice and political career continued to flourish. His colleagues included the future third, fourth, and fifth presidents of the United States. In 1779, he served alongside Madison on Governor Henry's Privy Council. Over the years, Madison, who knew Prentis well, kept Jefferson apprised of Prentis's various political appointments (see Madison, *Letters*). Prentis developed a warm friendship with James Monroe, who had been elected to the Virginia House of Delegates and chosen for the Governor's Council in 1782 at the age of twenty-four. The two men exchanged visits and letters for many years (see Preston). From 1777 to 1788, Prentis served as a representative in the Virginia House of Delegates, including a term as house speaker. In 1780–81, when Benedict Arnold led a British raid across the James River Valley to loot homes, burn warehouses, and liberate human property, Prentis commiserated with his compatriots, including Tucker, who lost many slaves to freedom behind British lines (Hamilton, "Revolutionary" 538). When Jefferson moved Virginia's capital to Richmond, Prentis traveled there often. In 1790, the General Assembly appointed him to committees that revised the new state's laws, including the slave codes. From 1788 until his death in 1809, he served on the General Court of Virginia, which held sessions twice a year in Richmond. He also helped to establish schools in Harrison, Monongalia, and Randolph Counties in 1787, lectured on occasion at the College of William and Mary, and served on various college committees. He viewed education as crucial not only to individual success but also to the project of nation building.

Judge Prentis was a passionate gardener whose four acres of pleasure gardens on the east and west sides of his colonial mansion were locally famous. Green Hill was bordered by Henry, Prince George, Nassau, and Scotland Streets. To the north and west of his lots, across Henry and Scotland Streets, Prentis used another twenty acres for farming and pasturage for his horses and cattle. The clean architecture of his flowers, shrubs, and trees pleased him, as did a delightful freshwater spring on his grounds. He conversed with Jefferson not only about politics but also about gardening, a joint passion that suited their self-construction as agrarian patriarchs. Like Jefferson, Prentis kept a "Monthly Kalendar and Garden Book" in which he chronicled the planting and harvesting of his vegetables and fruits, which included artichokes, Jerusalem artichokes, beans, Margaran beans, broccoli, cauliflower, currants, chamomile flowers, gooseberries, onions, parsley, strawberries, raspberries, spinach, parsnips, salsify, peas, and lettuce. He designed squares and borders, large gardens and small, giving his slaves careful instructions on how to dress borders, spread manure fertilizer, gather seeds, clean, prune, and weed. He experimented with rare and common varieties of fruit trees, vegetables, roses, flowers, and herbs. By the turn of the century, many members of Williamsburg's elite had become gardening enthusiasts. In 1799, Peter Bellet opened a gardening nursery and shop on Gallows Street, also known as Capitol Landing Road, where an adjacent canal enabled the easy transport of trees and other plants by boat. Prentis, whose gardens were widely praised and emulated, was one of Bellet's first customers. Prentis also exchanged plants and trees with his brother-in-law, Peter Bowdoin, in Northampton County as well as with Tucker and with other good friends and neighbors, the Skipwiths. When the gardens of Green Hill were damaged in a summer storm in 1795, Tucker wrote a poem for the occasion (Martin 169). The skills of Joseph Prentis's head gardener, Ellick, were widely recognized by neighbors, who turned to him for advice and assistance. During his term as governor, Jefferson hired another of Prentis's enslaved gardeners, Thompson, to help with the gardens at the Governor's Palace. The brilliant, free-thinking Jefferson did not develop a close friendship with the pious, convention-bound Prentis, eleven years younger, but like most members of Williamsburg's small elite, their lives had multiple interconnections. For example, Robert Skipwith was the brother of Henry Skipwith, Joseph's neighbor and intimate friend, and was married to the sister of Jefferson's wife.

Four of Joseph and Margaret Prentis's eight children, Joseph, John, Eliza, and Mary Anne, survived into adulthood.[5] Margaret and Joseph doted on their children, worried incessantly about their health, and painfully mourned the four who died in infancy or childhood. Accustomed to being tended by enslaved women whom they called "Nanny" or "Mammy," the couple reproduced this child-rearing practice by appointing their slave, Rachel, as mammy. It was not uncommon for polite Virginia slaveholders publicly to discuss the plump breasts and ample

Bruton Parish Church on Duke of Gloucester Street. Photograph by Kari J. Winter.

milk of their slaves and to lease or lend nursing slave women to families
with newborn infants. Such degrading intimacies were part and parcel of
the peculiar institution.

The Prentises had many relatives and close friends in the neighborhood. Two of the judge's closest friends, Skipwith and Tucker, lived near
Green Hill, as did his relatives, the Greenhows, who lived in a com-
modious house filled with elegant furniture, an organ and spinet, and
numerous slaves on Duke of Gloucester Street. They had a shop near
the Bruton Parish Church. The judge's sister, Sarah Waters, and her family lived on Duke of Gloucester Street, and sometime after the Revolution, Joseph Prentis's brother-in-law, Robert Saunders, purchased the
neighboring house and lots of Robert Carter III on Palace Street. Married to Sarah Bowdoin (b. 1768), a sister of Judge Prentis's wife, Margaret, Saunders had served in the Revolutionary War under General Na-
thanael F. Greene and had developed an acquaintance with the Marquis
de Lafayette. (Saunders's namesake son would visit Lafayette's family

in France in 1850.) The Prentis children thus grew up surrounded by aunts, uncles, and cousins. Although family members scattered to various Virginia cities and plantations in the early nineteenth century, they corresponded, visited each other, and vacationed together at Fauquier Springs, a spa in Warrenton, Virginia, that was acclaimed for its restorative waters. It featured two posh hotels that could accommodate nearly a thousand guests as well as cottages owned by luminaries such as Madison and Monroe.

Devoted to liberal arts education, Joseph provided his daughters as well as his sons access to his large library. Like many wealthy Virginians, he imagined himself as a benign patriarch dedicated to spiritual values and contemptuous of luxury. "Implicit in the paternalistic ethos was the denigration of materialistic motives in all of life's pursuits" (Oakes 6). Yet like most of their peers, the Prentises had trouble matching praxis to philosophy. They habitually outspent their income by indulging in home improvements, rich furnishings, fine clothes, jewelry, dinner parties, and balls. Many an evening was whiled away dancing, singing, eating, and drinking fine liqueurs from crystal goblets. With slaves at their beck and call, the Prentises kept horses, cows, a phaeton, a gig, and two carts. They had expense accounts with craftsmen all over town, including jewelers William Waddill and John Rowsay; John Houston, a jeweler and watch repairer; Jane Charlton, a milliner; Daniel Fergusson, a silversmith; Benjamin Bucktrout, a carpenter; John Smith, a baker; Thomas Sands and William Piggot, carpenters; James Galt, a silversmith; Humphrey Harwood, a brick mason; and others. The precariousness of their finances was exacerbated when the Revolution destabilized markets and currencies, plunging even the wealthiest planters such as Robert Carter III to the brink of financial ruin. In the 1780s, many genteel estates crumbled, partly as a consequence of the generation's habitual overspending and addiction to credit and partly as a consequence of a severe depression in tobacco prices. The latter helped to fuel antislavery sentiments because many planters "found themselves owning more slaves than they knew what to do with. 'I have more working Negros,' complained George Washington, 'than can be employed to any advantage in the farming system'" (Howe 53). In 1791, Carter, the cousin of Joseph Prentis's guardian and one of the largest slaveholders in Virginia, was inspired by dissident religious fervor and humanitarian compassion to attempt to free all of his five hundred slaves.

Like many of his contemporaries, Joseph Prentis contemplated the possibility of financial ruin. In June 1790, he grew sufficiently anxious that he decided to put Green Hill up for sale. Either he could not obtain his desired price or he found another way to ease the financial strain, and he retained the property. In 1796, he sold thirteen acres of his pasturage lands to Edmund and Elizabeth Randolph, but he lived at Green Hill for the rest of his life, raising his children in a world of extreme wealth and destitution, order and chaos, gentility and violence. When skipping or sauntering down the broad Duke of Gloucester Street with their dogs at their heels, Joseph Jr., John, Eliza, and Mary Anne passed small homes, churches, taverns, blacksmiths, shoemakers, and the courthouse. Continuing down the street to the apothecary or a bookshop, they could glance through the open doors and windows of a milliner, a wigmaker, and Raleigh's Tavern, where they may have recalled their father's stories about how his famous peers had met privately in the tavern's Apollo Room to pass resolutions despite threats of arrest by Governor Dunmore.

Green Hill, the family home of Judge Joseph Prentis. Photograph ca. 1877. Courtesy of the Colonial Williamsburg Foundation.

St. George Tucker House. Judge Joseph Prentis's friend and fellow judge, St. George Tucker lived with his large family in this elegant house abutting the Palace Green. Photograph by Kari J. Winter.

During the late eighteenth century, slaves accounted for about 40 percent of Virginia's approximately eight hundred thousand residents. In the Prentis household, about ten people were held in bondage at any given time—nine in 1782, eleven when the Revolutionary War ended in 1783, and twelve in 1784, for example. Such numbers were typical for prominent urban families. Only twenty-three Virginia planters owned more than 200 slaves at the time; the wealthiest, Carter, owned 445 (Tate 21). Virginia's Revolutionary generation was keenly aware of the paradox of holding slave auctions in intimate proximity to their agitation for the Rights of Man. Politicians and legislators have subsequently debated what the founders intended by the sentence, "All men are created equal and are endowed by the Creator with the unalienable rights to life, liberty, and the pursuit of happiness," but no one could prevent the sentence from being taken to mean what it said. The sentence had the power to evoke a revolutionary dream wherever and whenever it was uttered.

From conversations between their father and Tucker, the Prentis children absorbed the era's contradictions in a direct, verbose manner. Tucker, the scion of a prominent merchant-shipping family, had immigrated to Virginia from Bermuda in 1772 to read law at the College of William and Mary. Intelligent, articulate, and amiable, he rose quickly in the legal profession and solidified his social status by marrying a well-connected widow, Frances Bland Randolph, in 1778. Through her, he gained control of three large plantations and more than one hundred slaves.[6] In the 1790s, Tucker, who had become a professor of law at William and Mary and a general court judge alongside Joseph Prentis, delivered a series of lectures whose purpose was to demonstrate the incompatibility of slavery with democracy. In 1796, he submitted to the Virginia General Assembly *A Dissertation on Slavery: With a Proposal for the Gradual Abolition of It in the State of Virginia*. He took his epigraph from Montesquieu: "Slavery not only violates the Laws of Nature, and of civil Society, it also wounds the best Forms of Government: in a Democracy, where all Men are equal, Slavery is contrary to the Spirit of the Constitution." Although he imagined that abolition would take a hundred years, Tucker denounced slavery as nefarious, hypocritical, and atrocious. He considered

> the Abolition of Slavery in this State, as an object of the first importance, not only to our moral character and domestic peace, but even to our political salvation. . . .
>
> Whilst America hath been the land of promise to Europeans, and their descendants, it hath been the vale of death to millions of the wretched sons of Africa. The genial light of liberty, which hath here shone with unrivalled lustre on the former, hath yielded no comfort to the latter, but to them hath proved a pillar of darkness, whilst it hath conducted the former to the most enviable state of human existence. Whilst we were offering up vows at the shrine of Liberty . . . we were imposing upon our fellow man, who differ in complexion from us, a *slavery*, ten thousand times more cruel than the utmost extremity of those grievances and oppressions, of which we complained." (Tucker v, 7)

As his biographer, Philip Hamilton, explains, Tucker "wished to eliminate slavery while not infringing the property rights of his fellow slaveowners. In his plan, he soothingly explained, 'The abolition of slavery may be effected without the *emancipation* of a single slave; without depriving any man of the *property* which he *possesses*, and without defrauding a single creditor who has trusted him on the faith of that property'" ("Revolutionary" 536). Despite his affirmation of property rights, his extremely gradual approach to abolition, and his articulation of blatant racism, the Virginia General Assembly reacted to his abolitionist proposal with virulent fury and tabled it without formally considering it or even referring it to committee.

Tucker would continue throughout his life to appease his conscience by voicing antislavery polemics, but he refused, both in his legal cases and in his personal life, to take concrete measures to free slaves. While Washington and Robert Carter III decided to manumit their slaves in their wills, Tucker followed Jefferson's path of denouncing slavery in philosophy but never in practice loosening his grip on his imagined right to own, buy, and sell human property. Indeed, just two days after submitting his proposal for abolition, Tucker engaged a Petersburg slave trader to sell four of his slaves—a mother and her three daughters—because he needed the cash. Well aware that the ruling class derived its power from land and slaves, he supported legislation to expand rather than diminish slaveholders' power. He "played a significant role on and off the bench in shaping" a community consensus affirming patriarchy, slavery, and white male citizenship as the social norm (Doyle 422). "Possessed of more than one hundred slaves, Tucker resisted the appeals of relatives to manumit in his will even favored household servants" (Doyle 423). Devoted to domestic patriarchy, the judge micromanaged the lives of his children, stepchildren, and much younger second wife. He professed revolutionary ideals of liberty and equality while clinging to ancient forms of deference and hierarchy.

In the 1790s, Joseph Prentis sat on the bench alongside Tucker and Joseph Jones in Virginia's district courts to hear a series of freedom suits brought by black, Indian, and racially mixed slaves. The judges denied most claims, awarding freedom primarily to those plaintiffs who looked Indian or white. In a legal opinion, Tucker explicitly demanded a higher burden of proof from dark plaintiffs than from fair-skinned petitioners. He established, with the collusion of Prentis and Jones, a "sliding scale of evidence based on skin color, hair texture, and facial variations" (Doyle 432). Between 1790 and 1800, these three judges awarded emancipation to nineteen Indians but only seven Negroes. The judges invoked past racist practices to find "a solution to the quandary posed by slavery and revolutionary ideals. It achieved a conservative balance between rights of liberty and property" (Doyle 433). Nefarious though slavery appeared to them, they were committed to preserving the inherited advantages of white men within the existing social stratification. As legal theorist Austin Sarat observes, "Law operates as much by shaping the way people understand the world as by coercing or rewarding them; that is, law's power is primarily ideological. [It] shapes society from the inside out by providing the principal categories in terms of which social life is made to seem largely natural, moral, cohesive" (134). Within the judicial system, Tucker and Prentis worked to articulate an ideological resolution to the tension between their era's rhetoric of liberty and practice of slavery in a manner that would promote the affect of genteel humanitarianism without threatening the property rights of white men.

In the spring of 1801, Margaret Prentis fell ill during a visit to Richmond. She declined for several months, too sick to return home. She wrote to her husband and children of her longing for them and for the flowers and fruits of Green Hill. She died in August, leaving her four surviving children motherless at the ages of eighteen, thirteen, ten, and five. Her desolate husband wrote a note in the family Bible: "22 yrs 8 mo. 12 days I have lived at Green Hill as a married man ought to live. 'Sleep on in peace; obey thy makers Will / Then rise unchanged; and be an angel still'" (Rockefeller Library). He buried Margaret in the northeast corner of his beloved garden and invited one of her sisters, Susan Bowdoin (b. 1773), to move from Northampton County into his household to help care for the children. The children, especially the girls, found comfort in the enduring presence of Rachel, their mammy.

Among his many worries after his wife's death, Prentis was anxious to ensure the enlargement of his daughters' minds. When Eliza was six he had given her as a New Year's present a copy of *The Rational Spelling-Book; or, An Easy Method of Initiating Youth into the Rudiments of the English Tongue*, published in Dublin in 1796. He inscribed it, "This book was presented to Eliza Prentis by her Papa, because she is a good little girl, and is fond of reading. January 1st 1798." Proud of the gift, Eliza wrote on the inside cover: "Elizabeth Prentis, her Book given by her PaPa." Four years later, she passed the book along to her little sister, who inscribed it in turn, "Mary Anne Prentis, Spelling Book presented her by

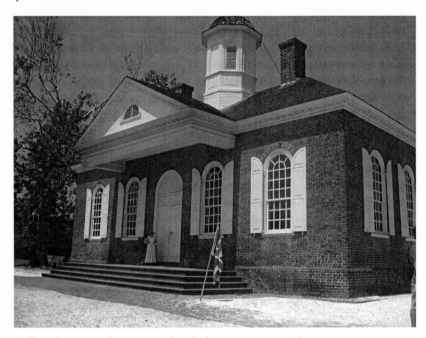

Williamsburg Courthouse on Duke of Gloucester Street. When court was in session, Joseph Prentis walked a few blocks from his house to the courthouse, while St. George Tucker simply walked across his front yard. Photograph by Kari J. Winter.

her Sister Eliza Prentis. April the 2, 1802."[7] Joseph Jr., Eliza, and Mary Anne studied diligently to master the liberal arts. Following his father, Joseph Jr. began reading law. Eliza grew into a young socialite obsessed with fashion and gossip, while Mary Anne became a dreamy, melancholic girl who longed to be useful to her family and society. She turned toward religion and to the devout Rachel for solace when she was haunted by illness, loneliness, and disappointment. As she grew, she developed a strong sense of concern for the sufferings of the poor and of slaves, but her compassion was intertwined with the high-handed self-pity and self-absorption of her class.

In contrast to his siblings, John chafed under polite constraints. He styled himself as "saucy Jack Prentis who is full of fun and play" (John B. Prentis to Joseph Prentis Sr., September 4, 1808, WPFP). An indifferent student, he neglected his books, preferring to develop his own opinions and to spend time outdoors with his dog, Fidel, and his black and white

Raleigh's Tavern on Duke of Gloucester Street. Photograph by Kari J. Winter.

playmates. The judge reproached John for his fondness for blacks, but the boy persisted in enjoying their company and in preferring physical to intellectual activity. Driven by a mixture of openness to others, skepticism about his family's values, feelings of inferiority, physical high spirits, and self-contempt, John developed a stubbornly egalitarian, antiaristocratic sensibility that enabled him to enjoy playmates of all colors. At the same time, when he felt out of sorts or inferior to his older brother, he may have found pleasure in the presence of playmates over whom he could exercise tyranny with impunity.

Although the role of spinster aunt and substitute mother could be awkward and stressful, Susan Bowdoin devoutly fulfilled her duties as mistress of the house. When she found the judge overbearing or disagreed with his views on parenting, finances, religion, or politics, she usually managed to keep her opinions to herself, as well-bred women were expected to do in the presence of men except insofar as self-expression manifested itself as polite banter or pleasing wit. She sustained an extensive network of social relations and encouraged the religiosity of her nieces and selected slaves, including Rachel. In April 1805, Lelia Skipwith Tucker, the second wife of St. George Tucker, described the Prentis household as a comfortably woman-centered space: "Yesterday we had a party at Mr. Prentis's, exactly to my tastes. About fifteen Ladies of my particular acquaintance, and not a gentleman, except a few little boys. You know I like now and then an assembly of petticoats, all quite at their ease" (Lelia Skipwith Tucker to Fanny Tucker Coalter, April 1805, Brown-Tucker-Coalter Collection).

The Prentis family hosted lavish parties, displaying a standard of elegance made possible by enslaved labor. In April 1806, William Wirt, a young lawyer whom President Monroe would appoint as U.S. attorney general in 1817, attended the wedding of a member of the Prentis family at Green Hill.

> I went last night to Miss P——'s wedding. The crowd was great, the room warm, the spirit of dancing was upon them, and the area so small that a man could not lift a foot without the hazard of setting it down upon a neighbour's. But then, by the way of balancing the account, there was a group of very gay and pretty girls. Miss P. herself, never looked so lovely before. She was dressed perfectly plain, wore her own hair, without wreath, laurel or other ornament. She had not a flower nor an atom of gold or silver about her: there was a neat pair of pearl pendants in her ears, but without any stone or metallic setting. Her dress a pure white muslin:—but she danced at least a hundred reels, and the roses in her cheeks were blown to their fullest bloom. You know she is a very pretty girl; but Sally C., who was also there seemed to bear off the bell. . . .
>
> But to the wedding. I went with the intention of seeing my friends, merely peeping into the supper-room, and coming home in an hour or two at farthest. But I got there about eight o'clock, and the dancing-room was so thronged as to be impenetrable without an exertion of strength which would have been very inconvenient to me in so warm a room, and much more inconvenient to those whom I might overset in my career. So, I watched the accidental opening of avenues, and it was an hour and a half, at least, before I had kissed the bride. . . .
>
> It was past eleven when the *sanctum sanctorum* of the supper-room was thrown open—although I don't know but that the designation of the *sanctum* would be better applied to another apartment in the house—and it was near twelve when it came to my turn to see the show. And a very superb one it was, I assure you. The tree in the centre cake was more simply elegant than any thing of the kind I remember to have seen. It

was near four feet high: the cake itself, the pedestal, had a rich—very rich—fringe of white paper surrounding it: the leaves, baskets, garlands, &c., &c., were all very naturally done in white paper, not touched with the pencil, and the baskets were rarely ornamented with silver spangles. At the ends of the tables were two lofty pyramids of jellies, syllabubs, ice-creams, &c.—*the which* pyramids were connected with the tree in the centre cake by pure white paper chains, very prettily cut, hanging in light and delicate festoons, and ornamented with paper bow-knots. Between the centre cake and each pyramid was another large cake *made for use*: then there was a profusion of meats, cheese-cakes, fruits, etc., etc. (Kennedy 133–35)

Wirt concluded, "All the grandees of the place were there." George Fisher, who had clashed with the "grandees of the place," including William Prentis, in the 1750s, noted the danger faced by anyone in Virginia who defied the power of the tightly knit ruling class. John Randolph had warned him "against disobliging or offending any person of note in the Colony . . . ; for says he, either by blood or marriage, we are almost all related, or so connected in our interests, that whoever of a Stranger presumes to offend any one of us will infallibly find an enemy of the whole" (George Fisher 123). Despite the political upheavals of the American Revolution, Virginia remained dominated by a few dozen families who intermarried, partied, drank, gambled, and legislated together. They claimed extravagant self-indulgence a birthright and a matter of family honor.

Valuing his daughters' education but not imagining that they would need or want careers, Judge Prentis sent Eliza and Mary Anne to boarding school, where they prepared for marriage or their social debuts, whichever came first. The judge held serious aspirations for his sons. Joseph Jr. was sent to the College of William and Mary to acquire the finest liberal arts education Virginia could offer. He would assume his father's mantle by practicing law, organizing his domestic life as an agrarian patriarch, and upholding the republican ideology that equated virtue with civic activity on behalf of what men of his social class presumed was the common good. By 1805, he had taken up residence in Suffolk, where he established a law practice. He and his father stayed in close contact, with the father insisting that the young man rely on paternal advice for guidance in life. "With the benefit of Experience on my part, I am the better able to judge of that conduct, by which [happiness] is most likely to be

Inscription by Eliza Prentis in the Prentis family Bible. Courtesy of the Colonial Williamsburg Foundation.

attained," the elder Prentis assured his son shortly after he left home (July 5, 1805, WPFP). In letter after letter, he emphasized that virtue was more important than wealth: "Surrender your business, your most flattering prospects, nay my dear Boy even your Life itself; sooner than your character to be lost" (March 5, 1806, PFP). The advice reflected the father's cherished image of himself as a loving man of high principles, but in his personal and professional judgments, when it came to the conflict between human rights and property rights, the judge always came down on the side of property. Joseph Jr. followed his example.

Judge Prentis worried about his younger son's prospects, writing to Joseph, "I fear that John has not that steadiness of mind, and evenness of manners which will promise himself Happiness in Life" (August 10, 1808, PFP). Averse to intellectual work, John begged his father to secure him an architectural apprenticeship. Prentis finally agreed, and John set off for Philadelphia for a five-year apprenticeship with a Quaker architect. After her brothers left home, nine-year-old Mary Anne penned affectionate letters to them, letters that lay bare the emotional dynamics of antebellum gender and race. "It seems to have been a year since I saw [Joseph] going from the house on his way to Suffolk, and when will my brother tell me to look out for his return again to Green Hill. Oh my dear Brother what would I give if I had your shirts to mend and to stop the holes in your small cloaths. It would give me great pleasure to do anything for you. . . . We every day look at the blanks where our Dear Brothers used to sit, but they have both left us. We have not heard of Brother John for a long time but hope every stage to hear he is well" (August 1, 1805, WPFP). Pining at home for boys and men who were off on adventures in the wide world was a posture that girls and women were socialized to assume at infancy. Both Mary Anne and Eliza readily understood that their path to emotional fulfillment, social respect, and material comfort lay in performing services for boys and men. Mary Anne's investment in this role exceeded her sister's. Extroverted Eliza embraced the social life of a belle. In March 1808, for example, she breathlessly described for her brother, Joseph, a grand ball she had attended: "We have had a most superb, and brilliant Entertainment in the old city, it was a called a *Wickham Party* or a *Squeeze*. I am sure if you were to guess a month, you could not tell where. I will no longer keep you in suspence, it was at Cousin Greenhows, in the new dining room, and quite in the Richmond style. All the world was there it appears to me. It was a general invitation, everybody was invited, & Mr. Greenhow said he felt quite happy, at seeing nearly the whole town of Wmsburg at his house. It was indeed a most splendid Ball, but much too crowded to be very agreeable" (March 9, 1808, PFP).

Mary Anne, in contrast, never recovered from the loss of her mother, writing letters that usually struck a mournful chord of loneliness, longing, and eagerness to please. She reproached herself as she aged for her inability to maintain the expected emotional detachment from slaves. She worried that her love for Rachel in particular violated the boundaries that her society deemed appropriate. Her affection, born out of emotional need for a comforting stable maternal presence, never blossomed into concern for Rachel's independent happiness and well-being or an appreciation of what Rachel's life meant to Rachel. Nonetheless, even as an adult, Mary Anne longed for Rachel's presence whenever they were apart. One of the last lines she wrote before her death was "Mammy Rachel is with me" (March 25, 1827, WPFP). Mary Anne had been trained from birth to expect a level of devoted, selfless service from slaves that both mirrored and exceeded what men expected from their wives and daughters. The value of both women and slaves was socially defined by their success in pleasing and serving their masters. In a revealing letter to her brother in Suffolk, little Mary Anne described how influenza had sickened her father, aunt, and sister, concluding with self-pity, "The black people are all sick, scarcely one to make up a bed, or cook a mouthful of dinner. These are distressing times" (September 20, 1807, WPFP).

CHAPTER 2   Apprenticeship

Be merry Peter, and feare not thy Master,
Fight for the credit of the Prentices.
—Shakespeare, Henry VI

"Dear Brother, I embrace this opportunity of writing these few lines to you to let you know that I arrived at Norfolk safe" (May 1805, WPFP). So opens John B. Prentis's voluminous correspondence to his family. In May 1805, at the age of seventeen, he set off to study architecture as an indentured apprentice in Philadelphia, stopping in Norfolk to catch a boat that would sail up the Atlantic Coast to the Delaware Bay and into the city of Philadelphia. John's prose was saturated with the values of his upbringing: effusive sentiment, eagerness to please, and a strong sense of duty to family, God, and country.

John quickly discovered that compared to Williamsburg, Philadelphia was a bustling metropolis. He loved to stroll in the evenings or on Sunday afternoons along narrow streets and broad avenues, alone or with mates, imbibing the sights, sounds, and smells of the city's pubs, cafés, water-ways, bridges, mansions, parks, gardens, and orchards. He was smitten by the smart clothes of the well-to-do. He lived and worked with a suc-cessful Quaker architect, Charles E. Smith, whose house and business were located two hundred yards from the corner of Sixth Street and Vine. With the Pennsylvania Legislature directing considerable state revenues to public works projects such as canals, turnpikes, and bridges, architec-tural companies were thriving. Charles Smith and his adult son, John, used many teenaged boys as apprentices. The boys learned how to design and build, beginning with small projects such as windows, sashes, shut-ters, and roofs and moving on to sheds, houses, churches, bridges, and large commercial and civic buildings. Their milieu fostered pride in their work. Partly as a result of the ideology of work promoted by Benjamin

The first extant letter written by John B. Prentis to his brother, Joseph Prentis Jr., 1805. Papers of the Webb-Prentis Families, 1735–1942 (accession #4136). Courtesy of Special Collections, University of Virginia Library.

Franklin, many Americans had grown to respect and even admire manual labor and commercial sagacity.

John Prentis expressed youthful pride and ambition in a letter asking his father to look after his tools back in Williamsburg. On his return home, he asserted proudly, he would use them "to make a handsome liveing with my labour and industry" (August 24, 1805, WPFP). While Joseph Prentis Sr. imagined a good society as one in which genteel intellectuals led their inferiors—manual laborers—toward virtue, his younger son viewed hard work and productivity as the signs of virtue and merit. He embraced the image of tradesman in training. He missed his old dog, Fidel, entrusted to his sisters' care, and his horse, entrusted to the care of a slave, Charles, but Prentis was pleased with his situation in Philadelphia—his "snug little room" with a small desk for his papers, letters, and books. He adorned his walls with a looking glass, his father's portrait, and likenesses of other relatives and friends. His early letters emphasized his gratitude that his father had given him permission to pursue his chosen line of work. Although Judge Prentis had hoped that his son would pursue a more cerebral profession, he eventually had used his social connections to secure John a spot as an architectural apprentice. John understood how highly his family valued liberal education, but his tastes ran toward hands-on work. "Give my love to sisters Elizabeth and Mary Anne," he wrote, continuing with a characteristic combination of self-laceration and self-assertion. "Tell Mary that she must be attentive to her learning not to be as careless about it as I was. Though I now plainly see the effects of not being attentive and paying that attention that I ought to have done when I had it in my power. . . . [A]ll my time and attention is taken up in learning the true art and mystery of the Carpenters trade for I never feel as contented as when I have a tool in my hand or studying the draft book which shews me how work ought to be done" (December 6, 1806, WPFP). He excused the infrequency of his letters with the explanation that his long work hours left him little time to read and write.

Apprentices typically worked six days a week from dawn to dusk and were subject to their masters' rules, whims, caprice, and punishments. Not only were apprentices not paid for their labor, they or their parents usually had to contribute money toward their room and board. Exploitative as the situation may seem to twenty-first-century readers, apprenticeships in skilled professions were coveted. Only boys lucky enough to

Miniature portrait of Joseph Prentis Sr. (1754–1809), possibly the one hung by John B. Prentis in his small room during his apprenticeship in Philadelphia. Courtesy of the Colonial Williamsburg Foundation.

come from well-connected families or to procure the favor of powerful people could obtain plum apprenticeships. Delighted by his success in obtaining his position, John initially viewed Charles Smith and his wife as wonderful substitute parents. John effused to Joseph Jr., "Believe me brother that I am as contented and happy as boy can be who has neither parents nor relations near him but I can safely say that I have a master and Mistress who is the same as a father and mother to me for all the boys say if there is any partiality shown either side it is shown more to us than to there own children" (October 20, 1805, WPFP).

During his first frosty Christmas season away from Virginia, John exclaimed to his brother "how comfortable and agreeable is it, that when we return home at night from the cold and fatigue of the day, there to find always a good fire and wholesome supper prepared for us, and good master and mistress who I can say does everything in their power for us so that our time may pass . . . agreeable." He continued in a manner that indicates his transference of bonds of affection and authority from his birth family to his new substitute family: "Whenever any of us is sick or get hurt from a fall or have a cut of any sort there is always the greatest care paid to us and perhaps more than if we [were] with our parents. As for my part brother I would not exchange my place not for the best in the world for I am sure . . . I could not find a place that would have suited me better in any respect than this place" (December 22, 1805, WPFP).

For John, familial affection was inextricable from authoritarianism. Ira Berlin aptly observes that "slavery stood at the center of economic production, and the master-slave relationship provided the model for all social relations: husband and wife, parent and child, employer and employee, teacher and student. From the most intimate connections between men and women to the most public ones between ruler and ruled, all relationships mimicked those of slavery" (8). John followed almost every invocation of affection with a declaration of his commitment to obedience, duty, and virtue. In December 1805, for example, he followed his expression of affection for the Smiths with characteristic pieties: "I can assure you dear brother that I will do all that I can do to obey them in every respect and do my duty if possible, for there is nothing brother that would hurt my feelings so much as for Mr. Smith or his Son to say that I would not mind them and do as I was bid. No brother far from it I hope that will never be the case for if it was I am sure that my poor father never would forgive me. . . . I thank Providence that my tender Father and brother that they cultivated my mind when young to know the proper conduct to pursue and now I intend to follow [their] good advice for I plainly see there is nothing like being obedient and dutiful to your master" (December 22, 1805, WPFP).

Charles Smith and his wife were devoted Quakers. Smith had formerly been a preacher and still occasionally took a month off from his business to travel and preach. John began to attend Quaker meetings with the Smiths on Sunday mornings. Within a couple of months, he began using the pronoun *thee* in place of *you* in his letters and demonstrating the Smiths' gentle antislavery influence on his thinking and politics. Despite his palpable craving for his father's and brother's approval, John began to allude to disagreements and discontent within the Prentis family circle that mirrored conflicts within the American body politic. In December 1805, after expressing hope that his father would always find his letters "agreeable and satisfactory," John explicitly identified race and slavery as long-standing bones of contention within his family and within his heart and mind. "Thee always seemed a little displeased at my working with the blacks but I can assure thee it is not the case now for I have not seen one black man Apprentice since I came to the City of Philadelphia. What is there more injurious to our trade in Virginia than the blacks. How much better dear father would our country be if it was not for those kind of people for where they are no person has the courage of a man to work having the poor slaves to drive that has to do the work that they themselves ought to do. I find father since I have been here that there is nothing better than to take after the quakers who are a plain moderate respectable religious people they consist of the largest society in this City and is respected the most" (December 6, 1805, WPFP). This passage outlines several of the vexed issues of labor, race, and slavery in nineteenth-century America. As a child surrounded by black laborers, some of them highly skilled, John early on developed a habit of "working with the blacks" that displeased his father's sense of propriety and social order. John perceptively pinpointed the ethics of labor as the heart of the question of slavery. Not only did "the poor slaves" suffer from violence and exploitation, but slaveholders destroyed their own better qualities by resorting to domination over others when they should have been seeking within themselves "the courage of a man to work." An ambitious young man who desired not only the money but also the satisfaction and self-esteem that come from work well done, John understood that the presence of violently exploited laborers poisoned the social meaning of work. In Philadelphia, he imbibed Franklin's communitarian work ethic, which was everywhere visible and tangible. He also drank in the liberalism of his host family. As Isaac Kramnick argues, liberalism, "at its origin, is an ideology of work. It attributes virtue to people who are industrious and diligent and condemns as corrupt privileged aristocrats and leisured gentle folk" (1).

In short, among Quakers in Philadelphia, most of whom opposed slavery, John found a work ethic that suited his tastes and ambitions. He also voiced an inherited set of political positions that had been most persuasively articulated by Franklin but also infused Virginian public discourse during the early decades of nation formation. In 1774, for example, the Continental Congress had instructed patriots to "discountenance and discourage every species of extravagance and dissipation . . . and other expensive diversions and entertainments." As Rhys Isaac explains, "The obligatory renunciation of important customary forms of social intercourse expressed a growing uneasiness at effete luxury among all ranks of free men. . . . Indebtedness, attributed in part to extravagant living, was seen to be more deeply responsible for the failure of craft industries to develop in Virginia. The absence of such industry—and of the frugality and virtue that it was believed to promote—was in turn ascribed to the importation of African servile labor in place of 'freemen and useful manufacturers'" (247). Perhaps because John did not want to offend his father by adopting an accusatory stance regarding the older man's betrayal of Revolutionary ideals—his lifelong practice of extravagance supported by slave labor and indebtedness—John held out the possibility that blacks might be to blame for Virginia's lack of industry. He vacillated between condemning blacks as "those kind of people" whose presence benighted the country and describing them as "the poor slaves" driven to work by lazy, cowardly, unmanly whites. Such befuddlement—Was slavery the source of corruption, or were blacks themselves the problem?—was not unique to seventeen-year-old John. He was channeling the ideological contradictions that the Revolutionary generation had failed to resolve, a toxic stew that soon would fuel the colonization movement. Most advocates of colonization wanted to rid the United States of slavery by returning all people of African descent to Africa. Implausible as it was to blame blacks for the evils of slavery, many whites found blaming the victims more charitable and less confrontational—in other words, less threatening to the social order—than blaming the creators and beneficiaries of slavery.

Quakers had been fighting slavery in Philadelphia since the mid-eighteenth century. "By 1758, prominent Philadelphia Quakers Anthony Benezet and John Woolman had convinced the Philadelphia Yearly Meeting to direct members not to buy or sell slaves. The meeting agreed to punish those who bought slaves, declared that slave-holding members should give up their slaves, and denounced all aspects of slavery" (Harris 50). In 1780, Pennsylvania enacted a gradual-emancipation law, but its complicated rules "kept slavery in Pennsylvania for decades after the statute was passed. In addition, many of the freed slaves and their children were forced into a form of long-term indentured servitude that resembled slavery" (Gordon-Reed 457). Philadelphia's thousands of blacks labored under oppressive conditions but nonetheless possessed more hope for the future than did blacks in Virginia. Black Philadelphians had reason to believe that they would benefit from the fruits of their labor. Although the city roiled with racism, especially during outbreaks of yellow fever such as the 1793 epidemic, African American leaders Richard Allen (1760–1831), Absalom Jones (1746–1818), and others were powerful antislavery and antiracism activists who founded churches, a school, an African Masonic Lodge, and mutual aid societies. Allen published an influential memoir, *The Life, Experience, and Gospel Labors of the Rt.*

Rev. Richard Allen, Written by Himself, in 1793. Several black preachers, writers, and educators from New York spent time in Philadelphia, as did free blacks and slaves who excelled in many arts, crafts, and professions. Thomas Jefferson's slave, James Hemings, who had mastered the culinary arts during years of study in Paris, was one of the city's top chefs in the 1790s (see Gordon-Reed). Despite Philadelphia's strong antislavery sentiment and accomplished black population, John Prentis discovered that whites and blacks lived and worked in more segregated patterns in the North than in the South. He had lived and worked in intimate albeit perverse proximity to black men and women in Williamsburg but found no black people among his Philadelphia coworkers.

For the first year of his apprenticeship, John found his work exciting and rewarding. Distance and a growing confidence in the wisdom of his life choices enabled him to articulate strong critiques of Virginian society. He told his father that Philadelphia offered far richer opportunities for learning his trade than could be found in Williamsburg. He "would like very well" to visit "the old place, but never to remain for long in it for fear I should catch some of the lazy practices which men is too apt to get there which ruins them" (February 1806, WPFP). His letters began to elaborate a central motif: the corruption and laziness of white southern slaveholders.

> What is there father that ruins our young Virginians that by the time they are [illegible] grown they are such Gentlemen that they can neather do one thing or another thats like work for fear of hurting themselves or be laugh at for so doing. But must call one of there servants to do it which they will drive and order about as if the poor servant had no feeling; forget there own laziness and that these feelings are alike. I hope father that thee will not be the least offended at my saying of the Virginians what I do, but I really do think and in fact know that they are wrong for haveing slaves in the state for they will be the ruin of that large and increasing state it twas once. This cannot be said of the young Pennsylvanians and jersey boys they have no poor slaves to wait upon them, but can be greater gentlemen & spend there time happier and more agreeable than them that have all the waiteing upon that infant requires. I plainly find father by experience that a person who works and always have something to keep there minds employed are always happier than them that does nothing from one years end to another. For I can say that since I have begun to work that I have never spent my time so agreeable as I do now when I have nothing to do

but to rise with the sun and go to work untill the going down of the same. For it makes me very hearty and healthy and grow at such a rate that I have out grown all my cloathes. (May 6, 1806, WPFP)

To his brother, John wrote, "I am of the same opinion with yourself concerning our old Williamsburg friends and acquaintances for they are such a conceited sett that they are too lazy to [do] any thing, though I believe brother that there is some of my age if they were sent away from that place to be brought up That they might be made men of" (September 28, 1806, WPFP). He would not have "the least idea" of returning to Virginia except for the fact that Virginia needed architects.

An outbreak of yellow fever in the hot days of August and September turned John's thoughts to the fragility of life and the realities of human interdependence. In September, he watched as a fire spread from the second floor of an eight-story building to three other houses, which were "burnt to ashes." He observed to his father, "It was very handsome to see the fire companys going home with there engines and hose," and so he decided, with his master's permission, to join the Perseverance Hose Company of volunteer firefighters, which comprised carpenters between the ages of eighteen and twenty-five (September 1806, WPFP).

By the end of his first year of apprenticeship, John was still assuring his father that he was conducting himself properly, keeping good company, and obeying "my preceptor's commands." Emphasizing how hard he worked, he seemed to chafe at having to ask his father to supply the necessities of life. By his third year in Philadelphia, his letters began to seethe with resentment at apprenticeship's exploitative conditions. In 1808, he suffered an emotional crisis after returning to Philadelphia from a visit home. He fumed to his father, "I have too much pride and the spirit of a man to be imposed upon by anyone or tyrannized over. It is my wish to do nothing but what is right and what would meet your approbation. You have been at the trouble and expense of sending me far distant from home for the purpose of getting my trade perfected, which I shall try my utmost . . . to do." He asserted that he was "fonder of Mr and Mrs Smith and better pleased with them than I ever have been before," but the old man had grown "whimsical and childish." John had frequent run-ins with an older apprentice and with Smith's sons. John and most of his fellow apprentices were in despair over a two-year project that they detested. The work was rough and dangerous for the apprentices but highly profitable to Smith. John and his peers felt so "discouraged" that they talked about "following the sea." Finally, John alarmed his father by declaring, "If it was not from my pledging my word and honour with my sister and from my expectations of doing well . . . and to comply with my fathers wish [I would follow] a seafaring life in preference to the present by a thousand times and should not hesitate one moment in going if it was not for disobeying a parents command" (May 24, 1808, WPFP).

The judge responded with a letter that cut John to the quick, as his reply made clear. "Dear father, Yours of the 3d was handed me on the 13th inst at dinner by Mr Smith, a letter father which came like a thunder bolt to my poor heart. Never never do I hope that my father shall ever have an occasion to write such another as long as we shall be separated which time seems long to me. Little did I think it of ever occasioning my beloved parent so much uneasiness and trouble as he seems to express in his letter to his poor boy who has truly repented [that] he should have made use of the words that has occasioned such an answer as to cause his poor little heart to break with grief and sorrow to think that he had caused his father to write him so severe an answer." Assuring his father that he would always obey his master and mistress, John continued, "I can boast of never haveing an angry word spoke to me on my account by either and of being praised by my master as being industrious and the easiest boy to manage that ever he had. . . . I never should have supposed father that you would have said of me that I hated work. I always thought and expected that you had formed a better opinion of your son than to have imagined that he hated work it hurts me" (June 13, 1808, WPFP).

A few weeks later, John described himself as his father's "absent sun burnt child who is as brown as an indian full of life and spirit" (July 31, 1808, WPFP). He vacillated between high spirits and a tone of mourning over the death of a fellow apprentice, Thomas Stout, an orphan who had drowned in the Delaware River while swimming after eating a heavy dinner. Philadelphia was losing its charm. The summer of 1808 was the hottest in memory, and according to John, Philadelphians had experienced "82 sudden deaths from drinking cold water" (July 31, 1808, WPFP). Expressing more and more homesickness, John longed for the company of "an intimate friend whom I think very highly of," a "sweet object that lives not far distant" from Green Hill who had written to him often for two or three years before her letters tapered off (John B. Prentis to

Joseph Prentis Sr., September 4, 1808, February 12, 1809, WPFP). When she married someone else, John experienced an anguish that endured for several years.

Philadelphia was beginning to jar his nerves as a "noisy City" (John Prentis to Joseph Prentis Sr., February 12, 1809, WPFP) full of economic hardship and political strife caused by Jefferson's Embargo Act of 1807, which banned international trade to and from American ports. John suffered from various injuries and illnesses and witnessed alarming epidemics of yellow fever. He suspected that his father had heard complaints about his behavior or his associates. His father and brother had long been warning John to avoid bad company. In 1805, Joseph Jr. had advised John to stay away from "a certain female race," by which he could have meant either black women or prostitutes. John replied, "I thank thee for the caution you gave me. . . . Thank Providence that my mind is well guarded against such an unworthy and unhonorable character as them and God forbid that I should even live to see the day come to such a fate as that for I am sure it would not only ruin my Character for ever but break the heart of my tender and affectionate Parent. I hope my dear Brother that time will never come for if it was it would bring trouble upon my relations for ever and ever" (October 20, 1805, WPFP). In 1809, John responded to stern warnings from his father by admitting that ruin could come to "a boy my dear father placed a great distance from home for the space of some years especially in such places as this a large and extensive City where all kinds of characters may be found to ruin and lead to destruction . . . a tender youth whose mind will be bent any way without he has a tender father to give him admonition" (April 16, 1809, WPFP). But he protested that Smith offered good guidance; John honored and esteemed his master, and John's character was spotless and widely admired: "I have many friends and acquaintances about this place that I never should have had if it was not from my Character that I have gained throughout the people whilst in office in my society I acted to the best advantage to gain credit and always spoke my opinion with firmness" (April 16, 1809, WPFP).

Hurt, defensive, and somewhat incoherent, John would never have a chance to clear the air with his father. In June, while John was hard at work framing a store, the judge died. On Friday, June 23, 1809, the *Virginia Argus* published the obituary: "Departed this life on the 18th day of this month, after a long and painful illness the Hon. JOSEPH PRENTIS, of Williamsburg, late a Judge of the general court, aged 57 years. He possessed all the characteristics of an honorable man. . . . He left two amiable Daughters and two sons." The judge's will, written in 1807, testified to his self-image as a benign, loving patriarch and a trusting soul devoted to God, family, and community. He repressed mention of anything—such as slavery or familial conflicts—that might sully his understanding of his beneficent role in a beautiful universe ordered by God.

I acknowledge my most unbounded love, and confidence towards my two dear boys, Jos. Prentis and John B. Prentis, they are incapable of doing anything unworthy of themselves, or of behaving in any manner unworthy of that love and affection they bear towards their sisters Eliza or Mary Anne. I feel that conviction of their virtue, that I devise all my estate of every sort in truth to be divided by them into four equal parts, one for Jos., one for John, one for Eliza, and the remaining fourth for my Mary Anne. This will be sufficient direction for my boys, and altho' this paper may be viewed, as my last will, there will be no necessity to have it proved in court or to qualify as Exors thereto, without my boys may incline to do so. There need be no Inventory of my personal estate, unless my sons may think it proper to show that they have acted properly in the disposition thereof. It is my intention that my dear children shall equally share what property I may leave, as they are equally entitled, and most certainly share my love and affection.

It is my wish that such part of my Estate as my sons may chuse may be sold and the money applied towards the payment of all my Debts. This must be done as soon as can be after my death, and the surplus applied to the benefit of my dear children. This will not probably be of much importance because it cannot be considerable. My children have all of them been Educated in pious Habits and it has been more an object with me to instil into their minds a proper sense of their duty towards their God, and towards man than to acquire wealth for their disposal. The one is a never failing source of delight, the other fleeting and transitory.

I give to my friend and neighbor Mrs Skipwith as a proof of my affection and Love my spectacles. They are in themselves very trifling but as a Momento I know they will sometimes call me to her recollection, also the Chinese picture in the parlour. To my friend her Husband, I give my Ploughs Harrows [illegible]. I give to my friend Alex. Green my riding Horse saddle and bridle, he will value him as a proof of that regard which I have ever had for an honest and worthy man. The world abounds with these characters and they may be found without a lanthern. I know no man who merits the title in a greater degree than Alex. Green and I beg him to believe that I have often lamented his misfortunes most sincerely but my situation in life only allowed me to lament them, not to relieve them. My two sons will execute this trust with fidelity. If this paper is to be called my will and to go thro the usual formalities of Courts, I desire they may not be called on for security as Exors. My mind revolts at the Idea of requiring security from those for whom I have the most unbounded affection and love, and who have received from their Father such an education, and have such a proper sense of rectitude and integrity as to be incapable of deviating from it. I devise to them the care of their two sisters and I know they will value this bequest, as the most affectionate Brothers ought to do. It has pleased an all wise Providence to protract my life longer than I had expected, this period has been devoted in preparing myself for my Dissolution, and improving the minds of my children. The first event I trust will be marked by calmness, tranquility and resignation to the will of Heaven. The second object has had my constant and unwearied exertions, and I trust my efforts have not been un[suc]cessful.

I beg my dear children to recollect the anxious solicitude their Father has expressed so often for their Happiness. However unfashionable it may be to neglect the admonitions of those having more experience in life, yet I hope they will have the good sense and prudence to profit by these counsels. Pursue the path into which your dear Father has placed you. The road to Happiness and respectability is the road to virtue, your Happiness will be secured here and a state of bliss awaits you hereafter.

My Boys will not suffer their intercourse with the world to corrupt the purity of their Hearts. Hold fast those virtuous principles already inculcated in your Hearts, nor suffer the least deviation from the principles of integrity and Honesty. Recur to the many letters you have received from me, replete with advice calculated to make you men of Honesty and integrity and view them as tending to these great objects. Your Happiness is my Happiness and so long as my heart retains its motion, so long will the prosperity and Happiness of all my children, retain its seat there.

After my death let my body be kept until certain indications of death shall have manifested themselves unequivocally, then let it be decently interred near that of your dear mother, in a plain pine coffin without pomp or parade, a few friends may be invited to attend the ceremony of Christian burial, they may possibly benefit by the occasion. I feel disposed to say something as to my spirit. I do believe most confidently that it will go also to the regions of Bliss. I feel the conviction of my own insignificance and unimportance on a general scale, but through the intercession

and merits of my saviour Jesus Christ, who suffered for mankind, I derive
consolation impressed on my heart, which is the source of the greatest
delight. My spirit will return to him who gave it, and I shall be judged by
a merciful and good god in a happier world.
   Jos. Prentis
(Will of Joseph Prentis Sr., October 7, 1807, WPFP)

As a judge and legislator whose career had spanned three of the republic's foundational decades, Prentis had helped to constitute the laws
of Virginia, including its slave codes. Since slavery was an integral part of
the social system, participation in it did not sully his reputation. He had
formed enduring relationships with his peers, one of whom recalled him
after forty-five years of friendship as "an honorable man, an affectionate
parent, and a charitable and benevolent man, religious without fanati-
cism, undeviating in his moral and political course, and truly attached
to republican principles" (Binney 344). The judge's commitment to a
sentimental notion of self and family—his fragrant cloak of sanctity—required severe forms of internal denial and repression. Although an astute
lawyer, he attempted in his last will and testament, a legal document, to
exclude the (dirty, public, contestatory) legal system from involvement
in settling his estate. Ironically, this attempt to exclude the law gave his
trusted son, Joseph Jr., an ambitious young lawyer, the legal latitude to
manipulate the estate while maintaining a self-image just as pristine as
his father's.
   One of the deepest repressions in the judge's will was the omission
of any mention of the human beings enslaved in his household. William
Prentis, Joseph's father, had named slaves in his will; Joseph's uncle, Robert, mentioned slaves. But Joseph Sr.'s tender conscience precluded any
mention whatsoever of them. They would be sold alongside nonhuman
pieces of property at the estate sale over which Joseph Jr. would preside.
Perhaps the judge could not bring himself to name the aspects of his
life that threatened the beautiful dream he wanted to uphold. As Saidiya
Hartman observes in relation to both the patriarchal family and slavery,
"Kindness and affection undergirded the relations of subordination and
dependency. As a model of social order, the patriarchal family depended
on duty, status, and protection rather than consent, equality, and civil
freedom" (*Scenes* 89).

Judge Prentis's fear of being buried alive was a popular nineteenth-century phobia that Edgar Allan Poe would cast in "The Fall of the House of Usher" as a symptom of cultural unease regarding the suppression, or living death, of women in the patriarchal house. To allay his anxieties, Prentis reassured himself of the goodness of a God who shared his values and would judge him mercifully. His expressions of humility and his desire for a simple burial without "pomp or parade" suited the personality inherent in his writing. His genteel lifestyle had been saturated with an elegance and luxury that enabled as well as contradicted his humane, unassuming persona. In his loving manner, he stated his expectation that his will would continue to direct his children's lives. He described the letters he wrote to his sons throughout their lives as a deliberate bequest—a premeditated archive—through which he intended to remain present.

Joseph Jr. had established himself as a lawyer in the town of Suffolk, which had more demand for legal services than did early nineteenth-century Williamsburg. After the capital moved to Richmond, the formerly vibrant metropole was becoming a quaint village. The exhilarating Revolutionary days of their father's early career had faded into legend. Although Virginians still controlled the White House, the American centers of population, power, and culture were shifting northward to New York, Philadelphia, and Boston. On January 13, 1810, six months after his father's death, twenty-seven-year-old Joseph married nineteen-year-old Susan Caroline Riddick. John sent congratulations from Philadelphia, but questions about how the estate was to be settled had higher priority than the marriage. Responding to Joseph's question some months earlier about whether John was concerned about dividing up the family's slaves, the younger brother wrote, "On what is to be done with the slaves, I have made myself easy on that head." He was concerned only about one slave, Hannah, and he thanked Joseph for "for your kindness in keeping the said slave untill I return." Having dispensed with the matter of dividing slave property, he continued by voicing pieties about the value of marriage: "I congratulate you my dear fellow of much pleasant health and happiness wishing you may enjoy that real conjugal affection that ought allways to be found with a happy couple. It tis a very serious period in a mans life in passing through to meet with a virtuous prudent affectionate companion. . . . Wealth or beauty does not constitute happiness one may be exhausted with extravagance and the other may be taken and vanished through pride. Remember me to my new Sister. I only wish she may be a prudent affectionate wife to her deserving companion" (February 4, 1810, WPFP). John then mentioned that he had "left my old master and got to work for myself. . . . I expect you will send me the means of leaving this City but how or when I shall leave it I know not." Facing a critical period of transition from apprenticeship to independence, John needed money, but Joseph was inclined to be tightfisted.

In April 1810, ten months after their father's death, the four siblings endured the spectacle of their childhood home put up for sale. Joseph did not appear to suffer from nostalgia for either the house or his father's beloved gardens. His dreams focused on the possessions he hoped to gain from the sale: twenty-six slaves. As Walter Johnson observes, slavery was profoundly related to fantasies of the self. When slaveholders "talked about and wrote about buying slaves," they "dreamed of people arrayed in meaningful order by their value as property, of fields full of productive hands and a slave quarter that reproduced itself, of well-ordered households and of mansions where service was swift and polished. They dreamed of beating and healing and sleeping with slaves; sometimes they even dreamed that their slaves would love them. They imagined who they could be by thinking about whom they could buy" (78–79). The precision of Joseph's list of the types of slaves he desired reveals that he devoted significant time to imagining elaborate details of the good patrician life and the ideal paternal self who would wield immense interpersonal power. The *Williamsburg Enquirer* advertised the estate sale on April 24, 1810:

ADVERTISEMENT The subscriber is authorized to offer for sale, the neat and convenient HOUSE, Garden and Appurtenances in Williamsburg; lately the property of Joseph Prentis, Esq. deceased, with several adjoining LOTS OF LAND, under enclosures, and some adjacent LAND, containing in the whole, from twenty to twenty five acres, for which Negroes of the description herein after mentioned will be taken in payment. An undoubted title will be made to the premises, by the executor and devisees of the late Judge Prentis. He is also authorised to purchase a number of SLAVES of the following descriptions: one Blacksmith; two house Carpenters; two brick makers; one Brick layer; two men used to a saw mill; six expert axemen; four plantation men; a good Cook; a dining-room servant; a driver and hostler; a washer-woman; a dairy-woman; a lady's servant, and a seamstress.—Any person who is willing to purchase the above mentioned Houses and Lots, and will undertake to furnish Slaves of the above description, will be allowed a generous price for them, and paid in cash, or in undoubted bills on Philadelphia, at not more than ninety days sight, for whatever balance may remain due after deducting the price of the houses, lots and premises, first above mentioned.

JOHN BROCKENBROUGH.

Joseph's fantasies were not realized as quickly as he hoped. Green Hill and its gardens were sold to a family acquaintance, Evelina Louisa Barbe Skipwith, the wife of Fulwar Skipwith, who had been a U.S. consul in Paris, governor of West Florida, and slaveholding planter in Louisiana. The judge's friend and neighbor, Henry Skipwith, negotiated the sale on behalf of his sister-in-law, and he paid not with slaves but with cash— "£925 current money of Virginia," to be precise (Bill of Sale, April 20, 1812, qtd. in Mary A. Stephenson, "Lots" 21). Joseph and John Prentis were present at the closing. The bill of sale asked the purchaser to preserve as a graveyard the "square of ground in the north East Corner of the Easternmost Garden" where Joseph and Margaret Prentis were buried.

Before finding a buyer for the house and land, Joseph arranged an estate sale for the remainder of his father's fungible property.

On Monday, the 31st of July, will be sold, At the Dwelling-House of the late Joseph Prentis, in the City of Williamsburg, The PERSONAL ESTATE of the said deceased. The Sale will be continued from day to day until the whole, or a greater part of the personal Estate is Sold. There will be some valuable Household and Kitchen Furniture and Plate for Sale; and it is probable several House Servants will also be Sold. There are several Milch Cows, two Horses, and a neat single Phaeton and Harness quite new.

The Sale will be made on a credit of nine months, to bear interest from the date, and if the payment is punctually made, the interest will be remitted.—Bond and approved security will be required from the purchasers before any article which may be sold is delivered.

JOSEPH PRENTIS, Exc'r.

Williamsburg, July 1

(*Williamsburg Enquirer*, July 1, 1809, PFP)

Judge Prentis had owned ten slaves: Hannah; Rachel and her daughter, Lucy; Ellick; Pinah; Ben; Leah and her daughter, Sally; Effy; and Pompey. These ten human beings whom the Prentis children most likely had known all of their lives were sold to six different people at the estate sale along with other items. From his father's estate, John apparently desired only Hannah—and cash. According to Joseph's records, John paid for Hannah with $100 of his inheritance, and he did not receive any other noncash items from Joseph Prentis Sr.'s estate. The archive does not reveal if she served him as a mother substitute who cooked, cleaned, washed clothes, and otherwise did his bidding, or if she was a young woman from whom he extracted additional services. Joseph used $200 of his inheritance to retain Rachel and Lucy. For $250 each, Henry Skipwith bought the gardeners Ellick and Pinah to go with the gardens on which they had labored with great success for decades. Ben, a strong healthy boy whose parents went unnamed by Joseph Jr., was sold to John Y. Tabb for $300. Tabb also purchased Leah and Sally for $300. Effy was sold to John Taliaferro for $80; the low price suggests she was a child or an elder and/or may have been sickly. Pompey was sold to Ben C. Waller for $250. It is not clear why Joseph, who had hoped to obtain twenty-six new slaves from the sale of Green Hill, did not attempt to keep the rest of his father's slaves. Breaking up enslaved families and communities was one of the most infamously cruel aspects of slavery, and it did not fit well with the self-image of benign paternalism, yet Joseph clearly imagined that new slaves would suit him better than familiar ones, and he readily cast aside whatever qualms he had about ripping apart the existing community.

The judge's other possessions testified to his love of luxury. His debts equaled four-fifths of the value of his assets, apart from his house and land. His neighbors far and wide were intrigued by the prospect of purchasing his lavish collection of furniture, china, linens, and other goods. James Madison, Samuel Tyler, Robert Saunders, John Peyton, and Henry Skipwith were among the many prominent men and family friends who shopped at the sale. Joseph shopped for himself and his sisters; John acquired next to nothing. Joseph may have secretly sequestered some items for himself and his siblings; he and his sisters kept most of the family library, for example, and most of the books were not mentioned in the estate sale ledger, although sixty-five individual titles, one complete set and two "broken sets" of magazines, and a "parcel of old books of no value" were itemized in the estate's inventory. Comparing what Joseph acquired with what his sisters got illuminates the hierarchical family dynamics as well as the material culture of turn-of-the-century Williamsburg.

Joseph Jr. purchased from his father's estate

1 large basket
7 wine glasses
1 rim & cartons
1 cream bucket and spoon
a mustard pot
a pair sugar tongs
12 silver table spoons
2 silver ladles
11 teaspoons
1 silver can
1 bed, bedstead & co. complete
1 clothes press
1 silver rim
1 paper press
12 windsor chairs
1 lot tinware
1 set tongs & finder, 2nd choice
1 set tongs & finder, 3rd choice
1 knife box & knife & fork
1 mortar and pistle
1 pair sealer & weights
1 grater & decanter
2 sculpture peices
clutter [illegible]
1 bread table
liquer café
Chimney ornaments parlour
4 pr. sheets
6 linen diaper towells
8 cotton towells
1 sm. cotton table cloth
1 wash basin cracked
1 set tea china
1 table
7 walnut chairs
12 mahogany chairs
5 windsor chairs
a pair moneyscales & weights

1 chaffing dish
1 lot tea china
4 waiters (3 wood)
1 lot dishes & plates & tureen
1 pair flat candlesticks
1 tea kettle, iron
2 tubs
1 green bedstead, 1st choice
a baking hoe
2 spits
1 pot & 2 pr. pot hooks
spice mortar and pistle
1 Bile metal skillet
1 grid iron
1 spoon & frying pan
1 pair blankets

Mary Anne acquired

1 pr. candlesticks & snuffer stand
1 sm. waiter

Eliza acquired

1 sugar bowl
1 large waiter
1 press for papers

Eliza and Mary Anne jointly purchased

1 bedstead & co complete (small room)
1 pair blankets (Account Book, PFP)

The Prentis siblings retained less than a quarter of the total goods sold to shoppers at the estate sale.

The execution of the remaining estate did not proceed smoothly. As the settlement dragged on, Joseph wrote memoranda to himself that reveal grief and bewilderment as well as a self-aggrandizing assumption of control over the estate and over his sisters. In 1811, he entered in his Suffolk account book,

Memo

    The death of my dear father having produced a thorough revolution in his beloved family, it has become not only my duty, but inclination to take care of my beloved infant sisters, whom I have adopted as my children. My residence and circumstances in life forbid that I should keep the establishment. I am of opinion under the Will, that his sons have the power to dispose of his real estate.—My brother and self have accordingly sold Green Hill, and the Gardner Ellick to Henry Skipwith, for the sum of £1000—which was, adjudged by every body a most advantagious sale—The price of Ellick £75 is credited on my account of administration—The proceeds of the Sale of G.H. has been disposed of in the following manner, ¼ I have paid to My brother John, ¼ to my sister Eliza, and have taken their discharges—¼ credited on my guardian's account with my sister Mary Anne, and which will be ready for her when she has the legal ability to demand the same and the remainder ¼ belonging to Myself, I have retained. (Account Book, PFP)

Although his sisters were legally minors—Eliza was twenty and Mary Anne fifteen—Joseph's insistence on infantilizing them indicates how the role of loving patriarch enabled him to repress recognition of the financially self-interested and emotionally overbearing nature of his behavior. The difference between his records of the amount he received for Ellick—$250 and £1000 minus a £75 credit to himself for administration—could indicate confusion resulting from the instability of international currencies or could show that Joseph, like many bookkeepers in his day, still did mathematical calculations more readily in shillings and pence than in dollars and cents. It also could indicate that Joseph was keeping more money for himself than he told his siblings. In any case, the family's anxieties were intensified by Jefferson's embargo on British goods, which would escalate into the War of 1812. Joseph did not finish selling off his father's assets and paying his debts until January 1813. The court then determined that each sibling should receive the equivalent of $770.03 in slaves, goods, and/or cash from the sale of the house and lands of Green Hill and $240.44 from the rest of estate, but it would take Joseph another fifteen years to finish paying his siblings their shares.

    Despite strains within the family system, the Prentises remained besotted with rhetoric of family values. Joseph continued to function for decades as an emotional anchor for his siblings, or so the archive suggests;

our sense of his centrality may be magnified by the fact that he and his descendants saved the letters they wrote to him, whereas most of his letters to them and their letters to each other have vanished. In any case, "family" was increasingly constructed as "a model and a metaphor for the youthful nation. Republican leaders held up the family as an incubator of civic and political values—of virtue and affection—deemed essential to the welfare of the republic" (Amy Taylor 8). Like its companionate terms *love* and *freedom*, the ideological elixir of *family values* increased in potency during the course of the early nineteenth century. The Virginian ruling class was in full retreat from the Revolution's natural rights ideology. As Philip Hamilton observes, "Domestication and sentimentalism began to spread soon after most Virginians retreated from reform" (*Making* 545). To sweeten their betrayal of their former ideals, the cultural elite elaborated the forces of sentimentality—racial paternalism and the cult of true womanhood—that strengthened the bonds of the family, black and white.

CHAPTER 3 Brotherly Collusions

> If most books on the topic of American subjectivity have focused on
> the possessive individual, it would be fair to say that mine examines
> the collectively haunted individual: the individual who does not exist
> unless in an ongoing, reciprocal relationship with an other in which the
> boundaries between self and other, past and present, alive and dead
> are constantly being negotiated. The collaborative self is produced and
> perpetuated only through participation in an economy of emotions in
> which affections circulate in the form of gifts to bind disparate persons
> together into subjects able to recognize themselves and act on the world.
> —Mary Louise Kete, *Sentimental Collaborations*

Possessing one slave and a few personal items, twenty-two-year-old
John B. Prentis felt dispossessed, bereft, and anxious about his future.
Aching with desire to possess his dream of the good life, he decided that
Richmond, a familiar city in which his family was known and respected,
offered the best prospects for professional success. A picturesque town
on gentle hills, Richmond had supplanted Williamsburg as the capital of
Virginia in the late eighteenth century and would become the capital of
the Confederacy in 1861. On Prentis's arrival in 1810, it was burgeon-
ing into a cultural, commercial, and manufacturing entrepôt connecting
Virginia's rural plantations and farms via roads and waterways to the eastern seaboard and the Atlantic world. Produce, manufactures, slaves, and
travelers passed in and out of boats, wharves, warehouses, and wagons
clustered along the James River. The Virginia General Assembly met in
Richmond annually from December to March, and party passions were
fueled by the city's competing newspapers, the *Richmond Gazette* and the
Richmond Whig. The city had grown to ten thousand people, more than
half of them black. About one-fifth of the black residents were free. Alliances among free blacks, slaves, and poor whites, whether commercial,
social, sexual, religious, or political in nature, troubled the ruling class.

Prentis was intimately familiar with Richmond's history of racial strife. On August 30, 1800, Virginia governor James Monroe alerted John's uncle, Petersburg mayor William Prentis, that a slave insurrection was in the works. Monroe had received reports that between five hundred and five thousand slaves were conspiring to revolt under the leadership of Gabriel, a tall, scar-faced man who was a skilled blacksmith owned by tobacco planter Thomas Prosser. Two slaves betrayed the conspiracy to their master, who in turn notified the governor. Monroe called in the state militia, which squelched the revolt before it was launched. On October 11, Monroe notified William Prentis that Gabriel's conspiracy had been repressed. News of the conspiracy unleashed a bloodbath of white rage. "Area courts tried approximately seventy men and convicted forty-four. Twenty-six or twenty-seven were hanged in public executions; others were either pardoned by the governor and his council, or their sentences were commuted to transportation outside of the United States" (Sidbury 8). After eluding capture for a month, Gabriel was hanged in Richmond on October 10, 1800. Governor Monroe established a public guard to protect the city from further insurrections, but white Virginians continued to exude racial anxiety in newspapers, letters, diaries, speeches, and acts of violence. The Richmond City Common Council debated a stream of legislation aimed at limiting the rights of free blacks as well as slaves to sell goods in the city market; to drive wagons, drays, and carts; to ride in carriages; to drink in tippling shops; and to conduct "tumultuous assemblies . . . in the streets of our City on Sundays," among other measures. The legislators also sought to expand the elites' power to indenture "poor children whose parents were raising them in habits of idleness or vice, especially free black children" (Sheldon 34, 38).

On January 3, 1802, Monroe forwarded to William Prentis a letter warning of another slave revolt. The governor could not vouch for the accuracy of the rumor but thought it should be taken seriously. Mayor Prentis replied on January 5, requesting the appointment of an officer to supervise the guarding of Petersburg and the provision of ammunition for his militia. Enslaved boatmen who worked on the Appomattox and Roanoke Rivers were organizing a rebellion but were betrayed by a slave named Lewis. Monroe asked President Thomas Jefferson if the conspirators, who had been thrown in a penitentiary, could be shipped to Sierra Leone. Jefferson replied that the Sierra Leone Company accepted only freed slaves, not insurgents. Monroe then considered transporting

View of Richmond, 1819. Watercolor. Courtesy of the Virginia Historical Society.

the men to the West Indies. The Virginia Assembly enacted draconian legislation, banning education and hiring out of slaves and requiring freed slaves to leave the state or face reenslavement unless they petitioned the legislature for special permission to remain. (For Monroe's correspondence, see Preston.) However, Virginia laws regarding slavery were in a constant state of turmoil and contestation, and the ban on hiring out was short lived and difficult to enforce.

To the elite's dismay, Richmond's labor force remained transnational and multilingual, and the number of free blacks continued to rise. German and Irish immigrants exerted significant influence on the urban landscape, but the majority of Richmond's workers were slaves of multicultural African, Caribbean, and American origins. In many parts of the Americas, only the elite could afford to own slaves; in Richmond, however, "approximately two-thirds of the households had slaves" (Sheldon 30). They labored either directly for their masters or as hired hands, with their wages usually going primarily or completely to their masters. Slaves worked alongside both free blacks and poor whites as barbers, blacksmiths, butlers, carpenters, clothiers, confectioners, cooks, coopers, fishermen, gardeners, grocers, hucksters, maids, milliners, porters, prostitutes, sail makers, saloon keepers, shoemakers, valets, waiters, and washerwomen. They built roads, bridges, canals, and houses and worked in ironworks, brickworks, and tobacco factories. The relative autonomy and mobility integral to many of these forms of employment heightened slaveholders' racial anxieties. Black women typically performed types of domestic work that granted them little mobility, but black men's relative freedom of movement as sailors, boatmen, and draymen enabled them to steal, transport stolen merchandise, carry news between rural and urban blacks, and engage in political conspiracies, organized crime, and other subversive activities. Freedom of movement always threatened slavery's efficacy, and slaveholders chronically worried about it. In 1807, for example, a newspaper essayist writing under the nom-de-plume Paternus protested that Richmond was endangered by the presence of "at least 1,000 black men regularly employed either in bringing produce to the city on the canal or in transporting goods from the basin to Rocketts on drays" (Sidbury 172).

John Prentis soon sent a vexed letter to his brother, Joseph, who, John fumed in a rare moment of candid resentment, had always treated his younger brother like a stranger. Looking for a business partner, John worried that no one could be trusted, implying that experience had cast doubts on even his brother's honesty. Hoping that success in the commercial world would prove his worth and virtue, he warded off low self-esteem with belligerent pride, casting his lot emotionally with the white male working class. His letter roiled with rage, disappointment, betrayal, longing, pride, love, hope, and ambition.

> I frequently my dear fellow suffer a gloomy moment to pass with me
> as a very surprising and at this period uncommon *instance* remains with
> us. During my youthfull days of a faithfull apprenticeship writing to my
> relations was an arduous task. My occupation destroys the use of the hand
> entirely of writing which I dislike much. The little correspondence that
> ever has been between us has always been with as much [illegible] from
> you to me from myself in answer the same as two men strangers to each
> other transacting business together. It is true we have been a long time
> weened from each other. . . . On our meeting each other it tis allways
> with the pleasing sensation of joy and gladness. Yet we cannot unbosom
> ourselves confide with each other our pleasures, future prospects not the

least sign of pleasure and felicity. We both always appear distant and cool of counseling together and when we did our opinions were different,

You never knew or learned from me my different intentions about business, and then my dear fellow we both misunderstood each other entirely and we remained in the dark because I did not feel myself under obligations of some in Williamsburg where I ask no favors. (November 7, 1810, WPFP)

John rarely called such explicit attention to fissures and pain within his family. He craved his brother's approval and financial assistance but was too proud to demand his fair share of their father's estate and too emotionally dependent to let the crevice of cool distance become an unbreachable chasm. He again fantasized about escaping to the adventure of a life at sea, admitting, "It is true I applied for a berth under Captain Bright in the Cutter but there was no vacancy. I had some little expectation of going to New Orleans though I was persuaded to remain near my old abode." Frustrated and angry, he explained how much he would benefit from assistance: "I have a very pretty prospect of doing business next year on my own factory. If I can possibly do it I certainly shall if I could find a friend to assist me in the beginning. I must if I can possibly find out any means to do it purchase myself a likely boy to learn the business though prices is very high here my chance will be [illegible] in the country." Eager to obtain sufficient funds to purchase "a likely boy" to help him in the building trade, John buried his moral qualms about slavery. Using the logic of capitalism, he intended to leverage the short-term profit from a slave sale into funds to purchase a boy who would help increase John's long-term profit margin. John did not at this stage view slave trading as a full-time occupation; he was merely continuing the long-standing practice in his family and virtually all slaveholding families of selling or buying slaves when cash flow problems arose, when a labor shortage or overage was perceived, or when a particular slave had provoked anger or desire. Asking Joseph to be his "copartner," John explained his motive for slave trading in as matter-of-fact a tone as if the person for sale had been tobacco or an armchair. "If you have not sold the boy staying with Anderson I could sell him here for more than he will sell for there" (November 7, 1810, WPFP).

Joseph already had extensive experience in slave trading despite the fact that society viewed him as a genteel squire and would not have sullied his good name with the designation *slave trader*. In addition to selling his father's slaves and purchasing others for his home in Suffolk, Joseph as a lawyer routinely participated in court-ordered sales. Because slaves "were the South's most valuable asset and one of its most mortgaged forms of property" (Deyle 166), the South's legal system was deeply involved in every aspect of the peculiar institution. "The largest source of state-sponsored slave selling . . . came from sales ordered by southern courts of law. Not only did southern courts spend much of their time settling disputes over slave sales, but they were also responsible for initiating many of these same sales" (166). The interstate slave trade was beginning to boom in Virginia as a consequence of the insatiable appetites of planters in six new states—Kentucky, Tennessee, Missouri, Alabama, Mississippi, and Louisiana—for constant fresh imports following Eli Whitney's 1793 invention of the cotton gin. Between the Revolution and 1820, the U.S. enslaved population tripled from 500,000 to 1,500,000 (Rothman 10).

Agreeing by return mail to become John's partner in selling "the boy staying with Anderson," Joseph reproached John for his coldness, thereby reigniting John's emotional dependency. Joseph reaffirmed family bonds by mentioning that his wife, Susan, had just given birth to their first child, Margaret. John expressed "great satisfaction" with Joseph's letter and apologized obsequiously for his sentimental shortcomings: "My heart beats with greif to think that I should be the cause of makeing my one and only brother as much uneasiness as his letter appears to bear testimony. . . . Remember my dear fellow . . . I am willing to kneel before you and ask pardon and forgiveness of that heart which I know to be as free and clear of the least blemish as yours; Brother I cannot it tis impossible for me to express to you my feelings what is it that I have I would not part with to embrace you once again" (November 25, 1810, WPFP). His overwrought tone indicates the force of yearning for reintegration into the symbolic economy of the white patriarchal family. He could no more enact a decisive shift away from the oppressive structures of sentimental possessiveness than could the leading men of his childhood, including Jefferson, Patrick Henry, St. George Tucker, and Joseph Prentis Sr. Tucker had wondered in his *Dissertation on Slavery* "what . . . could have influenced the merchants of the freest nation . . . to embark in so nefarious a traffic, as that of the human race, attended, as the African slave trade has been, with the most atrocious aggravations of cruelty, perfidy, and intrigues, the objects of which have been the perpetual fomentation of predatory and intestine wars?" (13). Like Tucker, John found his answer not through a philosophical or political conversion but through ordinary acts of professional judgment and domestic sentiment. Focused on financial self-interest and family dynamics, he adapted to the state of the world. By abandoning his dream of social equality to pursue wealth, John found common ground with his brother. Joseph persisted in the posture of agrarian patriarch, while John positioned himself as an urban entrepreneurial capitalist, but the brothers shared "the American dream of upward mobility [that was] implicitly linked to land and slavery" (Oakes 7).

John had been attracted to the way northerners professed to value free labor over slave labor, but experience had taught him how brutal wage labor could be. In *Uncle Tom's Cabin,* Harriet Beecher Stowe depicts a common antebellum debate about labor in a conversation between Louisiana slaveholder Augustine St. Clare and his antislavery Vermont cousin, Miss Ophelia. St. Clare observes, "The American planter is 'only doing, in another form, what the English aristocracy and capitalists are doing by the lower classes'; that is, I take it, *appropriating* them, body and bone, soul and spirit, to their use and convenience." Miss Ophelia protests, "How in the world can the two things be compared? . . . The English laborer is not sold, traded, parted from his family, whipped." St. Clare replies, "He is as much at the will of his employer as if he were sold to him. The slave-owner can whip his refractory slave to death,—the capitalist can starve him to death. As to family security, it is hard to say which is the worst,—to have one's children sold, or see them starve to death at home" (195). While Stowe's novel argued that slavery was the more severe form of labor exploitation, she reminded readers time and again that the economic logic of capitalism was almost indistinguishable from the logic of slavery.

Having experienced exploitation firsthand during his Philadelphia apprenticeship, John was determined to raise himself above the ranks of the exploited. Despite illnesses and injuries, he supported himself by working for a Quaker architect named Winston who paid him "at the rate of 7 shillings per day which is more than he gives any other of his workman the journeymans wages generally speaking is from 4 shillings to 6." Embracing capitalism's exploitative logic, John observed, "My employer makes a considerable profit on my labor at the rate of 7 shillings therefore certainly the profit is greater upon the lower prices for which I can employ men enough to work for me, I pay out of my bills every week 2.50 for board which leaves me 4 shillings 5 to clear."

John retained enough of his family status, despite his manual occupation, to mingle in Richmond's highest social circles. He took particular pleasure in pursuing "ladies," as he told Joseph: "Being with you as it tis with me at my age allways ready to enjoy the pleasure of being with the charming society of the young females especially where there is a little fondness, I spent a very agreeable day with one who passed through this place. . . . I dined at the Governors with her" (November 25, 1810, WPFP). The governor with whom John dined was John Tyler, a graduate of the College of William and Mary who had long been familiar to the Prentis family. Tyler would be elected U.S. vice president in 1840 and would become president when William Henry Harrison died a month after his inauguration.

After a year in Richmond, John fancied himself the embodiment of Benjamin Franklin's work ethic and philanthropic spirit: "My mind and body being so continually employed; Satisfied and contented being able with my own industry to gain the means of procuring the common necessaries of life which I enjoy to my own satisfaction whilst I do live without being beholden, Yet ready to assist any of the human family that lays fair in my power to do." He exuded anger over his ongoing disinheritance but continued to refuse to ask Joseph directly for money.

> In my own and very strong opinion I have lost that assistance which I might have gained if I had been so condescending as to beg showing I was under great obligations would do this or that any thing in the world disoblige myself and the like. I would then have been a clever fellow. . . . Yet my dearest of all friends and only brother . . . my heart mind and body is so strongly supported nourished with all the pure blood of youth bearing its full manhood the blossom and flower of youth it twas impossible to droop its head. Though often has it been downcast and embarrassed by the trivial reproaches when it has been too much enamoured and enraptured with the smiles of the American Fair.
>
> My pleasures my friend I suffer not to interfere with my business. The houses of pleasure and amusement are perfect strangers to me nothing but the noise of the hammer crying . . . has been my amusement and pleasure from Monday to Saturday night since my arrival in this place. The play house inside I never saw. The race feild I have walked through of a Sunday. I endeavor to be constant and steady to my employment. (August 18, 1811, WPFP)

The twists in tone revealed John's difficulties in negotiating his conflicting impulses, not only between anger and affection but also between
his attraction to Franklinian self-reliance and his childhood immersion in
luxury. He backed away from anger by attempting to joke that his strongest reason for disappointment in life was his inability to afford clothes
that would attract women. He consistently asserted a dedication to relentless work. Whether or not he truly avoided houses of pleasure, amuse-
ment, theater, and horse races, he found it important to distance himself
from the image of southern idleness as a means of casting himself as a
worthy beneficiary of capitalism's meritocracy. His self-proclaimed dedication to making money without the distraction of pleasures anticipates
Marx's observation that "self-renunciation, the renunciation of life and of
all human needs, is [capitalism's] principal thesis. The less you eat, drink
and buy books; the less you go to the theatre, the dance hall, the public
house; the less you think, love, theorize, sing, paint, fence, etc., the more
you *save*—the *greater* becomes your treasure . . . your *capital*. The less
you *are*, the less you express your own life, the greater is your *alienated*
life; the more you *have*, the greater is the store of your estranged being"
(Marx 117).

Joseph did not share his brother's enthusiasm for "the noise of the
hammer," or commerce and industry. Joseph cast himself in his father's
image, constantly outspending his financial resources while obtaining social prestige, power, and influence as an attorney for Nansemond County,
clerk of the county court, U.S. surveyor, and inspector of Suffolk. John,
in contrast, was split at the root, like the American body politic striving
to reconcile democracy with slavery. His participation in slavery helped
to reinforce the power of planter class, but he felt emotionally and politically aligned with capitalistic notions of the marketplace and with
the interests of "mechanicks," by which he meant white working-class
American men. Most southern planters were contemptuous of capitalism, horrified by working-class politics, and terrified by the specter of
"mob rule." John simultaneously resented and worked with the elites.
Enraged by Jefferson's embargo and by what he perceived as the ability
of "foreigners" to succeed more readily than native-born Americans, he
immersed himself in partisan campaigning during the months leading
up to the War of 1812. The progressive potential in his working-class
sympathies was mired in a brew of xenophobia, racism, and hypocrisy, a
toxic mix that ultimately crystallized in "Jacksonian democracy." John lost

the capacity and desire for honest self-analysis. Although he had often felt exploited as an apprentice, as a slaveholder and employer he imagined himself as a generous benefactor to his employees. "Young as I am at my age brother what a consolation it tis and pleasure that providence has [enabled] me . . . to put bread in the mouths of little Children whose parents [look] to me regularly of a Saturday night for their weeks wages" (August 18, 1811, WPFP). In a letter that further illuminates how his mix of personal insecurities and aspirations fueled racism, xenophobia, and militarism, John fumed to Joseph,

> Our City is much disturbed at present by the affairs of Government which has played the devil with Mechanicks. All kind of business being at a stand not knowing what kind of a fit our Honorable President [Jefferson] will be seized with next. He has gone as far as he can possibly proceed. The Union will be disunited unless he proves to the world that he possesses the Courage of a man. . . . For above all things I despise a coward. For a Nation to be imposed upon insulted her rights trampled under the feet of Tyrants. The peace harmony and industrious husbandry destroyed sunk in oblivion in every corner of our peacefull American land by some of the worst of Gods creation the foreigners. . . . Courage is wanting much the Foreignman their is careful varnished and fastened, whilst the poor good hearted American must kneel in the bottom step whilst his inferior in every point . . . is admitted to the uppermost step whilst he that is as good as powder in the defence of his country must remain at the bottom. (April 14, 1812, WPFP)

Inflamed by bitterness against the ruling class and the specter of foreign intruders, John linked his political sentiments to the financial interests of his own class, which he now disingenuously cast as the exploited bottom rung of society. He inhabited toxic contradictions: to become a "self-made man," he exploited (but denied exploiting) the labor of unmen—that is women, apprentices, and slaves. Like apprentices, white male wage laborers occupied a transitional status in his mind: they were not-yet men, not yet self-made. For the rest of his life, John usually referred to the men who worked for him, whether free or enslaved, white or black, as "boys." Thus, he embraced the logic of the American dream, which promised him citizenship in a meritocracy constituted by race, nation, and gender. White American men, he believed, would obtain their just desserts as long as nonwhites, foreigners, and women were excluded from the social body. In this sense, he aligned himself uncomfortably with the planter class. As Frank Powers shows,

> Since the American Revolution, Southern politicians had argued that black slavery and white freedom were inextricably linked. According to this outlook, racial slavery, reinforced by a gender hierarchy that denied women political and economic equality with men, separated unskilled manual laborers from the owners of productive property and thereby restricted political participation to white, male household heads that ideally were financially and socially independent. At home, Southern white men governed their dependents as would a wise and benevolent father. That experience instilled in household heads the "virtue" (a concept in American political thought that denoted selfless commitment to the greater good) and independence (construed as an assertive defense of one's rights) that would enable them to participate as responsible, equal citizens in governing the larger society. (16–17)

John was suspicious of property owners and patriarchs. A younger son who often felt second-rated, he was inclined to sympathize with manual laborers and women yet remained determined to assert his rights over them—the rights of a white man of property—thereby proving himself virtuous, responsible, and equal to or better than men such as his brother.

Still chafing under Joseph's ongoing failure to settle their father's estate, John proposed expanding their partnership by engaging in land speculation. He admitted without apology, "Money is my object and study." After describing how he could profit from speculating in land, he asked for a loan at a low interest rate, suggesting that Joseph, "acting as a guardian and a father," would be "very justifiable" in selling the "useless piece of property" belonging to their sister, Eliza, to invest money with John (April 14, 1812, WPFP). With that, contact and correspondence appear to have ceased for two years.

When the war against "foreigners" broke out in 1812, John served as an officer in the Richmond Light Artillery under the command of Captain Andrew Stevenson, a longtime family acquaintance. The son of a prominent slaveholding Anglican clergyman, Stevenson was a prosperous lawyer with an office in his Dutch-roofed house on the northwest corner of Nineteenth and Grace Streets in Richmond. Joseph Prentis Sr. had been one of the Virginia General Court judges who conducted Stevenson's bar examination and granted the twenty-year-old a license to practice law in 1805. During the war, Stevenson skyrocketed from a position as clerk of the Henrico County Court, the Hustings Court, and the Richmond Common Council to speaker of the Virginia House of Delegates, a role he fulfilled until 1815. John was drawn to the tall, patrician Captain Stevenson, who although only three years John's senior already possessed extensive wealth in land and slaves. A talented orator, Stevenson achieved popularity among soldiers and peers for his witty conversation and ardent sentiments, including proslavery fervor (Wayland 10).

During the war, John Prentis also formed a friendship, based on shared political and economic interests, with William Lambert, a spy on British military movements who decades later was elected mayor of Richmond. For them, *interest* was a word "rich in the connotations of an entire social system based on personal relationships—kinship, neighborhood, favors exchanged, patronage given, and deference returned. . . . A 'friend' was a person, whether of higher, lower, or equal station, related by expectation of a mutual exchange of services. In short, one's 'friends' *were* one's 'interest.' The militia and election systems were integral to this social order—and ready instruments of it" (Isaac 113). Throughout his career, Prentis's success would depend on working productively with an extensive network of friends and relations who were mutually invested in the social order.

In 1813, Prentis appeared for the first time on Richmond city tax rolls. His property consisted of one slave, Hannah, for whom he was taxed fifty cents. Shortly thereafter, John met Catharine Dabney at a party and began an unconventional courtship that led quickly to marriage. The Dabney clan, of French Huguenot extraction, had lived in Virginia for more than a century. Catharine's widowed mother owned twelve acres of land in Henrico County, and Catharine had several sisters as well as a half-brother who had served an apprenticeship in Philadelphia at the same time as John. John and Catharine were wed at the Shockoe Presbyterian Church on May 12, 1814, with the Reverend Stephen Taylor officiating. Prentis's turn to Presbyterianism functioned as a public form of dissent from the Anglican Church of his childhood.

Marriage motivated John to reach out to his brother after their long silence, though he remained awkward and reticent about sharing important developments in his life: "Dear Brother, In the first place my

Brother I must entreat on you and my Sisters not to disown me for my long silence as you all know full well the dislike I have to writeing or rather scratching; I must candidly Acknowledge I have been neglect-full on that head and beg forgiveness by assurring you that my Heart and Thoughts is often with you all" (June 1814, WPFP). Noting that "the Dark Cloud" of war "hovers around our country" and that it "may put us to sleep with many of our brave countrymen," he explained that the de-mands of his work and his service in the War of 1812 had left him always "either in a great hurry about my business or marching at the head of my Company down the street." He then attempted to find comic relief in slaves, miming Hannah's voice, one of the rare instances of any allusion to a slave's voice in the vast Prentis archive. John wrote, "My old Woman Hannah . . . at last has got home, she says at home with my Master Yes thank the Lord, the most delighted perhaps you ever saw any creature in your life I never saw her in better health." His portrait of Hannah as happy, healthy, loving, and grateful to her master not only was self-flattering but also reminded his brother of their shared ties to the past as well as to the present social order. The figures of slaves often served as intensely emotive icons that defined slaveholders' sense of community and solidarity in domestic proprietorship.

Having struggled to reestablish patriotic and familial bonds of kinship, John finally broached the subject of his marriage, a matter made delicate by his failure not only to invite his siblings to the wedding but even to in-form them that he was getting married: "I expect you was much surprised at hearing of my changeing my situation in life and I hope and trust to the end of my days that I may allways find it as agreeable as I have done since it took place. I feel myself perfectly happy in the Love of my Catharine; She has been much indisposed since we was married. I have been told since I was married that I ought to have asked your consent which I did not know before therefore if I have violated a law and did it unintention-ally you will excuse me and say *John* is an *Odd Boy* he will have his *way*." Eager for forgiveness and affection while still determined to do things his own way, John styled himself an "Odd Boy" to evoke both the category of "odd duck" and the expansively permissive adage "Boys will be boys." Applying the charged term *boy* to himself also may have been an uncon-sciously or deliberately ironic nod to his status as a perpetual minor in face of his older brother's paternalism.

John continued,

> When I first met with my wife she was then engaged to be married to as
> likely a young man and as worthy a young fellow as Virginia can boast of.
> It was at a place with a great many of my acquaintants young men who
> laughed very heartily at me for saying that I had a thought of courting a
> girl I was not acquainted with and the first time I had ever seen her. I was
> intimately acquainted with her admirer Personally acquainted with her
> half brother who was apprentice at the same time with me in Philadel-
> phia and never knew his sisters untill I met with them on the first day of
> February last past at a ball. I dance[d] several reels with Miss Catharine
> Dabney and could not get any of the boys to introduce me to her that
> Night; I immediately persevered and fell in the next evening with her
> Brother went home with him got an introduction to his Sister and on the
> 12 of May wound the Ball up the Business is all over and well off it.

John's style of courtship—his posture as a romantic rogue who outwit-
ted convention and stole a girl from another "worthy young fellow"—
emerged from a wider political sensibility. Amid the tumult of the War of
1812, it was fashionable for white American men to imagine themselves
as coarse outlaws who did not follow Old World conventions. After the
Battle of New Orleans in January 1815, Andrew Jackson would ride to
national power in the commanding persona of a rough frontiersman endowed to lead by God and nature rather than by the class-based privileges and pretensions of the traditional Europhile Virginian and New England elite. Simultaneously an antielitist champion of white workingmen
and a virulent white supremacist, Jackson capitalized on and promoted
the sort of populist tone that was incipient in Prentis's letters. It was one
of history's most deadly paradoxes that violent autocratic personalities
with profound contempt for law marshaled enormous political force by
labeling their form of despotism "democracy."

In 1815, John Prentis's household was taxed for

1 slave between 9 & 12
1 slave over 12
1 Bureaus, Secretaries, and Book Cases; mahogany, in whole or in part
1 Dining Table or separate parts thereof of Mahogany
Total tax: $2.05 (Richmond Personal Property Tax Books)

With two slaves and two pieces of mahogany furniture, the Prentises
were off to a promising start as a young couple, although they were far

distant from the luxury to which John had been accustomed in childhood. When the war ended in 1815, the hardships of military conflict
were supplanted by fierce industrial competition across the Atlantic
world. With the embargo lifted, the British waged economic warfare,
deliberately flooding American markets with manufactured goods that
crippled many emerging American industries. Catastrophically cold
weather in 1816 and 1817 devastated crops throughout the Northeast,
pushing many Americans to the brink of starvation. Throughout the upheavals, Joseph Prentis built his law practice in Suffolk and increased
his collection of "dependent" children and slaves—his family, black
and white. John distanced himself from the political aesthetic of manor
houses by dubbing his home a "cabin," a term associated in his childhood with the humblest dwellings, especially those of slaves. Despite
the modest nomenclature, John constantly improved and extended his
lot not only by acquiring more possessions but also by adding rooms
and outbuildings such as a carpenter shop and a smokehouse for cur-
ing meat. He often sent gifts of beef, beef tongue, and sausages to his
brother in Suffolk. Catharine kept chickens and pigs, tended the garden,
sewed and mended clothes, cared for the sick, supervised the domestic slaves, and sustained a network of social relationships. In short, the
Prentis "cabin" was a hierarchical site where power, sentiment, and material items were produced and elaborated just as surely as they were on
a planter's estate.

In 1817, the federal government commissioned John, who had obtained the military rank of captain, to imprison a group of pirates, who
plagued much of the Atlantic world, including the Tidewater coast. He
bragged to Joseph,

> I can assure you my good fellow that I have a plenty to do just now. I have
> had ever since the second of July had charge of the pirates in addition
> to my other business: I have a house close by mine where I keep them
> confined. I have a guard of 14 men to guard them 7 in the day 7 of a night
> I have some good muskets well charged.
>   The United States allows me a dollar per day and per night for my men
> that I employ, myself they allow 2 dll.50cts per day. I have to furnish the
> prisoners with provisions good coarse beef soup and herring at 40 cts each
> per day—The United States owed me the first day of this month two thou-
> sand four hundred and fifty dollars—since which a few days ago I received
> a thousand dollars. (November 9, 1817, WPFP)

He noted that the times were hard and his responsibilities enormous as he strove to keep the pirates secure and the city safe. "The pirates frequently endeavor to escape from me, three did make their escape from me once. My men pulled the guns I saved two out of three, I apprehended a mail robber some time since and got from him in money which he had in his pocket book upwards of two thousand dollars I have to attend his trial this month and the trial of the pirates being so many they will take sometime." Smugglers, pirates, and privateers had worked both with and against the U.S. Navy during the War of 1812. "In Tidewater, privateers presented a golden opportunity for merchant owners and investors to recoup losses incurred during the embargo and to stay profitable during the British blockade" (Linder 46). The U.S. Navy was expanding its presence locally and transnationally in response to predations by many forces, including Barbary pirates, who captured many American vessels during the war. In 1815, the U.S. dispatched two navy squadrons to the Mediterranean to negotiate peace treaties with Algiers, Tunis, and Tripoli. Whether flying under the flags of nation-states or of outlaws, mariners, merchants, and thugs competed voraciously for the treasures of the Atlantic's triangular trade. In 1819, the *Boston Daily Advertiser* ran a typical pirate story that inflamed readers' imaginations in enduring ways. Captain Benjamin Carrico was one of many mariners actively engaged in the West India trade. He sailed his vessels filled with passengers and freight among Boston, the West Indies, and New Orleans, routinely stopping in Norfolk to unload New England goods, Havana white sugar, and claret wine and to gather tobacco, flour, furs, and feathers from Richmond. On one such voyage, Carrico,

> bound for St. Jago de Cuba, after being two days out from the Balize, distant about sixty miles, in a calm, was boarded by an open boat with nine pirates, armed with guns, pistols, knives and cutlasses, who plundered the brig of money, plate, merchandise, wearing apparel, liquors, provisions, & c. & c. supposed to amount to five thousand dollars—these same pirates have often been seen in New Orleans, and no doubt will occasionally visit that city again. It will be well to have this affair published as soon as possible—they often threatened to set fire to the brig and destroy every soul on board.
>
> Dated at Sea the 30th July 1819.
> BENJAMIN CARRICO

The U.S. Congress commissioned small vessels of war to detect and pursue such smugglers and pirates. Their capture would become a financial boon to various parties, including John Prentis and other jail keepers in coastal areas.

Devoted to surveillance, policing, and speculation, John led an increasingly wild, rough existence. He told his brother, "I scuffle very hard to get through life." He was unnerved by turns of fortune's wheel, and his anxieties were increased when he witnessed the financial toppling of some of the most wealthy and powerful people with whom he rubbed shoulders: "I feel very much for some of my acquaintances who have lost their *all* after many years hard scuffleing. Men who was considered *wealthy* when I first came here is now reduced to poverty. . . . Mr [William H.] Cabell the former Governor is compleatly ruined" (November 9, 1817, WPFP). Although John and Catharine's financial situation was precarious, they increased their holdings in slaves, with taxes of $2.10 assessed in 1817 for three slaves over the age of twelve—probably Hannah, Absolam, and Abbot (Richmond Personal Property Tax Books).

Ill at ease with himself, John felt excluded from the family's intimate core. Just as he had neglected to invite his siblings to his wedding, his sisters often left him in the dark about major developments in their lives. In February 1817, Mary Anne wrote to Joseph asking permission to marry Captain Edward Chamberlain: "Oh my dearest father, friend, and brother I have much to say to you on a most important subject. My heart is so full that I can scarcely find words to convey to you my feelings. . . . If I know my own heart, I have certainly formed a sincere attachment." Eliza Prentis added a postscript assuring Joseph that Chamberlain was "honourable, disinterested, and I think, truly *sincere*. I think he is certainly a great deal too old for her, but then, it is not for me to say. . . . Ever since his return from the sea he has been constantly here, and I believe him a truly excellent man. He appears to have a very high standing in Norfolk, among his acquaintances. But however, Mary Anne has told him most positively, that she will never marry him, without your approbation" (Mary Anne Prentis and Eliza Prentis to Joseph Prentis Jr., February 6, 1817, WPFP). Joseph conveyed his permission, and within a month twenty-one-year-old Mary Anne married.

Mary Anne apparently said nothing about her romance to John, although she invited him to her wedding. He did not attend, much to her disappointment. He, in turn, was stung when she and her new husband visited Richmond without calling on him. After telling Joseph that "I am as busy at this time untill Christmast as I possible can be. My Work never goes on so well as when I am constantly with my hands at work," John fumed,

> What do you think of Mary Anne and her Husband being in the City and Every Person in the City called *Big fish saw them*. Myself and wife poor people haveing to work for our liveing to pass unnoticed relationship. Amongst my acquaintances it tis talked of And I have been told of it by so many different persons male and females. . . . I have never done nothing in my life to my knowledge to Sister to occasion such conduct. If I have I should like to have been acquainted of it. If I am guilty I want to be informed of it. *Mind you*, By No Person but *yourself* for fear I make the worst matter worse. I am very obstinate when I feel myself so grossly in- sulted. I know not what you may think of it. What I have stated is fact. . . . The Captain dined with a large party at the spring the other side of my house. (October 9, 1817, WPFP)

By casting the tensions between himself and his siblings as class con- flict—the result of the snobbery of "Big fish" against poor working folk like himself—John glossed over the specific bones of contention that existed between Mary Anne and him. She was emotionally invested in imagining a degree of separation between herself and the violence of slavery as well as the messy working-class world that John inhabited. John, for his part, was keenly aware of the bad faith and hypocrisy of the slaveholding elite who projected all of the viciousness of the peculiar institution onto the figure of the slave trader. Like his siblings, John had been part and parcel of Virginia's upper crust from the moment of his birth, but as a professional, he increasingly associated with the roughest members of society. "Southern Shylock," "Southern Yankee," and "Negro Jockey" were among the many insults "that marked [slave traders] as figu- rative outcasts from slaveholding society" (Johnson 24). Walter Johnson points out that proslavery writers such as Daniel Hundley "described the slave traders as a caste apart. . . . 'The miserly Negro Trader,' Hundley assured his readers, 'is outwardly a coarse, ill-bred person, provincial in speech and manners, with a cross-looking phiz [face], a whiskey tinctured nose, cold hard-looking eyes, a dirty tobacco-stained mouth, and shabby dress'" (qtd. in Johnson 24). John and other traders, jailers, patrollers, and overseers bloodied their hands in visible carnage and became scape-goats for the vices of a system created by the elite. "Scapegoating the traders was a good way to defend the rest of slavery" (Johnson 25).

Tender Mary Anne recoiled from recognition of the violent rough-and-tumble of her society's structures of race, gender, and class. Longing to inhabit a sweet romance in which loving women and devout slaves cared deeply for each other and for the men who dominated them, she was destined for a broken heart and a short life. Many of the Atlantic world's eighteenth-century revolutionary leaders had found slavery and tradi-tional class structures objectionable, but virtually all of them wholeheart-edly embraced patriarchal gender roles and sexual domination. Thomas Jefferson, for example, described slavery as "an execrable commerce" but was thrilled by the image of Sarah delivering her young slave, Agar (Hagar), to the elderly Abraham's bed to serve him as a concubine. In a Dusseldorf art museum in April 1788, Jefferson viewed Adriaen Van der Werff's painting of the biblical scene and effused to his romantic friend, Maria Cosway, "I surely never saw so precious a collection of paintings. Above all things those of Van der Werff affected me the most. His picture of Sarah delivering Agar to Abraham is delicious. I would have agreed to have been Abraham though the consequence would have been that I should have been dead five or six thousand years" (qtd. in Gordon-Reed 282). On the French side, the revolutionary Napoleon addressed women in 1817 with a sneer: "You lay claim to equality? But that is folly: woman is our chattel and we are not hers; because she gives us children and man does not give them to her. She is, therefore, his property just as the fruit tree is the gardener's" (qtd. in Burton 10). The chain of reason interweaving slavery, women, sex, children, and the fruits of the earth into one solid proof of man's natural right to possess property seemed un-breakable; therefore, Mary Anne and many other young women sought to sweeten the image with sentimental fantasies. She referred to Joseph as "dearest father, friend and brother" and romanticized the figure of an older seafaring captain who would recount stories about his exciting life of adventure while she tended his home and hearth. In contrast, the roughness of her brother, John, resisted romanticization or recuperation within her sentimental frame.

As patriarch, Joseph inhabited the epicenter of his siblings' longings, anxieties, and affections. Unlike his sisters, John could not find in the course of normative development another patriarchal figure (that is, a husband) to whom to transfer his craving for recognition within the sentimental economy. In letter after letter, he unabashedly and even abjectly petitioned for his brother's love and approval. "Dear Brother," he effused in 1818, "every letter which arrives from you since I was last under your roof causes a feeling to pass very *forcibly* through my *heart*, and leaves a sting there that cannot be removed. . . . O my Brother my *heart* is *full*. . . . [W]hat a pleasure quite delighted at hearing from Brother his wife and your prattling *Babes*." Having learned from a mutual friend that Joseph was sick, John declared, "Sleep is a stranger, my prayers and thoughts are offered up to *heaven*, to grant you health and prosperity. How often in *Imagination*, I am with you in my dreams alooking at *Susan* nurseing of you. . . . Nothing gives me more pleasure than when it is in my power to please you and pay attention to your request" (February 4, 1818, WPFP).

   That year proved especially hard for John. He faced difficult construction deadlines, complaining to Joseph, "I had to work my boys and journeymen untill Christmas Eve All alooking at me for *money*." He felt "pushed to the very eye lashes to get a large job of work done which is not finished yet" and was infuriated when "a Yankee" outbid him on a two-thousand-dollar contract (February 4, 1818, WPFP). Responding to Joseph's questions about the costs of home improvements, John offered to bring a work crew to Suffolk to build new windows, shutters, and doors for Joseph's house. Ten days later, John wrote in a similar tone, worrying about Joseph's health and about money. Enraged by what he saw as the elite's contempt for workingmen, John longed to redeem himself, in his brother's eyes above all, by growing wealthy; however, business was "duller now at this time than it ever has been." He vacillated between the view that wealthy people were vicious predators and the view that wealth was the product and sign of a life well lived—the stamp of God's approval. Grateful for the work his brother had given him, John effused, "If I am poor my dear Boy and a laboring man classed with a denomination called Mechanicks, you have always notice me as an only brother Never have you been ashamed to acknowledge me as such—What a great crime the world . . . cries out against *me* a poor Mechanick . . . in the City of Richmond, Where there is so many wealthy and great men lives who no doubt have picked the pockets of my Country and of many orphaned children" (February 14, 1818, WPFP). Representing wealthy men as vultures who preyed on the labor of the poor, John further lamented, "What a great Crime Poverty." He asserted that men in power denied him contracts not because he lacked skill as an architect but because he did not "command money." He both despised and submitted to the social hierarchy, understanding correctly the cultural equations among commanding money, commanding power, and commanding respect.

John begged Joseph and Susan to visit him in Richmond or to send one of their children. "O my brother what pleasure it gives me to hear from your little *darlings*. . . . [T]he thoughts of one day yet to come when I shall have my little nieces and nephews to play with and hear them prattleing. . . . O my brother Let us Love and our Love grow as we advance in age. This is too serious perhaps for you, it presses very much upon my Mind; write me as soon as possible for I do love to read your letters" (April 30, 1818, WPFP). He continued in the same vein two weeks later: "I have once more seated myself in my Little Cabin, To gratify myself in *one* of my greatest pleasures. During the *Hours* of affliction our hearts and thoughts are drawn very *Near* to the points and objects most dear to us, That *Thing*, Dear Brother I must say, called *Love*, that of Brothers and Sisters. I want to see you" (May 16, 1818, WPFP). Despite a violent headache that caused him to fear for his life, John described some "handsome green" shutters and doors he had designed for Joseph and his in-laws. The shutters and doors would enable the free flow of air while providing shade from the sun, wrote John, emphasizing their utility as he worried that his brother might not find his workmanship sufficiently "handsome." Catharine also sewed gifts for the children, which were included in the packet of housing materials, which John shipped via a riverboat the roughly seventy-five miles to Suffolk.

While indulging in dreams that the Prentis ship would come in—literally, from their Uncle Robert in Trinidad—John also contemplated the benefits slaves could bring him. He complained to Joseph, "I never hear of any news from *Trinidad* except from you, I am in hopes of good *Luck*, *Dame* Fortune may smile on us yet." He regretted that Hillary, a white man whom Joseph had recommended to work for John, had conducted himself "so bad in this place that he was oblige to leave it." He was better pleased with Hillary's slave, Charles, telling Joseph, "I should like very much for you to bargain with Hillary for his Boy *Charles* that is now liveing with me, I have tried him his price was too high 1000 Dll— . . . I want to make a workman of him for my own use" (April 16, 1818, WPFP). A month later, after informing Joseph that Hillary owed money to both John and a Richmond tavern keeper, John described Hillary as "constantly *drunk*, insulting and quarrelling." He asked Joseph to ask Hillary "if I must give Charles some cloathes and if he will allow it in his hire for the boy is naked now." Alleging that the naked Charles followed Hillary's example by getting drunk "whenever he can get enough liquor," John sent Charles to a rural plantation to be handled by an overseer because "I will never undertake to break a Negro of that habit where I hire him only by the month" (May 16, 1818, WPFP). Like many buyers of slaves, John might have emphasized Charles's "defects" to induce Hillary to lower the price.

Unlike his brother, Joseph did not usually concern himself with such material details as nakedness and drunkenness; he focused on ledger books and legalities. His ships did come in, often in the form of death and inheritance. In 1819, his father-in-law, Robert Moore Riddick, died, and Joseph was appointed to administer the estate after the death of the named executor, Thomas Swepson. Riddick was a wealthy man whose estate included seventeen slaves, the value of which Joseph calculated as $3,320. However, as was the case with many Virginian slaveholders, Riddick's debts exceeded his assets. John negotiated with his brother-in-law, Richard Riddick, to divide the slaves, listing the seventeen men, women, and children the elder Riddick had owned:

Maria a young woman 21 years of age	$325.00
Mary a child of Maria about 18 months old	80.00
Dempsey a fellow fifty five years old	100.00
Charlotte a woman thirty years old	275.00
Charles a son of Charlotte three years old	150.00
Edith an infant at Charlotte's breast	25.00
Caty a woman twenty eight years old	300.00
Frank child of Caty seven years old	225.00
Burwell [ditto] of [ditto] six years old	190.00
Sam [ditto] of [ditto] three years old	150.00
Cornelius [ditto] of [ditto] fourteen months old	75.00
Ciss a woman twenty nine years old	300.00
Tom Bray a fellow forty eight years old	350.00
Jacob a small and weakly fellow forty two years old	275.00
Armistead a lad about eighteen years old	500.00
Jemmy called Jemmy Sapsiter sixty years of age very decrepit	00.00
Mingo about seventy years of age, very diseased, having lost one eye, and nearly blind in the other	00.00
(Ledger Sheet, PFP)	

Cloaked in the law, Joseph coolly generated formulas that transformed human beings into dollars. A baby was worth $25. Elders who had been worked almost to death were pronounced without worth, without value. In his accounting, years added value up to the age of twenty-one, after which prices diminished annually. Like most slaveholders, he valued men in their prime more than women in their prime.

Thus itemized, the slaves were hired out to neighboring farmers until they had brought in enough money to pay off their deceased master's debts, which took eight years (Riddick Family Papers). In 1827, when the Riddick estate was finally settled, Robert Riddick took Armistead, Frank, Cornelius, Cloe, Edith, Caty, Sarah, Charlotte, Moses, Jacob, and Sam. Joseph Prentis took Burwell, Charles, Shadrack, Maria, Mary, Ciss, and Tom. No accounting was made of the elderly Jemmy or Mingo, or at least no one bothered to account for these elderly men whose value Joseph had listed as zero zero zero zero. Perhaps they had died in the intervening years. Caty and Charlotte had given birth to new babies, who added value to the ledger sheets.

Enacting their expected gender roles, John and Joseph corresponded endlessly about business and money. "These *Articles* you know called wifes they are very useful for mine has just presented me with a little refreshment which enables me to write more," John joked to his brother. Catharine sewed clothes and made jam to send to Suffolk, while John made furniture and cured sausages and steaks for his brother's family. Joseph and Susan reciprocated with gifts of oysters and peaches preserved in brandy. Well-mannered antebellum women, Susan and Catharine exchanged recipes and expressions of affection; highlighted their household chores and health concerns; conveyed greetings to and from their circle of friends, relations, and slaves; reported on the travels of their male kin; and voiced religious platitudes. In their letters to one another, they did not discuss business, politics, literature, philosophy, aspirations, anger, rebellion, or dreams. Joseph and John, in contrast, interlaced business, politics, affection, and ambition. In the midst of the distresses of 1818, John effused, "Remember the words only, When shall we embrace each other again unfold our hearts to each other with more pleasure and freedom than ever. . . . In a word I must say the only love of Mankind is for my only Brother" (February 14, 1818, WPFP). He needed the sentimental discourse of white brotherhood to suture his increasingly fractured sense of self and community.

> I find it continually necessary to guard against that natural love of wealth
> and grandeur that prompts us always, when we come to apply our
> general doctrine to our own case, to claim an exception.
> —William Wilberforce

After his financial hardships of 1817–18 and the national economic crash
of 1819, the notion that poverty was "a great crime" began to fester in
John Prentis's soul. The specter of impoverishment threatened his ideas
about who he was and his roles as husband, brother, uncle, employer, and
benefactor. During his first eight years in Richmond, he had focused on
developing his trades as a builder, carpenter, landlord, and jailer. He occasionally bought and sold slaves to turn a quick profit, as did virtually all
slaveholders, but slave trading was a supplement to rather than a central
source of his income. While he would continue to pursue many different occupations and business ventures, after 1820, the slave trade would
consume the lion's share of his time and imagination. To succeed as a
speculator in human values, he would assess market demand, evaluate
commodity type and quality, and forecast prices. He preferred to purchase from individual owners, at court sales, and at estate auctions but at
times would buy at slave markets. He would evaluate the cost and speed
of various modes of transportation, choosing to transport some coffles
by land and others by boat. He would make informed decisions about
when and where to sell. Locally, he would conduct transactions whenever enticing opportunities presented themselves, and he would avidly
seek opportunities. The interstate slave trade, in contrast, was a seasonal
business. In the summer, John and his agents would travel around the
Upper South, especially Virginia and Maryland, to purchase slaves. In
the fall and winter, they would transport one coffle after another to the
Lower South. Their coffles usually would include forty or more slaves
who would be sold whenever and wherever John or his agent felt a good

price could be obtained: along the road, on plantations, or in the markets of Yorkville, South Carolina; Lexington, Kentucky; Montgomery, Alabama; Natchez and Clinton, Mississippi; and New Orleans. John would employ his wife, overseers, and agents to assist him in specialized aspects of the business and would capitalize on his social network to obtain access to commodities and to markets. He would campaign for politicians who would fight nationally and internationally to preserve the South's peculiar institution. He would cope with mutinies and runaways. As a midsized dealer in competition with Richmond's largest slave-trading firms, he would grow aggressively, anxiously, shamefully, bitterly proud of his success.

Residents of Virginia's most modern city, John and Catharine Prentis were not enamored of old-school agrarian gentility, but they were dazzled by the traditional allure of land and slaves. Southern politicians worked diligently to spread the so-called empire of liberty westward to revitalize and expand their agrarian, slave-based economy rather than concede to the urban, industrialized power of the North. John was first taxed for six acres of land in 1822, the year that the United States, under President James Monroe, annexed Florida from Spain. By this point, Richmond had grown into the South's fifth-largest city, and land acquisition was one of the surest ways to wealth. Over the years, John bought and sold many plots of land in Henrico and other counties. As an architect, he built houses, tenements, warehouses, and other structures on his lots. He employed many carpenters, enslaved and free, white and black, to construct buildings and make furniture. By 1826, he owned at least 100.25 acres, including two large lots in West Richmond, a half acre in Duval's Addition, and a large lot near Brook's Turnpike, also called Brook's Road, a major thoroughfare that angled north out of the city through a predominantly black neighborhood that during Reconstruction would become the heart of Jackson Ward, a black neighborhood subsequently graced by Victorian row houses, a statue of Bill "Bojangles" Robinson, and the Black History Museum and Cultural Center of Virginia. In one of his large fields, John grew herds grass, a variety of hay that could be used to feed animals or as packing material when shipping furniture and building materials to clients. Catharine tended chickens, pigs, and a vegetable garden on their home lot. They owned three prestigious lots on Church Hill, a bustling East Richmond neighborhood with views of the city and the James River, and appear to have resided on one of these lots, in the neighborhood of

St. John's Church, where Patrick Henry had declaimed, "Give me liberty, or give me death!" only to admit later that while "he could not defend slavery, he could not imagine living without slave labor" (Mason 21).

John's fear of poverty was not based on actual experiences of deprivation. Neither he nor Joseph suffered serious hardship from the crash of 1819. Joseph added one young slave and a second horse to his household possessions during that year, while John kept two slaves over the age of twelve and acquired a horse. Neither brother really had reason to despair about money. Both possessed portions of their society's most valued resources: land, slaves, and horses. John and his wife were strong, hardworking, and resourceful. They had no children to support. In short, they had every reason to trust their ability to survive and prosper. But fear of poverty was a potent seducer; it could be used to justify the most nefarious moneymaking schemes.

Had John Prentis lived in a society that did not condone trafficking in slaves, his dreams and ambitions would have been channeled in less violent directions. He stepped into slave trading in a manner that was au courant. Steven Deyle observes, "Between 1790 and 1860, Americans transported from the Upper South to the Lower South more than 1 million African-American slaves, approximately two-thirds of whom arrived there as a result of sale. Twice as many individuals were sold locally. During this period, slave sales occurred in every southern city and village, and 'coffles' of slaves (gangs held together in chains) could be found on every southern highway, waterway, and railroad. The domestic slave trade, in all of its components, was very much the lifeblood of the southern slave system, and without it, the institution would have ceased to exist" (4). White people in many professions desired slaves, but after Eli Whitney's 1793 invention of the cotton gin, the Lower South's appetite for slave labor was virtually insatiable. By 1820, farmers and planters in Georgia, Tennessee, Kentucky, Alabama, Mississippi, Louisiana, and Missouri were clamoring for slaves. More than 875,000 interstate sales occurred between 1820 and 1860 as the number of people enslaved in the Lower South soared. The enslaved population of Alabama, for instance, increased over those four decades by 393,000, while the number of slaves in Mississippi grew from fewer than 33,000 to nearly 437,000 (Deyle 42–43). Antebellum slave traders were not relics of an outmoded economy. "Just like northern capitalists, [slave traders] were acquisitive entrepreneurs engaged in a highly competitive business, who employed all of the latest marketing techniques and took advantage of the most recent forms of transportation and communication to increase their business. This was an occupation filled with risks, yet it could also pay tremendous financial rewards" (Deyle 6–7). By midcentury, when southern politicians were desperate to defend slavery, they would hit on the insight that slavery was capitalism par excellence. In his 1854 essay, "Slavery a Positive Good," for example, Benjamin F. Stringfellow would assert, "In the South no struggle between labour and capital can arise. Where slavery exists, capital and labour are one, for labour is capital. There the capitalist, instead of exhausting his labourer, must strengthen, protect, and preserve him, for he is his money" (69).

Participating in slavery was never an inevitable choice for John. Like most white Virginians, he repeatedly struggled to accommodate his conscience to human bondage. The antislavery voices of his youth never vanished; they mutated and gathered force, striking him hard emotional knocks time and again. Abolitionism sounded alarms not only in the northern press but also in his head, within his family circle, and even occasionally in the words of rabidly proslavery acquaintances such as Thomas Ritchie, the powerful editor of the *Richmond Enquirer*, who sometimes exclaimed, "We do not vindicate servitude; we wish no slave had touched our soil; we wish it could be terminated" (qtd. in Freehling 150). By 1820, all of the northern U.S. states and territories had abolished or were gradually eradicating slavery within their borders. During the Missouri Controversy of 1819–20, the long-standing national debate grew vituperative, pushing the North and South toward polarized positions. Many southerners found that investing patriotic pride in the "southern way of life" helped them conquer their self-disgust and loathing of slavery, which in any case was often indistinguishable from their loathing of slaves and free blacks. While northerners were bitter that the three-fifths clause of the U.S. Constitution gave slaveholding states disproportionate power, most whites in eastern Virginia, where the state's slave power was centered, celebrated the undemocratic political advantage they gained from slavery. After all, "Virginia's elite . . . controlled the new nation's highest office for 32 of the republic's first 36 years: truly a Virginia dynasty" (Freehling 147). The national debate over Missouri focused on "the question of Congress's ability to prevent the spread of slavery, and the slave trade, into the new states and territories" (Deyle 195). Denunciations of the slave trade as wicked, base, and cruel abounded in the northern press and to a lesser extent in the southern press.

But under the leadership of President Monroe, an old friend of Joseph Prentis Sr., the Slave Power won the debate. When the Missouri Compromise opened new territory to slavery, Richmond was the most felicitous place in the Upper South for a man willing and able to speculate in slaves. Any man who mastered the logic of the market could make thousands of dollars in just one season. The scale of Richmond's slave market was second only to New Orleans within the United States. With cotton planters in the ever-expanding Lower South "willing to pay hundreds of dollars more per slave than were owners in the older states . . . the market value of a slave in a place like Richmond was no longer dependent upon local demand" (Deyle 5). John Prentis was well positioned to capitalize on his city's hottest commodity. He had local, regional, and national connections. He was not squeamish about physical, gritty, or violent work. He liked being on the road. And unlike most speculators, who had to pay someone else to house their slaves until they had amassed a sufficient number to fill a coffle, Prentis owned a jail that could double as a "slave pen," a phrase that simultaneously evoked a yard for animals and a penitentiary for criminals. The proliferation of slavery depended not only on the imperial acquisition of new territories and the slaughter, removal, or confinement of Indian inhabitants but also on the growth of the American prison system.

In May 1822, John Prentis informed his brother that he had "a large gang" of Negroes imprisoned in his jail and was buying more at "every opportunity" (May 6, 1822, WPFP). Although Richmond's slave dealers tended to congregate "in the heart of the city's commercial district, along Fifteenth Street from Franklin to Broad, just two blocks from the state capitol and governor's mansion" (Deyle 153), Prentis's jail probably was situated on his lot in Jackson Ward, where a narrow street abutting his land came to be called Prentis's Alley or Prentis's Row. It was intersected by Charity, Baker, and Duvall Streets in a neighborhood packed with free black households as well as slaves' quarters. As early as 1817, John told Joseph that virtually everyone in the neighborhood, black as well as white, knew who he was and where he could be found at various times of the day. In 1852, the first Richmond City Directory listed twenty-six free black households adjacent to Prentis's Alley. The black residents worked as washerwomen, laborers, seamstresses, blacksmiths, shoemakers, and gardeners. His jail most likely included a complex of buildings that served various purposes as well as a fenced-in yard. It probably was not as large as that of one of his competitors in the business, Robert Lumpkin, whose jail complex in the 1850s "consisted of four brick buildings on about a half acre of fenced-in land. One building served as Lumpkin's office and residence, another as housing for out-of-town traders and buyers, another as a kitchen and barroom, and the fourth as a two-story jail for boarding those who had recently been purchased or were about to be sold (men on the bottom floor, women on the top)" (Deyle 115). Lumpkin generated most of his income from running his jail, whereas Prentis depended more heavily on buying and selling slaves.

Gun-toting guards kept a vigilant eye on prisoners and slaves. Prentis's jail no doubt featured an inventory of whips, chains, paddles, finger screws, and guns as well as an outdoor cage in which some prisoners were kept for particular humiliation. In 1856, Richmond native Samuel Mordecai recalled such a cage as an octagonal shape with "open iron gratings on three sides, about ten feet above the street, and the floor of this open prison was arranged amphitheatrically, so that each occupant could see, and, what was worse, be seen from the street" (Sheldon 32). City constables patrolled the streets, and blacks without papers proving they were free or passes from their masters could be thrown in jail or in the cage.

William Grimes, a Virginia-born slave who was imprisoned in several jails there and in Georgia, recalled one of his experiences in vivid detail in his 1825 memoir, *Life of William Grimes, the Runaway Slave, Written by Himself.* Enraged by news that another slaveholder wanted to purchase Grimes, Grimes's owner asked the constable to place Grimes in solitary confinement for three weeks. Grimes described his jail cell as "so foul and full of vermin, it was almost insupportable. The lice were so thick and large that I was obliged to spread a blanket (which I had procured myself) on the floor, and as they crawled upon it, take a junk or port bottle, which I found in the jail, and roll it over the blanket repeatedly. . . . My readers will here understand that this room had constantly, previous to my imprisonment therein, been occupied as a prison for negroes. They, no more than myself having a privilege of a change of linen, or water wherewith to cleanse it" (79). In 1832, Mary Blackford, a white woman from Fredericksburg, Virginia, recorded in her journal some of the daily horrors that occurred in jails while slaves awaited the march south. She

LUMPKIN'S JAIL.

Slave trader and jailer Robert Lumpkin ran a jail and slave pen similar to the one owned and operated by John B. Prentis. Both jail complexes were in Richmond's Shockoe Bottom. Lumpkin's Jail became a religious and educational facility for freedmen after the Civil War and is now the site of Virginia Union University. Engraving from Charles Corey, *A History of the Richmond Theological Seminary: With Reminiscences of Thirty Years' Work among the Colored People of the South* (Richmond: Randolph, 1895). Courtesy of the Virginia Historical Society.

described interceding on behalf of a mother "whose son, about to be sold south by a slave trader, was incarcerated in the trader's cellar. The mother begged her son's guard to let her see the boy one last time" (Varon 54). The jailer rejected all entreaties; the mother was not allowed to see her son until some weeks later, when he was taken away from the jail in chains. Blackford also recorded the lament of Betsy, a slave who was "kept in a slave trader's jail in which old and young were routinely cobbed—beaten with a board with holes in it. After hearing the cries of a young girl undergoing this torture, she lamented to Blackford, 'I sometimes think the world will not stand much longer, there is so much wickedness in it.' Her own children were soon sold away from her" (Varon 54).

To fill his jail or slave pen, Prentis, like most slave traders, hit the road. "Most interstate traders spent the summer buying slaves. Wherever slaves were sold in the Upper South—whether at court house estate sales, private sales on a slaveholder's land, or even in another trader's yard—interstate traders were there to buy them" (Johnson 48). John and other traders who had been born into the slaveholding elite had a distinct competitive advantage. About half of the slave sales in the South took place at public auctions or through court actions (Deyle 145), but John worked to find sales before they were publicly announced and even to induce owners to sell before they had thought to do so. He sent queries by letter and word of mouth to his network of well-heeled relatives and friends as well as a variety of middlemen such as tavern keepers. He typically would compose a list of the genders and ages he was seeking:

> If you will send any of your [slaves] up to me I will sell them for the
> very best price and remit you the money. Good servants is scarce with
> us at this time although I have some as good as any in Virginia. . . . I was
> offered 500 dlls cash for one of my female servants a short time since.
> And refused it. Unlikely slaves will never sell in this market women and
> children dull sale Young Women like them that *James* bought and young
> Men Boys that is large enough for plough Boys will always sell and at a
> good Price Young Men 350 dlls to 400 dlls. Women 250 to 300. (John B.
> Prentis to Joseph Prentis Jr., January 4, 1828, WPFP)

When he received word that a slave owner was looking to sell a particular slave or a group of slaves, Prentis or his agent would travel to view the "merchandise" and to negotiate with the owner. He often would go from plantation to county court to city court as well as to markets and manors in search of the best people available for the most reasonable prices.

As he became experienced in passing cool judgments, Prentis honed his skills at exhibiting his expert professional knowledge. In the masculine world of the slave trade, "being a 'good judge of slaves' was a noteworthy public identity, a world of manly one-upsmanship in which knowledge of slaves' bodies was bandied back and forth as white men cemented social

Old slave market in Richmond, mid-nineteenth century. Courtesy of the Virginia Historical Society.

ties and articulated a hierarchy among themselves through shared participation in the inspection and evaluation of black slaves. And as these white men watched one another examine and choose slaves, and as the slave-pen mentors helped inexpert buyers choose slaves, they daily reproduced and passed on the racial 'knowledge' by which southern slavery was justified and defended" (Johnson 137). Sometimes Prentis would voice genuine opinions; other times he would downgrade the "merchandise" to drive a hard bargain. Joseph Prentis Jr. might have wondered which way to interpret his brother's assessment of two slaves in 1828. According to John,

> I am afraid that you will not be able to get the value of your slaves being defective they are very dull sale here. If you will send them to Norfolk put them on boarde of the steam boate Capt Chapman say next Tuesday week which will be 15th of the month. One of my men servants will be on boarde from James town who will take charge of them and take them to my house safe. You shall be at no expence whilst they are with me

or for selling of them accept I should have to send away to some other state for sale. The amount of their sales will be small without deducting commissions. You may send them before if you think proper by inform- ing me of it so that my young man can be at the Boate to receive them. Capt Chapman will charge you 4 dollars for their passage that is 2 dlls each tell him they are for me and if they should come on that day he will put them under *Jack* charge when he takes him from James town where I have permitted him to go to see his wife. I have no doubt but what them slaves have tried you very much and I would not have such defective ones about me. Let your instructions be to sell them for what can be gotten for them much or little. It may be some time perhaps before I get a chance to dispose of them I will not let a chance slip. (April 5, 1828, WPFP)

John's brutally dismissive categorization of Joseph's slaves as "defective" was standard practice among dealers. Like most salesmen, he took pride in spinning a sales pitch that pinned a financially advantageous identity on the slave. *Defective* is a categorical term that masks the particulari- ties that might place people, no matter how degraded, within a human story. John used descriptors that foreclose any sympathetic response to the slaves' bodies as sites of traumatic histories.

John relied on his brother for information and for slaves. For decades, his letters to Joseph contained requests such as, "I want to purchase some slaves could a few be bought down there Would that Tavern keeper who lives on the hill buy on commission what would it be. I have been at Mr. Frances [his agent] to . . . buy all that would suit us. He . . . allways goes up to the country where I believe the prices are higher Young Negroes will always sell here let them cost what they will with you I could make a handsome profit on them here, is my opinion if a proper arrangement was made with some one down there" (September 11, 1827, WPFP). John used other employees as well as slaves to deliver monies and pick up slaves. While completely dehumanizing and commodifying most slaves, John placed a great deal of trust in selected slaves such as Jack, a re- sourceful man who exercised significant independence and freedom of movement. Jack often traveled alone from city to city via waterways and highways, was entrusted with money, and was given full responsibility for transporting slaves back to John in Richmond. Jack played this role from the 1820s through the 1840s. An 1842 letter illuminates the hazards he faced when he traveled. Jack showed up at Joseph's house in Suffolk half-starved and out of money. Joseph fed him and loaned him money to return to Richmond, earning John's thanks for his "love and kindness to me as a brother and the goodness of your heart in befriending any person [of] any colour who told a fair tale about *me*" (January 4, 1842, WPFP). A black man, whether enslaved or free, would find his life endangered if weather or an unexpected event prevented him from reaching his destination on time or if he needed more money than anticipated for traveling expenses. Jack's survival depended on Joseph's recognition of his connection to John. John described "my man Jack" as honest and quick, adding with self-congratulation, "Jack cannot be beaten of his colour so long as he has to look at me" (January 4, 1842, WPFP).

John depended on assistants not only to achieve the scale of slave trading that he coveted but also to take over the trade when his time was occupied by his many other civil and business commitments. In the early 1820s, for example, he developed a sideline buying, selling, and breeding horses, which he sometimes advertised in the newspaper. He was enamored of horses, especially his favorite, Charles. Like slaves, horses not only were useful but also were status symbols seen as extensions of their owners. Rhys Isaac observes that the "role of the steed as an adjunct to virile self-presentation is revealed in the endless conversations the gentry had about their horses, in which they expressed the closest identification with the animals" (99). John lost money on horses, but his emotional investment in them exceeded his financial concerns. The "symbolic equation between horses and White masculine power" (Sidbury 66) was evident in Virginia's tax books, which listed first slaves and then horses as significant pieces of personal property. The government of Virginia depended deeply on its revenues from taxes on those two items. "In fact, by 1860, slave property had even surpassed the assessed value of real estate within the slaveholding states" (Deyle 60).

John also accepted various military commissions and government contracts over the decades, including sundry contracts to jail pirates and other criminals. In the mid-1820s, he was placed in command of a night guard or patrol. He complained to Joseph, "This night work is getting to me very disagreeable. . . . I have lost my *relish* for it. My *first* Lieutenant *Page* resigned sometime since *health injured*. This winter has carried off several of my *men*. I have not a *man* here now that was here when I took command. I attribute my health to the care that my wife takes of me. Our wages has all been reduced mine from *1200* Dllr to *700* Dllr per year which is not enough for me. I had rather have a great deal less and *day light*" (March 12, 1826, WPFP).

Because he had fingers in so many pies, John sometimes lacked the time to travel in person around the Upper South to buy slaves or to the Lower South to sell, relying on employees to undertake these tasks. His letters to Joseph were filled with references to his agents' comings and goings. In January 1828, he noted that Frances had just returned home from Suffolk on a Friday night steamboat in the midst of a rainstorm. As soon as the rain cleared at noon on Monday, "we shewed our stock in trade consisted of *nine* in Number and put the change in our pocket before night for the whole of them" (January 4, 1828, WPFP). Most sales in Richmond were held in dealers' offices or in large auction halls. Buyers examined male slaves behind a screen, where they were forced to undress and were poked and prodded. Examinations of women were usually more discrete and limited to hands, arms, legs, bust, and teeth (Johnson 148). "Every day, up and down the street (and along several alleys), red flags were posted, with slips of paper attached listing all of the lots to be sold" (Deyle 153). When John walked, rode Charles, or was driven to sales by Edmond or another slave in a barouche, he passed black porters and waiters bustling in and out of hotels and restaurants. He might have stopped to get a haircut and a shave from Mingo Jackson, a free black man who was one of the city's most skillful barbers, or to buy a peach or some peanuts from an Irish huckster before loafing in the shade of a magnolia tree with assorted gentlemen as they placed bids on human beings in a yard, on an auction block, or on the courthouse steps.

John also told Joseph that he wanted young men, by which he meant that he wanted both to buy young slaves and to hire young men to assist him in the slave-trading business before Frances began his southward trek.

> We have been buying and selling ever since here at home. Frances
> expects to leave here sometime this month for *Natches* or somewhere
> else uncertain what place on a tradeing expedition. We shall carry a small
> number and we have not got half that yet. We want young men. He is
> very busy himself a buying whilst I am attending to my other business I
> have been without any young man for sometime past I have them but *they
> could not stand me.* I got one about 2 or 3 days since that I shall be able
> to do something with I am much please with him. Frances and myself has

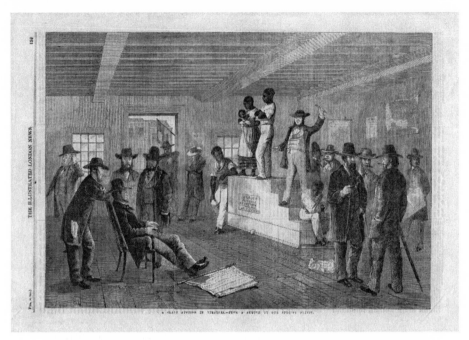

Slave auction in Virginia. Courtesy of the Virginia Historical Society.

settled all our accounts up to the first of January 1828. And we are still
going on without any difficulty. You [have] raised young men in your office
to the Law. I raise them in my office to make money by hard work as I am
speculating. I hope that Frances may always do well for my sake I trust
him a great deal with my money thousands at a time. I have tried to learn
him and instill into his mind Honesty is the best policy. (January 4, 1828,
WPFP)

Although John and Frances were employed in the wholesale theft of
other people's bodies and lives through both the local and the interstate
trade, John saw no irony in his use of the proverb. He often bragged to
Joseph about how well he treated his employees, but several passages
in his letters, such as the remark that he had trouble finding young men
willing to work for him because they could not stand him, suggest that he
was often cantankerous.

John's new young man was William Priddy, a poor farm boy whom
John imagined he had rescued by providing him an opportunity to escape

rural squalor and flourish in trade. The slave trade did indeed offer "men of ambition in the South an opportunity to make more money than they could earn in most other occupations available to them. At a time when a southern bank president's annual salary was $5,000 or less, even moderately successful slave traders could easily make twice that much, if not considerably more. And the larger firms outperformed the wealthiest cotton planters. A good annual income for southern yeoman farmers was $300, while overseers made $100–200 a year, and white laborers were paid even less" (Deyle 122). Priddy proved to be everything John dreamed, and he served as his right hand for the next fifteen years. John congratulated himself on Priddy's social transformation. "It is my greatest *pleasure* to be with W. Priddy at his native court house," he told Joseph. "To see the little barefoot plough boy *stared* at, to see the old men point him out, many a *hearty* shake of the hand do I get from them. Many a hearty welcome at their houses upon his account. Broad cloth cannot change him" (December 17, 1832, WPFP).

While John's slaves were waiting in his jail or "pen" for the coffle to be completed, Catharine prepared food, cared for the sick, and sewed two suits of clothes for each slave, the customary outfitting of slaves for sale in southern markets. John was proud of her industry, bragging to Joseph, "She has had a fine job of work makeing all the cloathes for my people two suits a peice. Our room was a compleat taylors shop for 10 or 12 days" (October 6, 1830, WPFP). John strove to buy as many slaves as possible for his coffles but would content himself with thirty or forty. Once he decided that a coffle was ready to depart, he and/or his agent would either load the slaves on a boat bound for a southern port or lead them on a grueling walk over land. The moment of departure was terrifying and traumatic for slaves. As Saidiya Hartman recounts,

> Sellie Martin, who was sold at age six along with his mother and ten-year-old sister, described the "heart breaking scene" when the coffle departed for market: "When the order was given to march, it was always on such occasions accompanied by the command, which slaves were made to understand before they left the "pen," to "strike up lively," which means they must sing a song. Oh! what heartbreaks there are in these rude and simple songs! The purpose of the trader in having them sung is to prevent among the crowd of negroes who usually gather on such occasions, any expression of sorrow for those who are being torn away from them; but the negroes, who have very little hope of ever seeing those again who are dearer to

them than life, and who are weeping and wailing over the separation,
often turn the song demanded of them into a farewell dirge." (*Scenes* 36)

Sale away from family and community inflicted a trauma that many
slaves feared more than death; indeed, they often viewed sale to the
Lower South as a death sentence. Some enslaved people killed themselves and their children rather than submit to being sold. For abolitionists, "the slave trade epitomized American slavery at its worst, and tales
of families being divided, children torn from their mothers, and humans
on an auction block simply could not be defended" (Deyle 184). Foreign visitors were appalled by the sight. "When the Englishman George
Featherstone encountered a slave coffle in western Virginia, he claimed
he 'had never seen so revolting a sight before,' and the British author
Harriet Martineau called a trip to a slave auction in Charleston 'the most
infernal sight I ever beheld'" (Deyle 185). Even many southern slaveholders found the spectacle of sales unpalatable. Mainstream as well as
religious southern newspapers sometimes soundly denounced the slave
trade. In 1822, for example, a letter to the editor published in a Kentucky newspaper condemned "the diabolical, damming practice of SOUL-
PEDDLING, or the purchasing of negroes, and driving them like brutes to
market" (qtd. in Deyle 224–25).

When John Prentis decided to ship slaves within Virginia, he often
made arrangements with Captain Chapman, whose boat sailed frequently
between Virginian ports. For longer journeys, Prentis paid for passage on
a variety of large vessels. Shipping was more expensive than other modes
of transportation but reduced travel time to New Orleans from more than
two months to about three weeks (Deyle 99). When Prentis transported
coffles over land, he and his agents forced the slaves to walk ten to fifteen
miles each day, sometimes more in good weather. Wagons were used to
transport supplies and sick, pregnant, or lame slaves. Such disabled or
weakened slaves were common, although Prentis, like most slave traders,
strove to keep their numbers to a minimum since strong healthy slaves
were the most profitable. Late at night, the coffle would stop to cook
dinner over a fire before going to sleep in tents or on the ground. Drinking "fresh" water was feared because it could produce "fevers"—yellow
fever, smallpox, malaria, and dysentery. When possible, people on the
march drank alcohol straight or laced their water with alcohol to make it
safe to drink. Drinking boiled water or tea also reduced the likelihood of

illness. Mosquitoes, gnats, flies, and ants provided seasonal torment, and the possibility of encountering snakes, bears, wolves, and wildcats was worrisome. At dawn, the slaves would gulp down whatever breakfast they were allotted before the march began. Prentis sometimes prided himself on not using fetters or ropes to bind the slaves; the lack of "confinement" most likely made him feel relatively humane and increased the slaves' capacity to walk long distances with greater efficiency and less likelihood of injury or disfigurement. He and his agents depended on surveillance, guns, and whips to keep the slaves in line while they marched, usually barefooted and in rags. Their new outfits were reserved for market days. Former slave Polly Shine recalled the pain of these kinds of marches: "Our master would put us in the road ahead of them and they would be on horses behind us as we traveled and they would follow and we had to travel pert, no laggin behind if we did, he always had whip that he would tap us with boy! When he hit us across the legs we could step real lively and I don't mean maybe either" (qtd. in Hartman, *Scenes* 37). John Prentis sent such reports to his brother as, "William has left me some days since to look for a market in fine health and spirits high for hard difficult undertaking. He left home with 41 slaves all loose not one confined any shape or form. All of them *walkers* except three, Two waggons with two fine horses." He proudly added that he had purchased another slave "the very morning [William] left here. I am still in the market" (October 6, 1830, WPFP).

When the coffle reached a market, the slaves were sometimes allowed to rest and heal. Doctors were brought in to tend to illnesses and wounds. The slaves were washed and dressed in a set of new clothes. "The traders shaved men's beards and combed their hair, they plucked gray hairs or blackened them with dye" (Johnson 119). The slaves received extra rations heavy in fat—bacon, milk, and butter—so that they would not look emaciated. "To keep the slaves' muscles toned, the traders set them to dancing and exercising, and to make their skin shine with the appearance of health, the traders greased the slaves' faces with 'sweet oil' or washed them in 'greasy water'" (Johnson 119). In Natchez, Mississippi, the slaves would be auctioned off at various sites, "from the river landing to the front steps of the fashionable Mansion House Hotel. But the main slave-trading center, especially after 1833 when the city prohibited public sales by slave traders within the city limits, was a collection of rough wooden structures just outside of town. Originally known as 'Niggerville,' by the late 1830s this market was more commonly referred to as the 'Forks of the Road.' Every year at least four or five large traders operated out of these stands, and one resident remembered seeing as many as 800 slaves in that venue at one time" (Deyle 153). Auctioneers cracked lewd, racist jokes and indulged in dramatic antics to keep the white crowd laughing while slaves were forced to dance, submit to inspections, and look lively. In Lexington, Kentucky, gentlemen could buy slaves in Hawkins and Bassett's Shoe Store as well as at the typical array of street auctions and private sales (Deyle 153). In New Orleans, dealers would enter a "neighborhood where today Chartres Street meets broad, boulevarded Esplanade—a few short blocks from the levee, past the cathedral and the gin houses and the sailor's tenements that served the nearby docks" (Johnson 2). In the city's large markets, the "streets in front of the pens were lined with slaves dressed in blue suits and calico dresses. Sometimes the slaves paced back and forth, sometimes they stood atop a small footstand, visible over a crush of fascinated onlookers. As many as a hundred slaves might occupy a single block, overseen by a few slave traders whose business was advertised by the painted signs hanging overhead: 'T. Hart, Slaves,' 'Charles Lamarque and Co., Negroes'" (Johnson 2). John Prentis and his agents witnessed the architecture of the markets and the laws regulating the trade change significantly from one season to the next. "Far from being ever-present in cities like New Orleans, the slave market was a quarantined space, legally bounded by high walls to 'prevent them from being seen from the street' and banned from many neighborhoods throughout the antebellum period. The state of Louisiana outlawed the trade entirely during the period of panic that followed Nat Turner's 1831 rebellion, and the city of New Orleans (like cities across the South) taxed it at the same high rate as pawn shops, cock pits, and race tracks" (Johnson 24).

Neither high taxes nor slave revolts deterred John when the prices were right. He did not mention Turner in his letters to Joseph, but in the season after Turner's rebellion, John specified that he was not on the market for "men."

> I got home 20th of October . . . leaving Mr. Priddy in the south who still continues the same William to me as formerly. I left Home with 38 slaves a less number than I had ever calculated to have left home with. I have been busily engaged since I came home apurchasing of a small lot which I want to leave home with the last of this month. [Can I] get the favor of you to find out whether any of those who are in the habit of purchasing

slaves in your neighborhood has any on hand or if there is any in your
neighborhood to sell. Enquire of Mr. Waters. I want all *sorts* except Men.
The prices for young Women, Boys 12 years of age, Girls 12 years of
age, a Woman with her first or second child: This may be disagreeable to
you. Read it to Mr. Waters and ask him to answer it *forthwith*. The 2nd
Monday is your court day. Will there be any sales on that day? I have
partly concluded to go to Louisa court house on that day. I could dispense
with that trip to see you all, especially if I could kill two birds with one
slave. . . . Hurry if your traders has some on hand will sell at a fair price I
will see Suffolk pretty soon they may waite for me; Waters will be so good
as well as yourself not to say one word or whisper the contents of this letter to Graddy the small man, Mr. Tates' agent. (November 5, 1832, WPFP)

Soaring prices led to fierce competition for slaves during the 1830s. Bacon Tait, one of John Prentis's main competitors in Richmond, ran a large
boardinghouse for slave traders alongside a jail for their slaves, advertis-
ing in the *Richmond Whig* that he would provide slaves with "general
cleanliness, moderate exercise, and recreation within the yards during
good weather, and good substantial food at all times." He promised that
their "confinement shall be rendered merely nominal, and the health of
the Negroes so promoted, that they will be well prepared to encounter
a change of climate when removed to the South" (qtd. in Deyle 115). In
addition, Prentis competed with the large slave-trading firm of Silas and
R. F. Omohundro, which also owned a trading depot.

In the years after Nat Turner's rebellion, Prentis specified several
times that he wanted all sorts of slaves except men, but most traders
found adult male slaves the most profitable commodities. "By 1860, the
average price for a prime male hand in New Orleans had reached more
than $1,800, an amount equal to more than $30,000 today" (Deyle 59).
Prentis's unusual avoidance of enslaved men might indicate that he had
developed a niche market, the most infamous of which was the market
in "fancy women." Slave traders "were notorious for raping the young
enslaved women under their control" (Deyle 126–27). Prostitution and
rape were so popular with slave traders that one large-scale dealer, Isaac
Franklin, considered establishing a brothel in Richmond "for the Exclusive benefit" of men involved in the trade (qtd. in Deyle 127).

John peppered his correspondence with romanticized anecdotes of
his travels with Priddy. As a team, they fit the profile described by Steven Deyle: "Despite all of their aggressive competition and cutthroat
practices, the masculine lifestyle of the trade left many speculators to

develop deep and sincere friendships with one another. . . . Slave traders frequently lived together on the road and stayed in the same boarding houses. They also experienced a certain camaraderie and male bonding as they boasted, cursed, drank, gambled, and shared women together" (127). John cherished his and Priddy's ability to move fluidly from Virginia's finest parlors to the rough woods. Anticipating a wedding party at a country mansion, he told Joseph, "Mr. Priddy will be in the height of his glory in the ball room, especially when we shall be on the floor together. . . . What will you think of *me* and my way of liveing; when I shall say the truth to you my Brother that from the 9th day of September 1835 to the 24th day of January 1836 that I lived in the woods, kept in my waggon and enjoyed as good health as I ever did in my life whilst strutting out and walking from 10 to 15 miles per day. Tell your boys that their Uncle to your knowledge made his little all as hard as the next man and . . . whilst the ground is covered with snow and frozen whither he shall take his axe on his shoulder and go to his little forest and fell some of its best timber trees to build my houses. I have plenty of old brick left from last year!" (January 5, 1836, WPFP).

During most trading seasons, as soon as Prentis and Priddy returned home from one trip, they began planning another. John took breaks only when he felt that prices were unfavorable or when he was exceptionally busy with other business ventures. Cotton prices dropped as a result in part of the Tariff of 1828, signed into law by President John Quincy Adams, which aimed to protect northern industry from low-priced foreign goods by imposing a tariff on imports. Labeled "the Tariff of Abominations" by southerners, the law raised the cost in the South of items produced in the North. It also led cotton prices to plummet when Britain, having lost money from its reduced exports to the United States, reduced its importation of U.S. cotton. The tariff contributed to Adams's defeat by Andrew Jackson in 1832. When the newly elected President Jackson failed to address South Carolinian concerns sufficiently in his revised law, the Tariff of 1832, his vice president, John C. Calhoun, resigned and split from Jackson to form the Nullifier Party, which campaigned on the platform that states had the right to nullify federal laws within their borders. Exclaiming "I am no nullifier," John threw his support behind Jackson. When Priddy had difficulty finding buyers in Alabama in the spring of 1833, John "tried to cheer his spirits up . . . by telling him that all his bad luck in slow sales *low prices* is nothing compared with Honesty, Our consciences being clear" (April 25, 1833, WPFP). John recounted to Joseph several stories of agents who stole from their employers. In one case, he had shared supper at the foot of a tree with a fellow dealer and his agent during a southern trek, only to discover on his return home that the agent "had absconded with 1300 dollars" (April 25, 1833, WPFP). Exuding anxiety about the thousands of dollars with which he entrusted Priddy, John emphasized to Joseph that "all them troubles my Brother is nothing when the heart is honest" (April 25, 1833, WPFP). His repetition of the word *honest* suggests the level of his anxiety. It was not unusual for agents to disappear with thousands of dollars. "After one such man swindled the Richmond auctioneer Hector Davis out of more than $10,000, another trader in that city warned, 'Bad agents will ruin Anyone'" (Deyle 121). At this stage in his career, if John ever meditated on the fundamental dishonesty, thievery, and destruction of human life on which his trade was predicated, he displaced his sense of guilt by imagining scenarios in which he might be viewed as a victim.

After the slow sales of 1832–33, John was alarmed the next season when slave prices skyrocketed while cotton prices fell. Concluding that the situation was "mad," he decided to withdraw from the slave trade until prices stabilized. He explained to Joseph,

> The high prices run mad. Prices of property has left me out of the market. President Jackson is putting things straight again. Money will come to its value. Mr. Priddy is in Alabama settleing up some of our outstanding credits. We done nothing last summer but *rested*; the high *prices* made us lay low and keep dark. We have concluded to *rush* this year as Crocket says go *ahead*. I had a letter from him the 6th of this month. He expects to be at home in March congratulating me upon our not tradeing as being *wise* and profitable in haveing no funds invested in slaves this season. Hard times amongst them, cotton in that country fallen from 16 cts per bsl to 8 or 8½. Many merchants hit. I shall expect to leave home on the 2nd day of February which is of a Sunday for the Eastern Shore Virginia to see if I can do anything. I will thank you and under many obligations to you for letters of introduction which if I mistake not you offered—If an opportunity occurs could you not enclose them to Norfolk to our relation or his brother. (January 22, 1834, WPFP)

John Prentis understood that the success of his business depended on his society's legal and political superstructure. Although he detested class snobbery, he knew he could depend on his own well-heeled kin to help uphold slavery's legal framework. Joseph was a delegate to the Virginia Constitutional Convention of 1829, where he helped to strengthen the state's slave codes. At the convention, a political faction representing John's proletariat sensibilities clashed with a group espousing Joseph's aristocratic views, as William Freehling describes:

> The eastern old guard—Monroe, Madison, John Randolph of Roanoke, Benjamin Watkins Leigh—bore the look of eighteenth-century drawing rooms. Their white wigs were scrupulously powdered. Their velvet cravats were fastidiously tied. Their knee britches and silk stockings were meticulously married. When their lordly leader, John Randolph of Roanoke, descended to endure the Convention, he came down from his imported English coach drawn by his imported English horses, snapping open his imported English watch to make sure he would suffer no extra moments among the riff-raff.
>
> Randolph smirked at the opposition. Westerners arrived not fit to ride hounds but fitted out for nineteenth-century enterprise. Their heads were topped with hair crudely cut. Their string ties were askew. Their homespun coats and pants were mismatched. They crudely dismounted from rudely bred horses and tramped into the Convention. (171)

John identified with the westerners' democratic aesthetic, but he was born of the old guard and depended on its members' complicity for the success of his work. He wanted to move fluidly among both factions. Joseph was solidly a member of the old order. In addition to serving in the state legislature and working as a lawyer and judge, he taught law on occasion at the College of William and Mary, helping to train the next generation of proslavery lawyers and politicians. His eldest son, Robert Riddick Prentis, followed the family's legal tradition, becoming a successful lawyer and eventually a proctor of the University of Virginia and clerk of the court of Albemarle County. During the Civil War, he would serve as Virginia's collector of internal revenue.

John did his best to negotiate his conflicting class loyalties. To keep slavery politically viable, he campaigned actively for his favorite proslavery politicians at the local, state, and federal levels. In addition to supporting Jackson, he promoted the career of his lifelong friend Andrew Stevenson. During the Missouri Crisis of 1819–20, Stevenson, a member of the Virginia House of Delegates, had opposed all efforts to restrict slavery in Missouri. Elected to the U.S. House of Representatives in

1821, he exerted national influence, rising to the position of Speaker of the House in 1827 during Adams's presidency and retaining the post for the first five years of Jackson's presidency. Stevenson ardently supported states' rights, southern power, and slavery. John considered it not only a matter of self-interest but also a patriotic duty to organize working-class men to vote for Stevenson when he ran for reelection in 1833, informing Joseph, "I have been engaged for sometime past in a *business* with all my heart for the love of country electioneering for Stevenson, our present representative in Congress. Our City tomorrow decides the question he comes from Hanover about 500 ahead of Mr. Robertson. I shall be up and a doing. I done all I could in Hanover, seeing them South Carolinians mustering at their Court Houses and carrying on as they did as if the General Government was a foreign enemy. B. W. Lee and all the talents of Henrico voted against us. The City may try to mass and I shall try and stir all the middleing class the working men to turn out. I am warm on this occasion; My Country, O my Country, good night" (April 25, 1833, WPFP). In the morning, he added a postscript about slave traders' woes: "I assure you without any jokeing that the prospects are very gloomy in the South respecting men who has thousands and thousands at Risque. One of my neighbors in that country has tried to sell at 1, 2, or 3 years credit; no sales effected. Mr. Priddy has not sold one. Great anxiety for his next letter not with me alone but with the traders in our City."

In 1836, Jackson appointed Stevenson to serve as the American minister to the Court of St. James's. Secretary of state John Forsyth informed Stevenson that the most urgent business of his diplomatic mission was to press "the claims of certain Americans against the British government for indemnification for a number of Negro slaves who had been seized and liberated by the British colonial authorities in the Bermudas and Bahamas" between 1831 and 1835 (Wayland 112). The British navy was working to stop the transatlantic slave trade, and slaveholders Stevenson and Forsyth were determined to defend "property rights." As the American ambassador in London, Stevenson devoted more correspondence to the African slave trade and the related issue of the right of search than to any other topic (Wayland 250n53). In January 1837, when he extracted approximately $115,630 from the British government to compensate southern slaveholders for the loss of liberated slaves, the *Richmond Enquirer*, whose editor, Ritchie, had known Stevenson all his life, commended him not only for defending the rights of individual slaveholders but also for establishing, from "a *national* point of view . . . a great and important principle" (Wayland 119).

As a politician, Stevenson forged crucial links between the various rungs of society—civil servants such as John B. Prentis; members of Congress; Presidents Jefferson, Madison, Adams, and Jackson; and foreign governments. In London, Stevenson and his wife, Sarah Coles Stevenson, a protégée of Dolley Madison, used all of their personal charm, social capital, and political skills to advance the American investment in slavery and concomitantly to remove international restrictions on the American trade in cotton, tobacco, and rice. Popular with the court and London's high society, the Stevensons were occasional guests of young Queen Victoria at Windsor Castle and attended her wedding to Prince Albert in 1840. Sarah Stevenson revealed the values of her class when she wrote to friends in Virginia, "It would be impossible for me to give you an idea of the excitement through which we have been passing. Such a whirl of splendors and gaiety, such riding and driving, so much to hear, to say, to do, such noise and bustle!" (qtd. in Wayland, 164). In contrast, her husband feigned extravagant self-pity when describing his career to his brother-in-law: "I presume you all think a Minister's life is one of leisure and ease. Far from it. It is one of labor, care and vexation, I may almost say slavery. . . . The continued round of dinners (public and private), parties, soirees and what not, to which we are doomed to go are enough to break one down. . . . [I]t is a great boor [*sic*]. I find it oppressive, tho' get along as well as I can" (qtd. in Wayland 158).

Jackson was an implacable authoritarian who gained fervent popularity among the majority of voters, almost all of whom were white men, by promoting white male democracy while vigorously repressing women, Indians, and blacks. Southern passions for land and slaves were inflamed by his aggressive policies of removing Indians and expanding slavery into new territories. When Cherokees were forcibly removed from Georgia and the state raffled off their lands in a lottery, Indian dispossession was celebrated in a popular song:

> All I want in this creation
> Is a pretty little wife and a big plantation
> Away up yonder in the Cherokee nation. (qtd. in Howe 414)

Jackson's racial militancy fostered "an epidemic of public violence that raged during his presidency" (Howe 411). "White supremacy, resolute and explicit, constituted an essential component of what contemporaries called 'the Democracy'—that is, the Democratic Party" (Howe 423). Violence breeds upon itself and spawns ever more hatred. Men filled with venom and eager to protect their "honor" not only committed atrocities against Indians and slaves but lashed out against political dissidents, abolitionists, women's rights activists, educators, labor activists, wives, daughters, and sons. In both the North and the South, mob violence was rampant and usually race-based, with abolitionists and free blacks the favorite targets. In 1835 alone, seventy-nine southern mobs "killed sixty-three people, while . . . sixty-eight northern mobs killed eight" (Howe 435). Violence broke out in the halls of Congress as well, with former congressman Sam Houston clubbing Representative William Stanberry in 1832 for alluding to "Houston's rigging of an Indian contract" and Congressman Preston Brooks of South Carolina beating Senator Charles Sumner of Massachusetts over the slavery issue on the floor of the Senate in 1856 (Howe 436). White supremacists would not tolerate other whites' criticism of their ideology or their corruption.

In addition to worrying about the health of markets and the long-term political viability of slavery, slave traders sometimes found their fortunes imperiled by outbreaks of diseases such as cholera and yellow fever. Their "merchandise" pursued infinitely creative modes of resistance and subversion. All slave traders dreaded slaves' capacity to undermine their value by being disobedient, talking back, going crazy, committing crimes, or running away. John Prentis often complained about runaways, yet he seemed to find the cat-and-mouse game of pursuit intellectually engaging and strangely pleasurable. When he described runaways, he revealed a particularized knowledge of individual slaves that he kept concealed at all other times. He narrated details about names, ages, heights, skin colors, hair types, facial features, emotional states, clothes, and life stories.

> I have this moment seen Mr. Somner from your Town who has a little Memorandum about a Runaway of Mr. Allens. Mr. Joseph Allen has his Boy now at this time at my House. I have strong suspicions that I know the Runaway in your Jaile. He is not a *boy* but a young Man a real Mulattoe a bushy Head of Hair; rather a down Look about five feet 3 or 4 inches named *William* formerly the property of a Mr. Garrett of King and Queen County Runaway from Him and went to Norfolk in the steam boat Capt. *Chapman* with forged free papers. Brought Back to Richmond and put

into my Jaile, sold out of [there]. Bought by Mr. Henry King who let him
stay with number of others at my friend Mr. *Wilkerson*, who hired him at
Mr. *Williams* tobacco factory. He has always been brought up to Waiteing
about the house Looks rather Delicate large eye brows. I do not recollect
any scars about him. He did have a pair of striped Pantaloons blue and
white *narrow striped* I think it was twilled Jeanes. He ran away about the
same time that Mr. Allens did. Also a black fellow of Mr. Wilkersons. Will
you oblige me so far as to get the Jailor to look into this *matter* for me and
let me hear as soon as possible the result. (September 11, 1827, WPFP)

John was far from unique in his manner of allowing his observational
and descriptive powers to blossom when slaves ran away. Runaway ads
were a long-standing genre in American newspapers. They aroused little
horror in minds accustomed to their stylistic conventions, but in the hands
of abolitionists, such notices became powerful fuel for antislavery sentiments. Foreign visitors also honed in on the gothic horrors of southern
newspapers. Charles Dickens, for example, observed many scenes of torture on a visit to Richmond and other southern sites in 1842. He penned
vitriolic indictments of the ways slavery saturated southern culture with
violence, and Americans as well as Britons read the famous writer's as-
sessments with dismay or rage, depending on their political persuasions.
One of his most powerful rhetorical devices was to reproduce excerpts
from runaway advertisements in which slaveholders bore witness to their
own sadism: chopped-off toes, mutilated ears, punched-out teeth, whip
marks, dog bites, collars, chains. Dickens excoriated southern newspapers for intermingling runaway ads with articles protesting the "abomi-
nable and hellish doctrine of abolition, which [the newspapers assert] is
repugnant alike to every law of God and nature. . . . The delicate mama,
who smiles her acquiescence in this sprightly writing as she reads the
paper in her cool piazza, quiets her youngest child who clings about her
skirts, by promising the boy 'a whip to beat the little niggers with'" (258–
59). Proslavery writers accused abolitionists of playing incendiary politics
by focusing on slavery's worst aspects. They cried foul, for example, when
the *Anti-Slavery Record* reprinted "a small woodcut drawing that was in
use at that time in the southern press to announce upcoming slave sales"
(Deyle 185). The *Record*'s editor responded, "Now, how does it come to
pass, that this said picture when printed in a southern newspaper is perfectly harmless, but when printed in the Anti-Slavery Record is perfectly
incendiary?" (qtd. in Deyle 185).

In September 1832, John Prentis set out to transport a group of slaves from Virginia to Alabama. In South Carolina, two men, Solomon and Ralph, who "sometimes calls himself Thomas," escaped. Both men were about twenty-one years old, about 5'10" tall, and "of dark complexion," according to detailed advertisements that Prentis placed in the *Richmond Enquirer* in July 1834, offering one hundred dollars for their apprehension and delivery. Prentis imagined that they had returned to their old neighborhood in Lancaster County, but they eluded him, and he was still searching for them two years later. Runaway slaves often received "plenty of help from neighboring slaves in escaping, hiding, and deciding when to come out" (Johnson 33).

Despite these escapes, John brought another coffle south in October 1832, selling some slaves on large plantations and others in small towns and cities. In December 1832, he told Joseph that he was in poor spirits because he was short of funds, but by the time he finished describing how he had lost the money, he sounded downright cheerful: "I wanted that money in Suffolk to lay out again. It was for the purchase of one of my Runaways who had a wife at Mr. [?]'s. I had upwards of two thousand dollars vested in slave property running wild in the woods this fall Not

100 DOLLARS REWARD. —Ran away from the subscriber, in September, 1832, in South Carolina, on his way to Alabama, two Negro men, namely, SOLOMON and RALPH. Solomon is about 21 years of age, dark complexion, very full eyes, about 5 feet 10 or 11 inches in height; and was purchased of Mr. Harvey, at Lancaster Court-house, Virginia, by Henry N. Templeman. Ralph sometimes calls himself Thomas, is about the same age, dark complexion, frowns very much when spoken to, is about 5 feet 9 or 10 inches in height; and was purchased of Doctor Kirk, Lancaster county, Va. by Mr. Templeman.—The above reward will be given for their apprehension and delivery to me, in Richmond, and all reasonable expences paid—or for their confinement in Jail, so that I get them again—or $50 for either of them. I think it probable that they have gotten back in their old neighborhood, from whence they were purchased.   **JOHN B. PRENTIS.**
June 13.   *Richmond, Virginia*

Facsimile of runaway ad, *Richmond Enquirer*, July 4, 1834.
Runaway ads often ran for several weeks after the dated posting.

all secured yet. My spirits has not left me as yet. I am still fat ragged and saucy. New York has a few hundred of my dollars" (December 10, 1832, WPFP).

John's profit margins suffered when his slaves ran away, but as a jailer, he profited from other masters' escaped and recalcitrant slaves. Ads for runaway slaves appeared often in the *Richmond Enquirer*, as they had for centuries in newspapers throughout the British colonies, sometimes alongside ads for runaway wives, sons, soldiers, and indentured servants. On May 12, 1829, Richard Walsh offered a ten-dollar reward plus all expenses to anyone who secured his runaway slave, Bob, in jail or delivered him to John B. Prentis in Richmond. On May 2, 1834, Joshua Alvis advertised for a runaway woman, Matilda, "to be delivered to Captain Prentiss' jail."

Searching for runaways made Prentis feel worthy of both pity and admiration, as he bragged to his brother:

William and myself had some rough times in the last of Feby and first of March in the woods thru cold sleety weather we stood it like good soldiers I left him about six miles beyond Yorkville South Carolina where he brought my last Runaway to me at night. In the morning ten days ride from home I started for my cabin and rode it in eight. The eight day at night I was snug enough at home with my old Woman. Horse nor his back *hurt* in the least from the saddle I average forty miles per day. (April 25, 1833, WPFP)

RUNAWAY

FROM the Subscriber, on the 4th inst., a negro man named BOB; about 5 feet 6 or 7 inches high, brown complexion, and a great impediment in his speech; hired by me from Mr. James Henry of King & Queen county, and formerly belonged to Washington Quarles of King William, where he will be apt to endeavour to make his escape; he was a runaway from the most part of last year, and once out of Henrico Jail.

I will give Ten Dollars reward, and pay all lawful expences for delivering the said negro to John B. Prentis, Richmond; or securing him in Jail so that I may find him.

            RICHARD WALSH.

May 8.

Facsimile of runaway ad, *Richmond Enquirer*, May 12, 1829.

$25 REWARD.—Ran away from the Subscriber, about the 25th Nov. Last, a Negro woman, named Matilda. She is a little above the common size of women of a brown complexion, and about 25 years old. It is thought that she may be somewhere up James River, or lurking above the Basin, as she was claimed as a wife by some boatman in Goochland. The above reward will be paid on her delivery at Captain Prentiss' jail, either by him, or by the Subscriber.   **JOSHUA ALVIS.** May 2.

Facsimile of runaway ad, *Richmond Enquirer*, May 2, 1834.

Prentis wasted no time wondering what motivated the runaways' desperate escapes or how they had survived the cold sleety weather, starvation, and terror. A month later, he boasted to his brother that all of the sales had worked out well. "The sort of seamstress one was the most unlikely sold for 500 Dls. The other two together 900 dls. My two runaway men, [Priddy] sold better I believe than he could have done last fall. The jail fees was something like 120 Dlr for both. After that I made something worthwhile" (May 31, 1833, WPFP). Prentis's assessment was not mere bragging; slaves often fetched higher prices late in the winter and early spring than in the fall. "The same person could sell for varying amounts from month to month with maximum prices offered during the height of the slave-trading season. . . . One study has found that, in the New Orleans market, slaves sold during the month of January brought prices 10.8 percent higher than those sold in September" (Deyle 57).

On January 28, 1830, the *Richmond Enquirer* reported that slaves aboard the *Lafayette*, an interstate slave ship bound for New Orleans, had revolted. The rebels were quelled after a hard struggle, and twenty-five of them were bolted to the deck until the ship reached its destination. Priddy was aboard the vessel with a coffle of Prentis's slaves. Downplaying the revolt as simply an unfavorable turn in his fortune's wheel, John assured Joseph that he was not discouraged and would not pause for a minute in his slave-trading work. Sick and medicated, he dictated to Priddy a letter to Joseph:

I have been from time to time determined to answer your kind and affectionate letter; but owing to my bad writing—and waiting, until my clerk got back from Orleans—I have neglected it until the present moment;

he returned upwards of a week ago; in as fine health as I ever saw him in my life. It is now night, and I am laying in my bed sick and been taking *calomel* with my William at my side, writing this and I dictate it—The mutiny, which you heard of was a bitter pill—and death blow to all that was on board, as respects the speculation; and dark and gloomy as the times were it required but the more fortitude, to bear under the pressure. William wrote to me constantly and regularly and sent me, all the money, he could get hold of. So you see sir, and I have the gratification, to tell you the fascinating charms of the Daughters of the Farros Table; or the sports of the ring; not fascinating Rowtell table or wheel of fortune; so called; did not roll my Bank notes into another pocket: I had to exclaim to my men on their return, well done good and faithful servants; as a proof of that—I sent one to his wife, on their return; as fast as a horse could carry him. As to my boy William, I can assure you that there was rolling, for I laid down my Public duties, for one night; I have a very fine young steed to match my horse Charles. In the morning he stood at my door, to a vehicle, with his neck bent, and his ears pricked forward, chomping at the bit—awaiting his two overjoyed passengers, one the darling son of his mother; myself delighted at being the bearer of an honest youth to his aged parents. Smack, went the whip; around went the wheels, and away went the horse. We stopped not to listen to neither friend, nor foe, until we got to the old gate post, where the watchful sentinel, the old gun hailed us, which brought the inmates of the house to look and from the actions of the old cur, they soon concluded that we had the watch word, which was friend. I can assure you the old fellow soon had a company around us, to have taken his prisoners, but he had not forgotten the hand which has afforded him a many piece of brass; What past afterward, I leave for you as a father to judge. As for myself I was full of Joy, and sick with Joy—Ten oclock at night and sorry sick—18th, a great deal better, nearly well. As we Jackson men generally go the whole hog, I am still in the market. I must ask the favour of you to inquire of the tavern keeper, whose name I know not, if there are any slaves in the market of any description, and for what prices they can be bought; they are very scarce here, and if there can be any bought in your part of the country I want to send after them. (May 17, 1830, WPFP)

Overjoyed by the safe return of his employees and with what he imagined as his own beneficent role in their lives, Prentis provided no evidence of being horrified or traumatized by the revolt. Rather than exuding fear, he appeared to relish the excitement and take pleasure as a victor after a hard battle. He would have had good reason to fear for his life. "By the 1830s, the killing of slave traders by their human cargoes had become so common that some whites in Virginia worried that it was having a negative effect upon the interregional trade, as well as on their most important export" (Deyle 255). If Prentis was worried, he did not share his anxieties with his brother. On the contrary, he cheerfully reminded Joseph of the bucolic domestic scene underwritten by slave trading: "My wife comes on bravely in the department of housewifery. The prospects of the garden are very flattering at this moment—a much finer one than I have ever had since we were married. It will save many a cent in Pocket. The prospects of the chicken coop is very flattering there is a continual musick in my yard, with the birds, and one hundred and twenty chickens, and a prospect for a good many more, having eight hens sitting" (May 1830, WPFP). He added a postscript underscoring his intention to proceed apace with his habitual business. "P.S. If the tavern keeper has any slaves on hand and could let me know through you, the ages and prices. I should know what to do. If I could get a small lot into this market in the course of two or three weeks I have no doubt, but what I could make something on them."

During the 1830s, when whites migrated in droves to the Lower South, "one out of every four slaves was forcibly removed" from Virginia to the lower states (Deyle 44). Prices for slaves boomed, as did Prentis's profits from slave trading. During a peak in the 1835–36 season, he itemized to Joseph "*The Cash*; We sold our slaves that you saw in my *yard* for Twenty five thousand eight hundred and fifty dollars [equivalent to approximately six hundred thousand dollars in the early twenty-first century], one half cash the other half 12 months credit bearing eight percent interest being the lawfull interest of the state. Mr. Priddy got to Orleans for our money haveing sold in a little town called Clinton Mississippi" (January 29, 1836, WPFP). However, the market sank after the financial panic of 1837, and "the price of cotton plummeted from seventeen cents a pound down to six cents, and the rate for prime male hands in New Orleans dropped from $1,300 to $700" (Deyle 56). Because his profits during good years were high and his business ventures were broadly diversified, Prentis was well positioned to ride out the market's ebbs. He was aided by his wife, who, he told his brother, "has astonished me in money matters and management." On his return home, Prentis purred with contentment at finding "all my servants well cloathed, smoke house full of meat, houses all tenanted" (January 29, 1836, WPFP). He had enjoyed the gratification of "two nights with my affectionate wife in my arms squeezed to my breast my *heart* would still *beat* a warm *heat*, yes, *thump strong*." Yet, he added, "this morning [I] waked with a stronger impulse and cried aloud for one that was still *absent*, my only *Brother*!! Yes my Brother. It shall release itself by scratching a few lines to him" (January 29, 1836, WPFP). Prentis's images could be read by twenty-first century readers as a sign that his desire for his brother was as sexually charged as his (alleged) satisfaction with his wife. We might wonder if John's boast about his sexual potency and pleasure in his wife's embrace was intended to assure Joseph that the widespread rumors about slave traders' sexual rapaciousness did not apply to him or that intimate months on the road with Priddy had no erotic overtones. Or we might marvel that a vicious slave trader could be a loving, grateful, sensual husband. Without discarding any of these possibilities, I would suggest that the passage might have a deeper meaning. After returning home from a spectacularly successful slave-trading trip, Prentis awakened crying, overwhelmed by a sense of absence. This absence gnawed at him despite his repetitious self-congratulations about his good life. He called the absent one "Brother." Perhaps his cry was provoked not by the absence of his biological brother but by the failure of his sense of human brotherhood.

During his first decade of slave trading, John B. Prentis had felt proud and gratified when Captain Edward Chamberlain, the husband of Prentis's sister, Mary Anne, spent a week with him in Richmond. After bragging to Joseph about his slave-trading profits, John described "a first rate gold pattern lever watch which I got Chamberlayne to buy *me* in Liverpool" (March 7, 1825, WPFP). By linking his acquisition of a gold watch to his profits from the slave trade, John unconsciously evoked a popular abolitionist song of the period, "The Negro Boy," in which the singer is an African prince who laments that his mind was once so enslaved by avarice that he traded "a fine boy" for a watch, a "poor simple toy." The song ends as a jeremiad prophesying that God "Whose voice in thunder's heard on high, / . . . In his own time will soon destroy / Th' oppressors of the Negro Boy." As the decades passed and his profits increased, Prentis may not have heard God's voice in the thunder of Nat Turner's rebellion or in the mutiny on the *Lafayette*, but he did begin to sense, as through a glass darkly, that his self-image was nightmarish. Bit by bit, the unspeakable entendres of "my family, black and white" would come to possess him.

CHAPTER 5   Family Values

> The government of a family, bears a Lilliputian resemblance to the
> government of a nation.
>
> —Mary Randolph, *The Virginia Housewife*

For John Prentis, the hardest part of being a slave trader was not figuring out how to deal with escapes and revolts; he found excitement in the chase, pleasure in the hunt. The hardest part was figuring out how to negotiate the tangled webs of "my family, black and white." He was a man of action who was best able to command men and speculate in human flesh when he did not pause for thought. When he confronted his family, black and white, his vexed tangle of needs, desires, fears, rage, and resentment grew so raw that he sometimes was compelled to slow down and reflect.

In March 1826, Prentis wrote to his brother, Joseph, to inquire if there were slaves for sale. Before getting down to business, John relayed the information that, according to their uncle, Robert Saunders, Rachel's daughter, Lucy, was distressed because she was being offered for sale to Ben White (March 7, 1825, WPFP). Saunders, who lived in Williamsburg, played a central role in conveying news, gifts, and business transactions among various members of the extended Prentis-Riddick-Saunders clan scattered throughout eastern Virginia. Lucy was married to a free man in Williamsburg, and having tasted freedom, she wanted to be free. Her husband, who may have been either white or black, could not afford to purchase her. John generally expressed contempt for free blacks but described Lucy's husband as a "very well disposed man sober and industrious," though he would "never be able to buy" Lucy (January 4, 1828, WPFP). Thousands of other poor white men and free black men saved enough money to purchase their enslaved wives and children. "In 1830 in the South, there were 3,684 black slaveholders, who owned a total of 11,916 slaves. . . . [T]he majority of these black slaveholders owned family members and lived in states that prohibited them from manumitting their relatives" (Deyle 245–46).

Saunders said he would try to do something for Lucy in six months, but John asked whether Joseph could "do anything for her." John would tell Saunders that he knew "nothing about it" but thought that Lucy belonged to Joseph. John explained, "I do not wish to purchase myself accept to sell again. Free negroes always do worst than slaves." He warned Joseph that Lucy's near freedom in Williamsburg had "ruined" her and she "now wants to be free; if she is your property Look sharp you don't loose her." John then articulated his core philosophy, a combination of traditional "family values" and capitalism: "*Charity* at home first a man ought always to stick close to his interest let his feelings be what they may." In other words, someone who wanted to practice "charity" should take care of his white family and avoid letting feelings get in the way of financial interests. Eliza and Mary Anne were intensely attached to Lucy's mother, Rachel, and John claimed to care about Rachel as well ("I have a great regard for the old woman and in need would assist her cheerfully"), but he expressed contempt for her freed son, Charles, and indeed for the concept of freeing slaves. "Her son Charles who has been *free* for a long time is good for nothing; I think that if I had *fifty dollars* [I would] give [it] away as charity instead of giveing off it to set a slave free" (March 7, 1825, WPFP).

John attempted to exile Lucy from his mind by itemizing the thousands of dollars he hoped to make from various categories of slaves. Although professing not to care about Lucy except insofar as he could profit from her sale, he found it hard to maintain a cool distance. Joseph and Saunders could not reconcile their paternalistic self-images with the violence of selling Lucy away from her birth community. Although Joseph was complicit in countless slave sales, he preferred to have John do the dirty work. The "crass commercialism" of selling Lucy "would expose the hypocrisy of paternalism" (Deyle 223). Rachel no doubt was doing everything in her power to circumvent Lucy's sale. Charles had obtained his freedom, probably through a combination of their efforts. Many slaves, especially long-term household slaves, were adept and resourceful at finding ways to avoid unwanted sales of themselves and their loved ones (see Johnson 30–37). The letters of the four Prentis siblings indicate that Rachel was the extended family's most valued slave. Eliza and Mary Anne likely would have been enraged if their brothers had sold Lucy away from the family.

Three years passed. Immersed in frenetic slave trading and other business activities, John procrastinated about dealing with the dilemma posed by Lucy, whom he could not avoid seeing as a distinctive human being. In *Slavery and Social Death*, Orlando Patterson shows that severing slaves from their bonds of kinship was a crucial component of enslavement. The Prentises had been trained from childhood to dismiss evidence of the significance of slaves' emotional needs and attachments. They had learned from the family of St. George Tucker, for example, that paternalism provided a convenient way to sidestep the "belief in universal freedom" and "dehumanize those African Americans [southerners] now profess to love" (Hamilton, "Revolutionary" 550). In 1804, Henry, St. George Tucker's son, had written a letter home describing the nightmares suffered by a ten-year-old enslaved boy, Bob, whom the Tuckers had separated from his mother in Williamsburg to send him to work at Henry's Winchester home. Although Bob appeared tortured by his mother's absence, Henry assured himself and his parents that "the American and African" were as different as "the civilized and savage . . . nay the man and the brute!" and that Bob's sufferings would be fleeting; his innate simplicity, affection, and docility would soon return (qtd. in Hamilton, "Revolutionary" 550).

In the case of Lucy, Joseph and John Prentis lacked Henry Tucker's cold decisiveness. John attempted to imagine her as a type of self-willed orphan by telling Joseph that "she has separated herself from her mother" (January 4, 1828, WPFP). Try as he might, though, he could not overcome the obvious evidence that Lucy was not a genealogical isolate but was a valued daughter, sister, and wife. Saunders continued to try without success to get his nephews to take definitive action. John pleaded with Joseph,

> Hear me for a moment if you please. If you should sell me Lucy I will not buy upon any other terms than that of her being my *slave* and will stand upon the same footing of all my other slaves upon no other *conditions* will I touch she has been free long enough and can be made one of the best slaves in Virginia I could not find one that would suit you better My advice to you is to take her home give her a room in the kitchen and make her attend to your children and their chambers She washes very well and understands Needle work. You cannot do better than to take her home

and try her. If she will not suit send her back to me I will either buy her or sell her for you just as you choose. Think on this subject if you please your feelings has been imposed upon long enough Why should you be deprived of the services of a good female servant or sell and then buy perhaps not get as good. . . . If you say the word I will send her down to you bag and baggage And if you will send any of your [other slaves] up to me I will sell them for the very best price and remit you the money Good servants is scarce with us at this time although I have some as good as any in Virginia and, I could, and, would make Lucy as good as any of them. (January 4, 1828, WPFP)

Joseph ultimately sent Lucy to John, but despite his harsh bluster, John did not immediately sell her. He either hired her out or sent her to work on one of his plots of land. In May 1830, he wrote to Joseph, "I have had to bring Lucy home this year, and she has had a fine son. She is very sick, and Mamma *Rachel* is here waiting on her" (May 1830, WPFP). Lucy was never again mentioned in their correspondence.

During Lucy's ordeals, Joseph Prentis finally wrapped up his father's estate, nineteen years after the judge's death. On January 12, 1828, Joseph Jr. gave his three siblings the last few dollars that he figured they were owed, carefully itemizing each allotment. John had received

1809	Oct. 4	negro woman Hannah taken at the appraisal	$100.00
	Oct. 19	Cash sent you to Philadelphia	50.00
1810	Mar. 26	check on the U.S. bank [illegible] for	100.00
	June 8	Cash this day paid you in Suffo[lk]	15.00
	July 7	Check on U.S. Bank paid you in Suffo. when you were going to Richmond to get work	40.00
1811	Jany 10	Cash paid you in full this day per receipt	465.03
			$770.03
1816	Jany 3	Cash paid you in part of your distributive share of the personal Estate of yr. father per receipt	120.00
1828	Jany 9	Cash in full paid you this day by your receipt	120.44
			$240.44

Joseph closed his ledger book with the note, "No interest was charged me by either sisters or brother. My [illegible] had always been very great, and now I thank God that I have finally paid off all the Legatees, and I feel much better satisfied" (Ledger, PFP). He had been careful to pay himself through the years for managing the estate, but he did not offer compensation to his siblings for the nineteen years' postponement of their inheritance—key years when all of them were struggling to find their way financially in the world.

One March midnight during the mid-1820s, before the estate was settled, John had sent Joseph a letter that reveals the emotional force of treasured childhood objects. John was unable to work because he was so entranced by some chairs that Joseph had sent, and John gushed, "Their was a great *Jubilee* at my house when the chairs arrived. It was equal to [the Marquis de] Lafayette's arrival [in Richmond in 1824]. I can assure you my brother that I have not experienced such a strong feeling of my *boyish* days since I have arrived to manhood. I actually, strange for me to *say*, spent one whole day in the house setting in *what*, why one of my fathers and mothers old arm *chairs presented* to *me* by my *Brother* which still makes it dearer to me. It caused me to ruminate back when I would set in it and behold the house that contained the first love that ever entered my heart and like to have been my Ruin" (March 22, [1824?], WPFP). The intensity of John's response, which moves from longing for parents and childhood to gratitude to his brother to bittersweet memories of youthful heartbreak, highlights the power Joseph controlled by neglecting to divide the property in a timely and fair manner.

Mary Anne Prentis Chamberlain had often found herself in financial straits over the years and with acute embarrassment had sometimes requested money from Joseph, always promising to pay it back even though he owed her money from the estate. By 1828, Mary Anne was at death's door, so the long-awaited inheritance no longer had much relevance. Her husband, Edward Chamberlain, was often at sea, and their only son often sailed with him. Afflicted by chronic emotional and physical ailments, Mary Anne sought solace in religion and the solicitations of Rachel. In late May 1828, she reported to Joseph that her husband and son were doing "a *very good* business" in the sugar trade, but she was beside herself with loneliness. "God grant that [my husband] may return speedily is my ardent prayer to heaven—Indeed I am by myself so much that I am almost *crazy*—How often do I wish that I had one of your dear girls with *me*." After inquiring whether Joseph had "heard anything of Brother John and his wife," she concluded with a plea to "excuse all blunders for my mind is not in a frame to compose a tolerable letter" (May 26, 1828, WPFP). Thirty-one-year-old Mary Anne died in New York shortly thereafter.

Her death did not disrupt her brothers' avid speculation in slaves, but they took the time to write an obituary so pious as to sound strangely impersonal and abstract:

> Her health had not been for several years such as to promise to her family and numerous and deeply attached friends, any considerable prolongation of that happiness which they enjoyed in the society of the deceased, and the attenuated thread by which hung so much of their earthly solicitude and affection, had, within a few months, told them that they must prepare for its early and perhaps sudden severance. Still the announcement that her spirit had winged its flight to another and we may hope, more blissful abode, was what they could not bear without poignant sorrow. The recollection of the many virtues and graces that through all the vicissitudes of this transitory existence, had daily enhanced her claims as a wife, a mother, a sister and friend, were too vivid—too deeply impressed upon their hearts not to overcome them with grief, for an event which, while it was their present loss, was her eternal gain. But resignation under the intentions of Providence, is enjoined by duties which those who recognize the obligations of religion, cannot disregard—and which ensures to the Christian consolation in every time of need. (Obituary, PFP)

Such was the stilted script of public mourning.

If Joseph attended to all of the instructions in his father's will, he would have had other duties along with the dispensation of personal property. His father had instructed his sons to reread his letters: "My Boys will not suffer their intercourse with the world to corrupt the purity of their Hearts. Hold fast those virtuous principles already inculcated in your Hearts, nor suffer the least deviation from the principles of integrity and Honesty. Recur to the many letters you have received from me, replete with advice calculated to make you men of Honesty and integrity and view them as tending to these great objects" (Will of Joseph Prentis Sr., October 7, 1807, WPFP). Before his death, Judge Prentis had confided to his elder son that he had low expectations of his younger son: "I fear that John has not that steadiness of mind, and evenness of manners which will promise himself Happiness in Life" (August 10, 1808, PFP). In contrast, Joseph Sr. had high expectations for Joseph Jr. When he was beginning to establish himself as a lawyer in Suffolk, the judge offered sage advice: "Your own Happiness is of more importance than wealth, and reject every means to get forward in Life, that may be at variance with the strictest Rules of Honesty, Morality & Virtue" (May 24, 1806, PFP). The fact that Joseph Jr. carefully preserved his father's letters suggests that he did treasure and reread them. But a chasm yawned between the judge's principles as a father and his practices as a consumer and slaveholder. Childhood at Green Hill had accustomed Joseph Jr. to a level of luxury based on a tight hierarchical order of race, class, and gender. His vision of happiness was inseparable from that order. By the time of Mary Anne's death, Joseph and Susan Prentis were managing a large Suffolk estate with several children, and it was not easy to imagine how happiness could be attained without wealth.

Having worked to uphold slavery during the Virginia Constitutional Convention of 1829–30, Joseph Prentis Jr. again found his state torn apart by vociferous controversies over race and class during the next two years. He responded with divided loyalties and painful ambivalences. As William Freehling aptly observes, "Nat Turner murdered slaveholders' domestic illusion" (180). The 1831 insurrection was "an anti-domestic coup" (181). Turner's army revolted against slavery's twisted family values by entering white homes and slaughtering white families. In response, "panicky whites briefly turned the Domestic Institution into an anti-domestic prison. Homes were abandoned. Women and children were garrisoned. Men marched in front of un-family-like forts, as if guarding jails. Having previously assumed, albeit with occasional qualms, that hearths and firesides were safe from midnight assassins, slaveholders now assumed the unmentionable reverse: that every domestic could be an executioner. Having previously assumed, albeit with some brutal lashings, that fatherly cuffs would keep slaves laboring, patriarchs now slaughtered dozens of suspected blacks, put bodyless heads on display, savagely reminded Cuffee of the price for not obeying Massa" (Freehling 181).

Prentis was alarmed by Nat Turner but was made even more uneasy by the ensuing debate within the Virginia General Assembly. In November 1831, Governor John Floyd argued that Turner's Southampton insurrection was no isolated incident and proposed to other southern governors that the entire South should take steps toward emancipation. In January 1832, for "the first and only time in the nineteenth century," "a southern state openly considered abolishing the institution of chattel slavery. For many white Virginians, this most successful of all North American slave insurrections shook their confidence in the slave system and its presumption that their 'people' were happy with their lot" (Deyle 40). Not only did delegates from western Virginia, where only a few whites owned slaves, propose abolishing slavery, but several prominent members of eastern Virginia's Old Order also sought slavery's demise. Thomas Jefferson Randolph, grandson of Thomas Jefferson, proposed gradual abolition on the grounds, as Freehling puts it, that "true patriarchs must save future families. In his speech in the Virginia House of Delegates on January 16, 1832, initiating the legislature's historic debate, [Randolph] predicted how his slaves would murder his grandchildren" (182). Floyd's nephew, delegate James McDowell Jr., agreed with Randolph, calling "this 'domestic institution' an inseparable union of 'danger and slavery'" (Freehling 183). Citizens flooded the newspapers with passionate editorials on both sides of the question. "In the end, the slaveholders in the state managed to thwart this challenge to their identity and their livelihood, but just barely, as the legislature came within fifteen votes of abolishing the institution" (Deyle 40). Thomas Dew helped to win the debate for slavery by arguing that although he hoped that the Upper South would one day become lily-white, slavery was biblically sanctioned and was a positive good, at least in hot climates. He suggested that antislavery views should not even be aired in public. He was no Jacksonian Democrat—far from it. As Freehling observes, Dew believed that "upper-class domination of poorer folk, black and white, was written into the Virginia government. Dew sometimes wrote color-blind domination into his proslavery argument" (191).

The vituperative public controversy left Joseph Prentis Jr. reticent and touchy about the slave trade. As if the inflammatory state debates were not sufficiently disturbing, black Bostonian abolitionist David Walker published an incendiary 1829 pamphlet, *Appeal to the Colored Citizens of the World*, that circulated throughout the anglophone world, including the South, despite efforts to repress it. Walker dissected Jefferson's *Notes on the State of Virginia* and excoriated Christians for supporting slavery. Abolitionist voices seemed to be gaining force everywhere. Just when he was most uneasy about slavery, Joseph grew ill, and his law practice suffered. Overwhelmed by debts that he believed he would never be able to surmount, he turned to his brother for help. John was feeling financially squeezed by the escape of two slaves, but he grabbed the opportunity to display munificence. He sent $276, for which Joseph thanked his younger brother profusely, exclaiming "it is a sum of a *magnitude which I never own[ed].*" He was "much relieved in mind at the prospect of having it in my power to pay off the most of the debts which I owe. The debts alluded to are such as are unavoidable, unmixed with a particle of extravagance on my part, or that of any of my dear household; but it is in part the consequence of my long continued ill health in August & September, and the expenses attendant thereon, together with the part reduction of the fees in my profession, and the diminution of business." He admitted that his sufferings were small compared to those of other people; indeed, he was not completely blind to the connection between the relief of his suffering and the infliction of atrocities on other people. He confessed, "It is true that my spirits were bad when I wrote you, and I fear that I complain too often of my situation, (which when compared with the condition of thousands of my fellow creatures is enviable) and that by so doing I commit much sin, but I am a poor frail mortal, and nothing, no nothing at all of myself. My dear Maria Louisa has gotten through the scarlet fever successfully and I thank God that she has. She is somewhat reduced. Susan has been much indisposed" (December 15, 1832, WPFP). Maria Louisa, Joseph and Susan's ninth child, died the following September at the age of seven. Three of their eleven children died as infants, and three more died in childhood or adolescence. Even for the wealthy, life was hard, and financial pressures could be intense. When the brothers felt a need to justify, to themselves above all, the sins they knew themselves to be committing, they meditated on life's hardships. Their letters often testified to their taste for luxuries, but when they felt guilty about the miserable condition of "thousands of [their] fellow creatures," they diverted their gaze to focus on their own hardships.

Overwhelmed by brotherly compassion, John gave vent to a torrent of feelings: wounded pride, self-contempt, love, and desperate desire for acceptance. As he barreled full-steam ahead in the slave trade, his anti-elitist rages were inflamed by the elite's contempt for the "lower orders." John's awareness that his activities as a slave trader were controversial within his extended family also aroused his bitter resentment.

> I am no writer or scholar enough to explain myself accept in plain plantation talk: We are Brothers. I have been the most wild and uncouth in manners.
> Our feelings no doubt are much alike in our reflecting moments how we shall get along in the world to *live* and be able to pay our way. It *distresses* me much at times, and God only knows how it is possible that such a creature as myself has gotten along thus far. It has been by his mercy and goodness; Notwithstanding all that with the dollars upon dollars that

has passed through my hands and still continue to pass and the prospect
of a large amount of a years work ahead of me to keep mind and body
employed I feel still poor in need and in want for fear that I shall come to
want. Paper money in my pocket the *Banks* good today tottering tomorrow the next day broke. Top payment 12 cents in the dollar. I have unfor-
tunately some of the handsomest pretty notes of that denomination that
you ever saw the Hundred Dollar Bills pasted up in Maria Louisa Baby
House would be an ornament for pictures. My spirits get low down to
the lowest ebb, untill I looke around me and take a retrospective *view* of
my fellow mortals and see their situation in life cloathed with misery and
woe. I feel thankfull for my condition; Give me health and strength. I will
try and scuffle to the last moment; although my feelings are often sported
with that I have no use for money. No *children* to raise rich enough; The
calls upon me for support of those that I have around me keeps me always
in motion. They are fair and honorable calls the people I have in my
employment the slaves I own there wants with me is great the feeding
and clothing. Sometimes miserably in thoughts, O, sometimes the happi-
est being in the world. (December 27, 1832, WPFP)

In this passage, John's use of passive verbs obscures who was sporting
with his feelings by suggesting that he had "no use for money" because
he had no children. He might have been insulted explicitly by other people, or he might have heard an accusing voice in his own heart or in his
wife's laments. He had amassed significant wealth—many plots of land; a
house, jail, and outbuildings; factories and rent-bearing tenements; three
horses and two carriages; a carryall valued at $30; and a barouche worth
$175. Aside from the slaves whom John purchased for resale, he and his
wife owned six slaves, who worked as maids, gardeners, ostlers, drivers,
carpenters, builders, and assistants in the slave trade. But to both her
and her husband's dismay, Catharine had never borne a child. Material
acquisition lost its luster and logic without heirs. Once John and Catharine Prentis had acquired more than they needed for their own survival
and comfort, why should they keep working so hard? To what end? What,
after all, was the meaning of their lives? What greater purpose justified
their daily struggles and cruelties? Privileged classes traditionally constructed property rights not only as a justification but as a mandate for
upholding exploitative social structures in the name of safeguarding the
family. Without children or heirs, John and Catharine stood in danger of
being unmoored from bonds of kinship. In this letter, he filled the ideo-

logical gap by substituting the "fair and honorable" claims placed on him by other "dependents" for the claims of children. Thus, his employees and slaves became, at least at the level of rhetoric, surrogate children whose needs justified the continuance of his professional endeavors. He predicted that he would find palpable comfort for his many emotional wounds if his brother would accept his gift.

> The act and deed which I expect to do this day if I am permitted to remain on this earth 12 months longer in my *sad* and *disconsolate* moments it shall and will shine a great light in my heart and imagination, it will make my pillow sweet and easy; O would my Brother consider it as a help, estimate it as such; comeing from that young Brother, whose ways and actions I know once was disagreeable to the whole of my connections. Peter Bowdoin who would not know his nephew John, my house that was always open to Robert Saunders junior, when Robert Greenhow would not endorse his *fathers* note for 1000 Dlls, I gave him a check on the Bank for 1000 dlls to go to France. My House, wife and self at this time is not *known*. The rideing of my horse is forgot. Several years trouble of collecting his rents, having the houses repaired, all *forgot* sunk in *oblivion*. His wife a-gone sons daughter, good bye you mechanick and slave dealer. I have lived to see the houses sold, plantation in the market. Encourage your boys to work. Let your boys know that they have got to work it is no crime to be seen at labor. Our Gentleman Prentis's of Petersburgh brought their pigs to a fine market, no laboring men amongst them, ashamed of me when in company, haveing the calling of a mechanick. (December 27, 1832, WPFP)

John's plea that Joseph accept the money lays bare a key dynamic in their relationship. Whenever Joseph accepted money from John, John interpreted his ability to give and Joseph's willingness to receive as a sign of Joseph's acceptance of John and of his lowly professions. His belief that his relatives' contempt for slave traders was a form of class snobbery was not mere self-delusion. Abolitionist Theodore Dwight Weld observed that slave traders "are not despised because they *trade in slaves* but because they are *working* men, all such are despised by slaveholders" (qtd. in Deyle 239).

All of the relatives whom John named were members of Virginia's slaveholding elite. His mother's brother, Peter Bowdoin of Northampton County, had died in 1829, so John's reference to his uncle represented an old wound. Robert Saunders Jr. (1805–68), John's cousin, had grown up near Joseph and John in Williamsburg and had completed a bachelor's degree at the College of William and Mary in 1823 and subsequently read law at the University of Virginia. Robert Jr. was courting and in 1828 would marry Lucy Burwell Page, the youngest daughter of former Virginia governor John Page, and was embarking on a prestigious career. He would hold a position as professor of mathematics at the College of William and Mary from 1833 until his death and serve terms as mayor of Williamsburg, vestryman of the Bruton Parish Church, president of Williamsburg's Eastern Lunatic Asylum, president pro tem of the College of William and Mary (1846–48), and a Whig representative in the Virginia State Senate (1852–58). During the secession debates, he was, by white southern standards, a moderate who supported slavery but opposed Virginia's secession and the formation of the Confederacy ("Saunders"). Robert Greenhow Jr. was yet another cousin from Williamsburg, where his father, Robert Sr., had been a merchant until about 1815, when he moved the family to a two-story octagonal home built in Richmond by Edmund Randolph. The home faced the Capitol and was staffed by twelve slaves. Not unlike John B. Prentis, Robert Sr. built a mercantile business, amassed twenty-one lots of city land, and owned farmland in Henrico County ("Greenhow"). He was elected to the Virginia Assembly and served for a period as Richmond's mayor. Robert Greenhow Jr., an interpreter and librarian for the U.S. State Department, wrote books about the western territories and was acquainted with many literary figures, including Edgar Allan Poe. Greenhow's wife, Rose O'Neale Greenhow, a feisty heiress, would become a celebrated Confederate spy during the Civil War. Finally, the "Gentleman Prentis's of Petersburgh" who were ashamed to be seen in John's company were the children of his uncle, William Prentis, a prominent printer and longtime mayor of Petersburg.

All of John's disapproving relatives were slaveholders, and all slaveholders at least occasionally bought and sold slaves. In other words, all slaveholders were part-time slave traders. Why, then, did John's cousins object to his profession? Steven Deyle explains, "More than any other facet of their slave system, the domestic trade troubled white southerners. For those who believed in their society's proslavery defense, the domestic trade always posed a problem, as it exposed the slaveholding class's failure to live up to its paternalistic ideals. Consequently, while the domestic trade was always perfectly legal, it was treated quite differently by southern society than the traffic in cotton, railroad stocks, or any other commodity. In fact, despite the widespread presence and importance of the domestic slave trade for the southern economy, its existence was often condemned or publicly denied" (223–24). Paternalism romanticized slavery as an affectionate, nonmarket relationship between benign patriarchs and the "dependents" who labored under their "protection." The undeniable horrors of family separations, slave coffles, and public auctions ripped the happy mask off of paternalism's face. Thus "slaveholders' defense of their slave system required that someone else had to take the blame for the cruel consequences of their actions. And that was what made the slave trader so essential. He became the perfect scapegoat for all of the system's ills" (Deyle 242). As legislators, lawyers, and judges, Joseph Prentis Sr. and Joseph Prentis Jr. were far more responsible for slavery's continuance than was John, but neither of them suffered the slightest ostracism within Virginia's elite society.

John further urged Joseph to "press your boys to work. The Mechanicks is the *Bone* and *Sinew* of the *country*" (December 27, 1832, WPFP). The unintended irony of this passage illuminates not only John's life choices but the vexed politics of Jacksonian populist politics, which Freehling summarizes as "pure egalitarianism for white males, pure servility for blacks" (164). During his years of apprenticeship in Philadelphia, John had objected to slavery because he believed it made white boys and men lazy. As a slave trader, he justified his investment in slavery with the claim that he worked hard, whereas critics of his profession were afraid of hard work. In short, he rejected class hierarchy while endorsing racial hierarchy.

If Joseph felt any twinges of guilt over accepting money made from the slave trade, John rubbed salt in the wound with a postscript: "If my brother acceeds to the above . . . [t]ry and find out some sales of slaves for me. I want to come down in that part of the world; I should like to buy some of the country traders out. I do not want men. I will give fair prices. I want and must have next month if money will get them: Do not go against your feeling or conscience about the slaves for me. It is not my wish. Would it be *treason* for Robert [Joseph's son, who was practicing law alongside his father] to make some enquiries. Let him write" (December 27, 1832, WPFP).

In May 1833, John overcame his resentment against his Northampton County relatives because he was planning a trip to the Eastern Shore and

wanted help from his cousin, Peter Bowdoin (1796–1875). John asked
Joseph

> to do a little writeing for me. Slaves is so extremely high here and in the
> vicinity that I want to try my luck on the Eastern Shore Va. At least I want
> to hear from there. . . . I do not know where to address a letter to our
> relation Peter Bowdoin or what sort of a man he is. . . . I could you know
> my Brother go there and find out and see all these things without make-
> ing myself known. To save a disagreeable trip by water and the spending
> of some money which is the root of evil, I must get the favor of you if you
> [are] *perfectly willing* so do. . . . [W]rite to him to this purpose. I your
> Brother wants to purchase about 30 or 40 slaves perhaps more depend
> altogether upon the price all kinds sorts and sexes not exceeding 25 years
> not one single one from its mother under 12 years. Under 12 the mother
> must be along with it. I am not anxious for men, plough boys. I want
> women first and second children there if young. Young women 18 yrs to
> 22 strong and likely for the feild. The prices for such I want to know. Bet-
> ter for you to understand, I put it this way. Young men from 18 to 22 what
> price so on, or I name them Young Women from 18 to 22, Boys from 12
> to 18, Girls from 12 to 18, a women first child, a women with 2 children,
> a woman with 3 children. What place is the best, a court house or county,
> what way is the best to get there, there is two line of Packets that runs
> from Norfolk, if there is any persons there who is a trader that has any
> on hand. This is the information I should like for you to get for me and
> request him to write me they answer at, Richmond Va. Do not forget to
> inform him somehow, *your way*, that John is not a good pensman, a rough
> Blunt sort of a fellow, plain as a [illegible] stem. (May 31, 1833, WPFP)

This letter reveals the ways in which John's profession positioned him
at the epicenter of Virginia's storm of contradictory family values. He
explicitly called on his white family connections to help him rip apart
black families and communities so that he and other whites could expand their investments in the beautiful patriarchal institution where the
slaveholder cherished his family, black and white. "Of the two-thirds of
a million interstate sales made by the traders in the decades before the
Civil War, twenty-five percent involved the destruction of a first marriage
and fifty percent destroyed a nuclear family—many of these separating
children under the age of thirteen from their parents. Nearly all of them
involved the dissolution of a previously existing community. And those
are only the interstate sales" (Johnson 19). Although John Prentis found

it advantageous to sell mothers together with their children under the age of twelve, he gave no regard to fathers and indeed did not want to purchase men.

How does one write a letter of introduction to persuade a gentlemanly relative to itemize, by categories of gender, age, and fertility, the human beings for sale in one's neighborhood? John suspected that this writerly predicament was beyond his ken. For him, words did not flow smoothly along well-worn conventional lines, as they did for Joseph. John's sentences spurted out clumsily, rough clamorous run-ons. He did not know when to pause gracefully or when to come to a full stop. He lacked a gentleman's mastery of turns of phrase that mask, conceal, and beautify. His second attempt to clarify precisely what it was that he wanted was uglier than his first. There was, in fact, no way to make the brutal realities of the commercial transactions sound polite. Stronger intellects, greater orators, and smoother writers than John succeeded in more or less persuading themselves and others that slavery's domestic arrangements were beautiful, but no one could write well enough to beautify the trade. In fact, southerners spewed venom on dealers, and some churches denied them communion. "The Huntsville, Alabama, *Democrat* dismissed them as 'more abject, more mean, more degraded below the standard of men than the poor human flesh in which they traffic.' [A] newspaper in Tennessee complained that 'these vile slave-drivers and dealers [were] swarming like buzzards around carrion, throughout this country'; and a Mississippi man simply remarked that 'if any of the worshippers of Mammon earn their gold, it is the slave-dealer.' The result was an almost universal public condemnation by southern apologists of the occupation of slave trader. As the Baltimore editor Hezekiah Niles complained, 'We cannot conjure up to our imagination a character more monstrous than that of a dealer in slaves'" (Deyle 238).

John Prentis's responses to social censure vacillated among pain, shame, bitterness, rage, and indifference. His letters rarely exhibited remorse about the violence and cruelty of his profession; instead, he often expressed anger at the slaveholding elite's affectations of moral superiority. He walked a tightrope between despising their patrician airs and priding himself on his well-ordered fiefdom. "William [Priddy, Prentis's agent] has come home safe and sound all straight as a shingle," he wrote in a typical vein. "I can say well done good and faithfull servant. My House is quite lively and cheerfull the Horses good faithfull creatures near their stalls in the stable. . . . My Wife joins me in love to you all" (John B. Prentis to Joseph Prentis Jr., [1833?], WPFP). Prentis insisted that he had earned his domain, unlike his incompetent, lazy, self-righteous critics, who could not even figure out how to hold onto the plantations they had inherited. He strove to find such critics contemptible to repress his raw longing for their love and approval, which sometimes hit him as almost unbearable.

In broad ideological terms, antebellum American disputes regarding race, gender, and class centered on the questions of who constitutes the family and what social arrangements would be most conducive to "the family's" happiness. The U.S. Supreme Court's 1857 *Dred Scott v. Sanford* decision explicitly framed the issue of slavery as a matter of defining who belonged within the human family. In his majority opinion, Chief Justice Roger Brooke Taney quoted the most troublesome words in American founding documents: "We hold these truths to be self-evident: that all men are created equal; that they are endowed by their Creator with certain unalienable rights; that among them is life, liberty, and the pursuit of happiness; that to secure these rights, Governments are instituted, deriving their just powers from the consent of the governed." He then opined, "The general words above quoted would seem to embrace the whole human family. . . . But it is too clear for dispute, that the enslaved African race were not intended to be included, and formed no part of the people who framed and adopted this declaration; for if the language, as understood in that day, would embrace them, the conduct of the distinguished men who framed the Declaration of Independence would have been utterly and flagrantly inconsistent with the principles they asserted; and instead of the sympathy of mankind, to which they so confidently appealed, they would have deserved and received universal rebuke and reprobation" (qtd. in Finkelman 61, 63; see also Fehrenbacher 350–51).

But the Supreme Court did not speak for the national body. In fact, the justices' words helped prepare the battlefields for civil war. A growing number of escaped slaves were publishing powerful memoirs and traveling abolitionist lecture circuits to expose slavery's atrocities. Free black activists, intellectuals, journalists, and preachers created alliances with thousands of white abolitionists in a massive transatlantic struggle against slavery. One of the earliest white abolitionists to serve as an amanuensis for a former slave was a distant Vermont kinsman of John

John and Catharine Prentis's favorite niece, Margaret Susan Prentis Webb (1810–82), holding her son, Joseph Prentis Webb (1843–92). Margaret's husband was Robert Henning Webb of Suffolk, Virginia. Oil painting by Oliver Perry Copeland, 1844. Courtesy of the Virginia Historical Society.

THE PARTING "Buy us too".

"Buy Us Too." In this engraving, an enslaved woman holds up her baby to a slave trader, pleading not to be separated from her husband. Courtesy of the Virginia Historical Society.

Prentis, Benjamin Franklin Prentiss, who in 1810 recorded, edited, and published an extraordinary first-person account of transatlantic slavery, *The Blind African Slave; or, Memoirs of Boyrereau Brinch, Nicknamed Jeffrey Brace*. About the same age as John B. Prentis, Benjamin Prentiss raged in the memoir's introduction, "When we look at the custom of European and American nations of purchasing, stealing, and decoying in to the chains of bondage the negroes of Africa, and the custom sanctioned by the laws of the several governments; that public and private sales are legal; that they are bartered, sold, and used as beasts of the field, to the disgrace of civilization, civil liberty, and christianity; each manly feeling swells with indignation at the horrid spectacle, and whoever has witnessed the miserable and degraded situation to which these unfortunate mortals are reduced, in the West Indies and southern states of United America, must irresistibly be led to ask—Does not civilization produce barbarity? Liberty legalize tyranny? And christianity deny the humanity it professes?" Prentiss concluded that everyone who "wishes to preserve the constitution of our general government, to keep sacred the enviable and inestimable principles, by which we are governed, and to enjoy the natural liberty of man, must embark on the great work of exterminating slavery and promoting general emancipation" (Brace 89–90).

By the 1840s, thousands of Americans held similar views. Great orators such as William Lloyd Garrison, Frederick Douglass, and Sojourner Truth were delivering thunderous jeremiads. Walt Whitman, America's most visionary poet, was on the streets peddling radically egalitarian family values.

> Swiftly arose and spread around me the peace and knowledge that pass all
>   the argument of the earth,
> And I know that the hand of God is the promise of my own,
> And I know that the spirit of God is the brother of my own,
> And that all the men ever born are also my brothers, and the women my
>   sisters and lovers
> And that a kelson of the creation is love. (33)

While many southerners were cultivating nostalgia for a golden age of (white) family honor and patriarchal order, many residents of New England were dreaming of creating a more just and peaceable world. As Ralph Waldo Emerson exclaimed to his friend, Thomas Carlyle, almost anyone "you met on the streets of Boston might produce from his waistcoat pocket a community project for the reorganization of society" (qtd. in Ludlum 262).

Among the most radical of antebellum dreamers were an eclectic assortment of intellectuals who viewed the patriarchal family not as an ideal but as the social foundation of oppression and misery. Communes devoted to developing egalitarian gender roles, sexual practices, and child-rearing practices sprang up in many places throughout America and Britain. During waves of religious awakenings, some converts renewed their commitment to the status quo, while others were inspired to smash the oppressive forces of slavery, alcohol, war, and patriarchal domination. Mainstream American religious and political ideologies upheld possession of private property as a primary article of faith as well as the foundation of the social order, but a vibrant assortment of dissenters viewed the human invention of and lust for private property as the wellspring of human misery. They noted that the concept of private possession provided the ideological and legal foundations for the dispossession of Indians, enslavement of Africans, and subjugation of women. In 1837, one particularly radical dreamer, Vermont native John Humphrey Noyes (1811–86), urged William Lloyd Garrison to renounce citizenship under a government that was "drunk with tyrannic power and rampant with cruelty toward Negroes, Indians and missionaries" (qtd. in Ludlum 247). Garrison's sons later credited Noyes with inspiring their father's radical antislavery stance. In his 1849 pamphlet, *Bible Communism*, Noyes argued that "the chain of evil which holds humanity in rein has four links: first, a breach with God; second, a disruption of the sexes involving a special curse on women; third, oppressive labor, bearing specially on man; fourth, death. The chain of redemption brings reconciliation with God, proceeds to a restoration of the true relations between the sexes, then to a reformation of the industrial system, and ends with victory over death" (qtd. in Ludlum 245). Noyes argued that love and sex would be liberated if men would practice "Male Continence" (coitus interruptus), thus freeing women from relentless childbirth. Traditional possessive marriage would be replaced by a cooperative communal home in which "men and women will mingle like boys and girls in their employments, and labor will become sport" (qtd. in Ludlum 246). After a sheriff was sent to remove the troublesome Noyes and his followers, the group relocated to Upstate New York and established the Oneida community.

In the 1840s, Horace Greeley published several articles in his *New York Tribune* advocating the formation of cooperative communities, and many prominent intellectuals experimented with such settlements. Ralph Waldo Emerson observed that during its brief existence, the Massachusetts communal experiment of Brook Farm had been "the pleasantest of residences. It is certain that freedom from household routine, variety of character and talent, variety of work, variety of means of thought and instruction, art, music, poetry, reading, masquerade, did not permit sluggishness or despondency; broke up routine. There is agreement in the testimony that it was, to most of the associates, education; to many, the most important period of their life, the birth of valued friendships, their first acquaintance with the riches of conversation, their training in behavior. . . . What knowledge of themselves and of each other, what various practical wisdom, what personal power, what studies of character, what accumulated culture many of the members owed to it!" ("Life" 264–65). Living communally enabled people to share the taxing chores necessary for survival, providing an efficient way to organize time and resources. Companionship could lighten, sweeten, and vary the quotidian grind of work, freeing some moments for the simple pleasures of reading, writing, art, music, trying new recipes, or walking with friends—leisure activities that were confined to the Sabbath and holidays for the many nineteenth-century wives and daughters who lacked large staffs of servants or slaves. In her 1898 memoir, *Eight Years and More: Reminiscences, 1815–1897,* antislavery activist and women's rights pioneer Elizabeth Cady Stanton recalled the hardships of running a nuclear household as a young wife. Her duties were so numerous and exhausting that all of her intellectual and artistic pleasures and aspirations "faded away in the struggle to accomplish what was absolutely necessary from hour to hour." She longed for a cooperative, communal household. Linking the fight against women's oppression to the fight against slavery, Stanton observed, "Emerson says, 'A healthy discontent is the first step to progress.' The general discontent I felt with woman's portion as wife, mother, housekeeper, physician, and spiritual guide, the chaotic conditions into which everything fell without her constant supervision, and the wearied, anxious look of the majority of women impressed me with a strong feeling that some active measures should be taken to remedy the wrongs of society in general, and of women in particular" (146).

Slaveholders, from the poorest owners of a single slave to the largest planters who owned hundreds, also sought to lighten their daily workloads by extending their households beyond the nuclear family. Unlike the "spiritual communists" who sought to increase the happiness of all members of society, however, slaveholders fortified the social hierarchies of race, gender, and class. They advanced the notion that "enjoyment" was the paterfamilias's special entitlement. White male citizens were uniquely possessed of the right to pursue happiness, to "harness pleasure as a productive force, and regulate the modes of permitted expression. Slave owners managed amusements as they did labor, with a keen eye toward discipline" (Hartman, *Scenes* 44). For slaveholders, slavery promised a romance of community that would cater to all of their needs, desires, and pleasures. For slaves, slavery made a mockery of the notion of human community. Its "family values" were brutally asymmetrical.

Slavery's brutality was clear in 1835 when Joseph Prentis asked John to help sell a slave who had been charged with a crime and was in danger of being killed:

> What could you afford to give, or what can be obtained, for a very likely black boy 18 or 20 years old? The prices here, as I am told, are from $750 to $800 and upwards the former sum has already been offered. It is probable that I shall be compelled to sell one of this description. He is charged with a crime about which there is great doubt, as I hear from others, for the case happened during my absence at Southampton court, the early part of the week. The boy is in jail for safe keeping, and I have satisfied the person yesterday, where he was, and invited a public prosecution against the slave.
>
> There are speculators at this moment here, and always agents, who are very anxious to buy.
>
> Before I concluded to sell, for I am so threatened with the entire loss of this boy, that he is confined at my expense for safe keeping, I wished to counsel with you, to know the prices, as I must of course desire, if forced to sell, to get all the money I can for him. If a sale is made, the boy must be sent far away, and would not be sold but on those terms.
>
> Your reply to this letter by the mail, after you shall receive it, will greatly oblige me.

In a postscript, as if it were an afterthought, Joseph informed John of the death of the husband of their sister, Eliza:

> Dear brother, I am not certain whether I apprized you of the death of Capt. [Samuel] Vickery, who died on the 2nd inst. His protracted illness had for many months held out no rational hope that he could survive. His pains and bodily sufferings were long and many; he died however

calm and composed, without a struggle, or a groan, as an eye witness told me, haveing full reliance on a blessed immortality.—Our widowed sister derives great comfort and consolation from the happy change which took place before his death and is indeed a balm to her aching heart. (December 1832, WPFP)

The death of his brother-in-law and his sister's state of mind took second place in Joseph's mind to the sale of "his boy," illuminating how much his investment in slavery had usurped other sentiments.

Vacationing with his wife at a wedding party in King William County, John responded to Joseph's distress in a manner that initially sounded cheerful and chatty, then grew coolly distant ("I am not in the market at this time"), and finally revealed rage that his aunt, Susan Bowdoin, had omitted him from her will. His brother-in-law's death evoked little attention for its own sake, but the association of death with inheritances provoked bitter memories.

Mr. Priddy has just arrive at my friend Pembertons House in this County and handed me your letter My wife and self haveing been absent from *home* some *days* on a wedding expedition. She has been as busy as hen with one chick. . . . My Wife is at the wedding house hard at work, Priddy in the porch in high chat with my friends daughter still fatigued with his ride from Richmond. . . . I would advise you to take for your young man the price offered as can be obtained say 750 to 800 dlls Richmond price. I am not in the market at this time. Mr Priddy informs that was the price when he left Richmond, *Cash*. I am building houses improveing my *Property* makeing tobacco *boxes*. (June 24, 1835, WPFP)

After cursorily alluding to his brother-in-law's death—"I feel for my *Sister She* is not forgotten"—John launched into a tirade about the will of their deceased Aunt Susan, evidencing no affection or sorrow over her passing. "If my *Aunt* had bestowed her little mite on my *sister* or her Poor Virtuous Connexions *instead* of *giveing* it to *curse* my *country* makeing it an *addition* to my country worst than the seven *plagues* that visited *Egypt*. I, I wanted nothing. . . . The last interview I had with her she spoke with *scorn* and such *coldness* of my father, that it *stuck* in my *heart*. . . . [I]t shall go down with me to my *grave*" (June 24, 1835, WPFP).

Susan Bowdoin, Margaret Prentis's sister, had helped raise the Prentis children after Margaret died, and her will appointed as her executors

Joseph Prentis Jr. and Dr. Robert Henning Webb (1795–1866), the husband of her great-niece, Margaret Susan Prentis Webb. Bowdoin left
legacies to the Bible Society and the Episcopal Education Society, which
elicited John's allegation that she had given money to her country in a way
that would plague it. She left Joseph $500; Margaret, $250; and another
great-niece, Mary Ann Saunders Riddick, her mahogany wardrobe. She
gave tokens to her nephew, Peter Bowdoin, and a friend, Susan Parker.
To her most cherished niece, Eliza B. Vickery, she bequeathed her dia-
mond ring and "all the rest and residue of my estate of every sort kind
and discription" (Will of Susan Bowdoin, March 8, 1835, PFP). She mentioned neither John B. Prentis nor his wife, Catharine, in the will, an emphatic sign that she disapproved of and felt alienated from them. John's
intriguing reference to his aunt's contempt for their father, which is not
referenced in any other extant document, offers a reminder that historical archives usually provide only veiled glimpses into women's sides of
family stories.

Ignoring everything John said, Joseph responded in a manner that un-
derscores the proclivity of slavery to upstage other family sagas. In his
personal and professional roles, Joseph was used to wielding enormous
power, but no role was as dictatorial and directorial as his role in the life-
and-death dramas of his slaves.

On the 19th inst. I wrote you by mail, and asked that you would reply
thereto by the return one, which came yesterday. I feel great solicitude
on this vexed and excited case about my negro, and want to know whether
the fellow would be bought by you, and removed away immediately to
distant parts, so soon as I gave the words. Speculators are here and give
high prices, but I want to sell when ready *to whom I please*, and not *be
compelled* to sell, to a certain fixed individual or individuals. The fellow
is still in jail, no prosecution set on foot. . . .

I am *threatened* with the destruction of my property if ever turned
loose, and in truth I am not disposed to set the boy at liberty again—he
would never be of the same value to me and I think as a good citizen I
ought to send him away. That he could ever be convicted of the charge
brought against him is thought by none, as far as I have ever heard.

The boy was put in jail on the 17th inst. at my costs for safe keeping in
my absence, and I have afforded every opportunity to have him convicted
by a public exhibition of the case in Court; having waited a reasonable
time for this object, I think it now due to myself that I should be making
arrangements which shall suit me, as to future action on the subject.

Do let me hear from you forthwith. (June 25, 1835, WPFP)

A fluid writer, Joseph exhibited a lawyer's mastery of logic, social standing, and piety. His phrasing ("I am threatened with the destruction of the property") was part and parcel of his attempt to reduce life to an account book. Yet the urgency and anxiety of his tone suggests that he was truly alarmed that the young slave's life was in danger. It is no wonder that he was enthralled by the drama and his own role in it. Slaveholders cherished the peculiar institution in part because it entertained them, in the most serious sense. It offered them their choice of roles to play, and on any given day they could assume multiple identities. Whether villains or rescuers, seducers or fathers, sadists or benefactors, they had enormous power to direct the performance and to imagine themselves as stars on life's stage, where the props and plots—the slapstick, the heartbreak, the babies, the chase scenes, the beatings, the murders—were real and consequential.

Not receiving John's response by return mail, Joseph immediately posted another letter:

The mail has arrived and no answer to either of my communications,
on the subject of my slave now confined in jail, in this place, which is a
great disappointment. As the person who of all others ought to attend to
the prosecution, refuses doing so, and as the slave has been in close jail
since the 17th inst. at my charges for expenses I think I have done all that
ought to be required of me as a man, or a public officer. I cannot think of
permitting the slave to remain in these parts, and I think it my duty to sell
him, to be carried far away.
      Will you on the receipt of this, come or send, some trusty well qualified
person to take charge of him?
      He must not be sold to remain as near as Richmond, but he must be
sent away to a far Southern Market and from whence he can never come
back here again. It is understood that I will cause this to be done and my
particularity in complying with what I undertake you well know.
      I am threatened with the destruction of the property if he is ever seen
by one individual, and there may be others, who might be disposed to
injure him, so that I want him carried off from jail, as early as possible.
There are negro speculators here, and the desire to get a likely boy is so
great that it is very annoying to my feelings, and therefore I want him sold
to whom I please.
      My conduct in this case has my conscience to approve my act, and that
is worth more than what others may say of me—Send to the P.O. and get
the letters I have written to you; this goes by a private hand, and I hope it
will reach you tomorrow night—You will find that I have been and still am

anxious for you to buy the boy as a speculator, and *not to keep him*—He cannot be sold on the last terms. If you should not be at home, I shall give such a direction to this, as will enable me to hear that fact immediately,— and be governed accordingly. (June 26, 1835, WPFP)

While Joseph explicitly fretted over the prospect of losing the value of his property, his palpable anxiety indicates a more complicated investment. Whether his pride was at stake because he resented the neighborhood's infringement on his power to do as he pleased or he did not want a death on his conscience, he appeared desperate to find a way to sell the young man to the Deep South so that he could never be seen or heard from again in Virginia. He did not offer any words of sympathy or comfort to John on the subject of Susan Bowdoin's will, nor did he respond to any of the other issues that John had raised in his letter.

While the Prentis brothers worried about their social status and ob-sessed about the possible imprisonments, punishments, and sales of their enslaved property, their widowed sister, Eliza, who lived in Norfolk, was "confined by indisposition" to domestic spaces and horrified by news of a "desolating scourge" of sicknesses decimating her intimate circle. Contemplating loss and affliction rendered her "deeply serious." "Alas my brother," she exclaimed to Joseph, "how many awful warnings, loud calls, and dark Providences are around and about us " (January 23, 1837, WPFP). Although she had inherited the bulk of Susan Bowdoin's (mea-ger) estate, Eliza was in financially straitened circumstances, living in a rented room with one hired servant, who was sick. Two weeks later, after receiving word that Joseph's mother-in-law had died, Eliza responded:

How shall I tell you, dear Brother, that our dear and excellent Mammy, who carried *us* in her *arms*, during the tender years of infancy, we shall see no more "face to face," until the great morning of the Resurrection. She closed her valuable life about three weeks ago—The summons came very suddenly, & unexpectedly, for her—but praised be God "she was *ready*." It is a great comfort to me, to think of the long conversations I had with her, twenty months ago, on our prospects for eternity. Her faith seemed to be strong, and without a cloud—& how sweetly she did seem to lean on Him, without any doubt of acceptance. I have been much af-fected at her death, as you may suppose. This is *not right*, if I could help it. But it seemed almost a part of my nature to love her—for she was truly a tried friend—a genuine and untiring friend, to my beloved parents, & all their offspring. She is associated too, with the last hours, & last sufferings, of my *best earthly friend*. She rendered me at that time, the most efficient services, for which I never felt, that I could be grateful enough—And more than all, she helped me to *pray* for his salvation. *Her* prayer also went up, with the strong cry which we were enabled to make, and which God graciously heard & answered. I can say no more my dear Brother, for I feel very much depressed, and am very unwell besides. (February 6, 1837, WPFP)

Slaveholders often espoused the self-flattering notion that slavery was constituted by love, but Eliza exceeded conventions by worrying that her love for Mammy Rachel was "not right." The force of her grief violated southern notions of racial propriety. Eliza offered her brother a synopsis of Rachel's lifelong service as compelling evidence of why she could not help but value and look up to the slave. Rachel had been a constant presence in Eliza's life, a "genuine and untiring friend" when the Prentis children lost first their mother and later their father. Eliza also had turned to Rachel for comfort when her husband died. Unlike her younger sister, Mary Anne, Eliza had been outgoing and vivacious as a young woman, but by her mid-forties she suffered, as Mary Anne had, from chronic physical ailments and depression. While devoted to tending the sick and writing condolence letters to bereaved friends and family, Eliza, like Mary Anne, appeared more attached to Rachel than to any other person on earth. Nowhere else in her correspondence did she express as much palpable grief as she did when Rachel died.

On June 3, 1837, a fire started in a Suffolk cabinet shop and quickly spread to the surrounding buildings. Much of the town was reduced to piles of smoke and ash, including the houses of Joseph and Susan Prentis and of their daughter and son-in-law, Margaret and Robert Webb. Learning of the disaster four days later, John dashed off a note to his brother, once again offering sympathy and cash: "My own *Labor* and that of *my people* shall be at your *service*. My *money* I have some *Little* half shall be yours you are my Brother no interest at stake at this moment We sprang from the same *Vine* We have set under the same Roof whilst your skin has been fair and polished mine has been *Burnt* and Rough. I feel for you all. Excuse Bad writing. My House is *free* for each and every Member of your family: If you have ever considered me your Brother I *beg* of you not to slight me now. If you want a friend speak freely. If you wish me to come and see you say so. All inconveniences must be laid *aside*" (June 7, 1837, WPFP).

Touched by John's offer and somehow preserving from the fire his treasured archive of correspondence, Joseph made a notation on the envelope before filing it with his papers: "My only brother offering me great aid & pecuniary assistance." Although his house had been insured, Joseph again needed money and sought help from John. By giving generously to the tightfisted, self-indulgent elder brother who had withheld his patrimony, John displayed a munificence that was as aggressive and competitive as it was affectionate. He asserted a superior financial sense that, in the logic of capitalism, suggested moral superiority. At the same time, generosity was viewed as a defining trait of southern gentility; indeed, many prominent slaveholders, from Thomas Jefferson to Confederate vice president Alexander Stephens, were so generous that they died penniless, possibly expressing an unconscious hope that acts of philanthropy would free them from the stigma of slavery's avarice. As his brother's benefactor, then, John gained stature as both a successful capitalist and a worthy southerner.

The fire intensified Eliza's sense of being overwhelmed by sin and her anxiousness about eternity. Ill and weak, she was still living in Norfolk, where, she told Joseph, she remained "under rather gloomy circumstances, at least different from any other period. Not knowing exactly, what to do with myself." She reproached herself for her "unfortunate disposition of looking too much on the dark side of the picture" (June 12, 1837, WPFP). Joseph offered no words of comfort. In December 1837, Eliza complained, "A long time has elapsed in silence—perhaps longer than at any period of our lives. Why is this?" She wondered plaintively "if you all ever think of me" (December 16, 1837, WPFP).

Silences were proliferating not only in the Prentis family but in the American body politic. By 1836, Dew's argument that slavery should not be debated in public gained sway in the U.S. House of Representatives, which imposed a gag rule to avoid discussing the thousands of antislavery petitions that citizens were sending to their congressmen. The southern Slave Power made even broaching the topic of slavery appear unpatriotic—a hostile threat to national harmony. The gag rule remained in effect until 1844.

In January 1842, John penned his last extant letter to Joseph, who had sent his son, John Brooke Prentis, to Richmond for a visit, possibly to

The last extant letter written by John B. Prentis to his brother, Joseph Prentis Jr., 1842. Webb-Prentis Family Papers, 1735–1942 (accession #4136). Courtesy of Special Collections, University of Virginia Library.

assist in the slave trade. John reported, "You wrote me three letters which you thought would be best to destroy. I have committed two of them to the flames the other I cannot account for in any other way than that I gave it to John to read he never returned it to me to my recollection." The three men apparently were conspiring in a matter that they wanted to keep secret. After describing the pleasure he had found in a recent trip to Suffolk to help his brother through yet another time of "trouble," John concluded,

> I have felt happy and comfortable ever since I embrace[d] you and perhaps for the last time no one can tell. . . . Your letter which bore the expressions of your gratitude for my visit, was my Brother a Balm and Gillead to my Heart; Although I was your Rough Brother you my Nice Brother, we have lived as Brothers, I hope we set an example for your Boys to live as Brothers;
> God in his infinite mercy and goodness has so ordained it to my lot to have none I am thankfull to him for it.
> My wife joins me in love to and every member of your family. (January 4, 1842, WPFP)

John's emphatic expression of thanks to God for not granting him children must have startled Joseph. For twenty-five years, John's letters had been filled with regret about his lack of children, passionate expressions of affection for his nephews and nieces, and signs of desire to secure suitable heirs. A sea change in his valuation of family apparently had taken place.

CHAPTER 6   Wills and Possessions

> Where are "things"? In amorous space, or in mundane space?
> —Roland Barthes, "The World Thunderstruck"

In the mid-1840s, the United States vigorously expanded its empire, producing a steady increase in the price of slaves. The momentous annexation of Texas as a slave state in 1845 produced a 21 percent increase in "the price of prime field hands in the New Orleans slave market" (Howe 700). John B. Prentis continued to capitalize on the boom markets until 1848, when the Atlantic world roiled with revolutions against despotism. President James K. Polk, adopting a characteristically American posture of self-satisfaction, declared to his emissary in Paris, "The great principles of popular sovereignty which were proclaimed in 1776 by the immortal author of our Declaration of Independence, seem now to be in the course of rapid development throughout the world" (qtd. in Michael Morrison 117). Henry David Thoreau, in contrast, raged against the U.S. militant tyrannies. Appalled by the Mexican War, which had caused the deaths of thirteen thousand American soldiers since 1846, Thoreau urged Americans to resist unjust government. Connecting the war to the desire to expand slavery, Thoreau declared, "Under a government which imprisons any unjustly, the true place for a just man is also a prison. . . . It is there that the fugitive slave, and the Mexican prisoner on parole, and the Indian come to plead the wrongs of his race, should find them; on that separate, but more free and honorable ground, where the State places those who are not *with* her, but *against* her,—the only house in a slave State in which a free man can abide with honor" (233). In Seneca Falls, New York, 240 women's rights activists, including Lucretia Mott, Elizabeth Cady Stanton, and Frederick Douglass, issued their "Declaration of Sentiments," modeled on the Declaration of Independence, asserting women's rights to citizenship and equality under the law. Margaret Fuller, foreign correspondent for the *New York Tribune,* underlined the ideological interconnections between all forms of oppression when she reported from Italy, "I find the cause of tyranny and wrong everywhere the same. I listen to the same arguments against the emancipation of Italy that are used against the emancipation of our blacks; the same arguments for the spoliation of Poland as for the conquest of Mexico" (165). The Brontë sisters in Yorkshire, England, Elizabeth Barrett Browning in London, and George Sand in France joined a host of transatlantic women writers in fostering a contagion of gender and class protest. In New York City, Horace Greeley, an abolitionist, women's rights supporter, and founder of the *New York Tribune*, responded with hyperbolic optimism: "Woman has grasped the pen, [and] few would now seriously deny that man has been instructed and the world improved by her writings" (qtd. in Isenberg 56).

In February 1848, a London press printed a German pamphlet, *The Communist Manifesto*, written by two radical young dreamers, Karl Marx and Friedrich Engels. "A spectre is haunting Europe," they observed in their opening sentence, "the spectre of Communism. . . . Freedman and slave, patrician and plebeian, lord and serf, guild-master and journeyman, in a word, oppressor and oppressed, stood in constant opposition to one another, carried on an uninterrupted, now hidden, now open fight, a fight that each time ended, either in a revolutionary reconstitution of society at large, or in the common ruin of the contending classes" (78–79). Ralph Waldo Emerson, writing home from London in April 1848, observed, "People here expect a revolution. There will be no revolution, none that deserves to be called so. There may be a scramble for money. . . . When I see changed men, I shall look for a changed world" ("Life" 316). Emerson failed to recognize the power of revolutionary dreams during times of starvation. Potato crops had been failing since 1846, and the wheat harvest failed in 1847. Over the course of 1848, riots and revolutions occurred "in almost every European city with more than 50,000 inhabitants. The occasion for the revolutions was hunger. . . . Soup kitchens were the prelude to revolution" (A. J. P. Taylor 25).

In the American South, politicians such as John C. Calhoun sounded alarm bells against the democratic revolutions in Europe and the emancipation of West Indian slaves by the Second French Republic. Proslavery southerners ratcheted up their financial and emotional investments in the peculiar institution, while a small but significant number of black southerners escaped from slavery and lived to tell their tales. In Richmond, Henry "Box" Brown was working in a tobacco factory when his wife, Nancy, and their children were taken to an auction house and sold. He last saw them in a slave coffle of about 250 men, women, and children being transported from a slave jail, possibly the one controlled by Prentis, to North Carolina. The next March, defying slave catchers and the Fugitive Slave Act, Brown nailed himself into a wooden box and was mailed to Philadelphia. His creative act of self-emancipation electrified abolitionists with delight and slaveholders with dismay.

During this period, John B. Prentis's physical and mental health were declining. Catharine posted a gloomy letter to Suffolk informing Joseph of the poor state of his brother's health:

> I scarcely know what to say respecting [John's] case, for he seems to have a complication of diseases. In the fall he seemed to suffer with a cold, sometimes better & sometimes worse, he would not be intreated to do anything for himself nor call Medical aid, the latter part of January his feet commenced swelling, I then told him he would not suffer any body to do anything for him, and I would send for a Doctor whether he would suffer him or not to prescribe when he come. The day after this he was taken down to his bed and unable to help himself the Doctr then had a chance and relived him after being confined about 5 or 6 weeks, he was taken again in April his feet swelling & a great discharge of Blood from the mouth, where it proceeds from I cannot say; his physician thinks it is not from the lungs—at times while he is sleeping, the blood will flow until his shirt and bed clothes are soaking wet to be changed immediately, although he is reduced and weak, it does not appear it is from the loss of blood, *you know* he will have his way, although thus afflicted, he will walk as slow and deliberate in a hard rain about his business without coat or umbrella, when I call to him and warn him of his imprudence he answers me by saying it is not going to hurt him. (May 21, 1848, WPFP)

Catharine's image of her dying husband proceeding slowly and deliberately about his business in a cold, hard rain, his feet swollen and his mouth spewing blood, resonates as an appropriate denouement for a slave trader.

When John's health failed to improve over the summer, Joseph sent his son, named John B. Prentis in honor of his uncle, to Richmond. Young John traveled to Richmond via a boat filled with southern gentility, including the governor-elect of North Carolina, who inquired after young John's family. John's missives home illuminate his uncle's difficult personality. The dying man could barely speak but used his last ounces of energy to fight his doctor's advice.

John B. Prentis died on September 13, 1848. When his nephew read his last will and testament, he was scandalized by its strange twists and unspeakable entendres. Shock waves rippled through Richmond.

John B. Prentis's Will

Richmond, May 14, 1848

I, John B. Prentis now seated in my old chair in the office cleaned shaved and cleane shirt on, uncommon for the middle of the week, being Wednesday. Being but a few days since I was at the burial of one of my friends and neighbors, Mr. Benjamin Franklin, who died suddenly in perfect health, the said John B. Prentis now in perfect health, sound in mind and body, having had it in contemplation for some time past to write or make what is called my last will and testament. Having intermarried with Catharine Dabney of said city, who I loved truly and sincerely, we being both very poor, by our industry and perseverance with the assistance of the will and consent of Divine Providence, having been so fortunate as to accumulate some of this world's goods, chattles, land, and tenements.

It is my wish and desire to give and bequeath to my good and affectionate wife the whole of my real and personal estate, after my debts are paid, which is the first that must be done—to accomplish which object my wife who I hereby leave my whole devise, appoint her my sole executor without any security whatsoever to be required of her. The intention of my writing now is for my dear and affectionate wife to have and inherit every earthly peice or peices of property real or personal that can be found in my possession when God thinks proper to call me to my long home. There will be no use of a public sale, my wife must sell any of the property that she may think proper, personal or real to pay all of my debts. The balance that is remaining will be hers at her own disposal. My dear wife the first request, wish and desire is that at your death you will recollect my Little Pig Emily Agnes Haroaway McCabe the daughter of John C. McCabe by his first wife, who died in our house. It was the will of Divine Providence that we should have no offsprings. She is now living with us upon our love and affection for her. Provide for her after my death and make her your only Fool on the earth. Think how often you have heard her call me who sleeps in Death her shoate. I want you at your own Death to give and bequeathe to her every species of property that you may possess when you leave this world it is my wish and desire that you should comply with. This my first request that you should leave it in writing as I have done. I want none of my connexions or of yours, to have any of the fruits of our labor, with the exception of Little Emily Agnes Haroaway McCabe, who is of your connexion. Think of me and fulfill my dying request to my little foundling. It is also my wish that you should at your death, in the event of the death of my little Pig Emily Agnes Haroaway McCabe, my request is that you will devise and bequeath, if it meets your will and consent the whole of the property both real and personal that you may die possessed of to the children of Charles Stebbins which he has now or may have by his present wife Charlotte Walden who he married at our house. It being my wish that John C. McCabe shall not inherit or in any manner become possessed of any portion of my property either real or personal. It is my wish and desire also that at your death you should emancipate and set free the mulatto girl Margaret Jackson now living with us, who I bought with her mother Fanny from Mr. William Lambert and her increase and to give her from your estate one hundred dollars. In the event of Margaret Jackson's death, she having a child or children, it is my request to you that whatever increase she may leave may be emancipated and the one hundred dollars to be divided equally between the children she may have, and if she leaves but one child then the hundred dollars to be given to that one child. My boy Edmond that was born at our house of a female servant named Mary who I bought of Mr. Andrew Stevenson I desire you also to set free at your death, if he behaves himself well to you and to give him out of my estate fifty dollars.

As concerns our burial place, we must buy a lot on Shockoe Hill burying ground for ourselves. No one whatsoever friend or foe do I ever wish to be buried in said lot with the exception of Emily Agnes Haroaway McCabe and the Stebbins mentioned in this will.

I am now still as at the beginning sitting in the old chair in my office, and having compleated writing of my last will and testament of my own free will and accord, perfectly sound in mind and body, do hereby declare before God above no person being present, I do of my own free will and accord acknowledge this paper to be my true and genuine will. As witness my hand and seal this day and date written above. May God have mercy upon my poor soul.

John B. Prentis

SEAL

Witness—

J. J. Wilson

Wm Lambert

Chs. Howard

(Richmond Chancery Court Wills)

In this evocative piece of writing, Prentis both revealed and concealed a great deal about his life and personality. The letter opens with a strong sense of place ("in my old chair in the office") and of embodiment ("cleaned shaved and cleane shirt on"). The clean shirt, a departure from quotidian habit, attested to the seriousness of the occasion. Sixty years old, Prentis had been party and witness to an enormous amount of violence and death. Was he haunted by the horrors he had committed, by the specters of his victims? In his telling, it was the passing not of slaves but of a friend and neighbor "who died suddenly in perfect health" that provoked his urgent awareness of his mortality. His sense of foreboding proved prescient, because although he claimed "perfect health" on the day he wrote his will, he, too, went to the grave a mere four months later.

With poetic felicity, the name of Prentis's neighbor as well as the concluding sentence of his opening paragraph indicate the extent to which Benjamin Franklin's autobiography functioned as a model of self-understanding for white American men. The most famous and influential sentence in Franklin's autobiography is the concluding sentence of his opening paragraph: "Having emerged from the poverty and obscurity in which I was born and bred, to a state of affluence and some degree of reputation in the world, and having gone so far through life with a considerable share of felicity, the conducing means I made use of, which with the blessing of God so well succeeded, my posterity may like to know, as they may find some of them suitable to their own situations, and therefore fit to be imitated" (3). So indeed, in imitation of Franklin's narrative of rags to riches, Prentis summarized his life story: "Having intermarried with Catharine Dabney of said city, who I loved truly and sincerely, we being both very poor, by our industry and perseverance with the assistance of the will and consent of Divine Providence, having been so fortunate as to accumulate some of this world's goods, chattles, land, and tenements." If, as Stephen Carl Arch argues, the genre of autobiography can be defined as "any narrative written or told by one person in which that person struggles to tell the story of how he or she came over time to be an independent, often original, agent," Prentis's will is not an autobiographical act (6). Rather, it is a testament to a life imagined and modeled after Franklin's. Franklin encouraged this reading of his memoir, which was not so much a testament to his individuality or particularity as it was a postulation of "a general pattern of development . . . from poverty to prosperity," a representative story of everyman that posits as a universal norm the ideas that men's actions in life are motivated by a desire to possess and that their success can be measured by counting their possessions (Seed 38). Indeed, rather than positing an idea or ideal of an original, essential self, Franklin suggested that imitation was not only inescapable but productive and pleasurable.

By imagining himself not as a son of privilege but as a "very poor" young man whose way to prosperity had been paved by merit, Prentis positioned himself as a true American, a participant in and beneficiary of democratic meritocracy in which hard work and its attendant moral qualities of perseverance and frugality formed the ethical way to wealth. He was responding to northern representations of Yankees as hardy laborers who were proud to earn a living the American way, by the sweat of their brow, unlike effete southerners, who basked in the Old World luxury enabled by the vice of slavery. In addition, he was striking back at the old order's contempt for laboring men. Competing valuations of labor had infused American sectional politics since the Revolutionary era, when Vermont's fiery Matthew Lyon, for example, took the floor of the U.S. Congress and accused Virginia's John Randolph of being "a person nursed in the bosom of opulence, inheriting the life services of a numerous train of the human species" (qtd. in Mason 35). Prentis had long been torn between pride in his Franklinian work ethic and financial success and rage, distress, and shame at the way he had felt censured in turns by his father, his brother, his sisters, Susan Bowdoin, and eventually "all of his connexions." He strove throughout his adult life to secure his brother's affection and approval but finally, in his last verbal act, distanced himself from and implicitly condemned the hypocrisy of a ruling class that censured men like him for their hands-on role in the gritty filth of slave trading while revering men like his father and brother who sustained a perfumed height above violence. Prentis knew that the manicured hands of the ruling class wrote the laws and other mechanisms of power that created and sustained slavery. He knew that his hands were rough and bloody, while his father and brother usually managed to veil their complicity under the cloak of beneficent paternalism. The fact that Joseph often needed to borrow money had long been a source of galling satisfaction to John, but in his final act, he ended his "generosity" to all of his legal blood kin.

Determined to align himself with working white men, John had spent most of his adult life attempting to ignore the injustice of slavery. He wanted to see himself as "fortunate" because God and hard work had enabled him to "accumulate some of this world's goods, chattles, land, and tenements." But as a workingman who often felt snubbed precisely because he labored so hard, some force of resistance to social hypocrisy seemed to compel him to recognize and reward, however inadequately, the labor of the white women and slaves who had helped make him rich. After striving all of his life to feel at home in his birth family, he finally abandoned the effort and gestured toward the possibility of an alternative family formation, albeit certainly one every bit as vexed, perverse, and hierarchical as the one into which he had been born.

Catharine was fifty-two-years old when John wrote his will, and the two had been married for thirty-four years. John's repetitions of sentimental endearments toward her "who I loved truly and sincerely," "my good and affectionate wife," "my dear and affectionate wife" are consistent with the tone that he almost invariably had used to described his wife in letters to his brother. John's decision to leave his entire estate to Catharine reinforces the interpretation that his love for her was deep and sincere. Historian Kirsten E. Wood shows that "southern widows' share in and authority over their husbands' estates declined" from the colonial era through the nineteenth century (15). By the time Prentis wrote his will, Virginia law required that the widows of childless men receive a minimum of one-third of their husbands' property. The number of husbands who "bequeathed their wives more than dower law required" declined throughout the nineteenth century, and "increasing numbers excluded widows from executing their estates" (Kirsten Wood 17). In comparison to his contemporaries, then, Prentis placed an unusual amount of power as well as money in his wife's hands.

As Prentis's will proceeds, however, it becomes increasingly difficult to read it within the confines of Franklin's urtext, capacious as those confines may have been. Franklin was generously forgiving of his own and others' errors in life, especially those of a sexual nature. He detested sexual hypocrisy, as his courageously witty satire of the sexual double standard in "The Speech of Polly Baker" makes clear. When he fathered a son, William, out of wedlock, he preserved the mother's anonymity and raised the boy himself. Years later, when William followed in his father's footsteps by fathering a "natural" son, William Temple Franklin, apparently with a London prostitute, Benjamin took his grandson into his home and raised him as a cherished child. Prentis may thus have found in Franklin's life plenty of room for deviation from Victorian sexual mores.

However, Prentis's will is so riddled with contradiction and excess that it defies the limits not only of what is exemplary but also of what is utterable in antebellum America. "Race" above all defines those limits, and the Prentis foundlings came in several shades and hues. The proliferation of the foundlings opens the possibility that Prentis stressed how much he loved his wife precisely because his provisions for heirs would highlight the many sexual and emotional asymmetries of their conjugal life. As Mary Louise Kete argues, the discourse of sentimentality functions "to reattach symbolic connections that have been severed by the contingencies of human existence" (15). Sentimentality undermines dissent by celebrating "the domestic, the familial, and the possibility of consent" (Kete 3). Wood makes a similar point about the rhetoric of sentimental love that took root among Virginia gentry in the mid–eighteenth century and blossomed fully in the antebellum era: "Expectations of familial affection and domestic harmony certainly had the potential to silence complaint by making it seem unloving or even deviant" (73). A directive from no less an authority than St. Peter could be invoked to justify such silencing: "Above all, love each other deeply, because love covers over a multitude of sins" (1 Peter 4:8). In any case, Prentis's invocations of love worked to secure his wife's collaboration with his will. He reminded her that a dignified, virtuous, and affectionate wife tolerates and accommodates her husband's weaknesses, sexual and otherwise. As a prudent wife, Catharine Prentis most likely turned a blind eye to John's fancies, refusing to know what she knew.

The trope of chaste wives and lascivious slaves was culturally entrenched. Christianity, like most world religions, sowed and fertilized sexual hypocrisy and violence by representing sexuality as inherently dirty and shameful. Embracing a racialized angel/whore binary enabled men of the master class to sustain their imaginary muse, their capacity for admiration and faith, at the same time that they indulged in multiple forms of nonreciprocal self-gratification. The dichotomy projected men's conflicting internal impulses and desires onto women in a manner that granted men permission to believe in their righteousness while committing acts that could range from mutually pleasurable to ferociously sadistic. It is possible, of course, that Prentis did not have sex with the enslaved members of his household or indeed with any of the thousands of slaves with whom he interacted during his years of slave trading. His decades-long habit of giving money to his brother indicates that he found many forms of gratification in playing the role of benefactor. Treating favored slaves with solicitude may have been a way to assure himself that he was a benign and discerning patriarch who would generously reward the (few) subjects who were worthy, with the implication that the rest were unworthy. However, as Clarence E. Walker observes regarding Thomas Jefferson and Sally Hemings, sexual relationships between masters and slaves were "neither unusual nor aberrant, but normative" (14). Furthermore, "not all sexual encounters between black slave women and white men were rapes. *In a world where there was no such thing as consensual sex*, the relationship [between masters and slaves] can be located on a continuum of sexual practices" (Walker 14; emphasis added). Women of all races maneuvered within, accommodated themselves to, and/or resisted their era's normative practices with varying degrees of satisfaction, dismay, and distress.

Emily Agnes McCabe, the mother of John's "Little Pig Emily Agnes Haroaway McCabe," had died in the Prentis household on July 25, 1837, when the girl was four years old. John's explicit, emphatic exclusion from his will of the girl's father, John Collins McCabe (1810–75), suggests a hostile relationship between the two men. McCabe, a relative of Catharine's, was financially struggling and unsure what profession to follow. He appeared in Richmond's Personal Property Tax Books in 1836 and 1837 as the owner of one slave, for whom he was taxed twenty-five cents, and no other personal property. He worked in a bank, studied medicine, and indulged a passion for writing, publishing poems and prose in various magazines as well as a book of poems, *Scraps*. He developed a friendship with Edgar Allan Poe, who had returned to Richmond, the place of his mother's death, in 1835 to edit the *Southern Literary Messenger*. In the year that Poe married his thirteen-year-old cousin, Virginia Clemm, and raised the *Messenger*'s circulation by 700 percent, McCabe's young wife sickened and died. Shortly before her death, McCabe submitted a poem, "The Consumptive Girl," that appeared to be a reflection on his wife's illness, to the *Southern Literary Messenger*. Poe rejected it on the grounds that it "is not, by any means, a fair specimen of your talents" (Poe to McCabe, March 3, 1836). In 1837, Poe left Richmond to take an editorial position in Philadelphia, and McCabe departed to prepare for the Episcopal priesthood. He abandoned four-year-old Emily in the Prentis household and apparently never contacted her again. He married Sophia Gordon Taylor on August 7, 1838, a year after his first wife's death.

Prentis detested McCabe, but the reasons for this animosity remain buried. Prentis never mentioned Emily or her father in his letters to Joseph. The Prentises may have had reason to blame McCabe for his wife's death. Perhaps, like Poe, McCabe struggled with alcohol and drug addictions; as a medical student, he would have had easy access to opium. He may have had a proclivity toward domestic violence. Given Prentis's lifelong dedication to moneymaking, McCabe's financial improvidence no doubt rubbed Prentis the wrong way. McCabe's older brother, the Reverend Dr. James Dabney McCabe (1808–75), a prominent Methodist clergyman in Richmond, was a friend of the Prentises despite John's distaste for religion. The phrase "my little foundling" raises the possibility that Emily, who was fifteen years old when Prentis authored his will, may have been his natural child, an impression fostered by the level of impassioned sentiment in his prolific if idiosyncratic endearments. In any case, while the mysteries of her origins remain clouded, the girl remained in the Prentis household as an adopted daughter, and John treated her with singular affection.

Prentis's provisions for Charles Stebbins raise the possibility that Stebbins may have been another natural child of Prentis's, but more likely Stebbins was a young agent for whom Prentis developed the type of keen fondness that he had held for William Priddy, who appears to have left Prentis's employ in the 1840s. Charles Stebbins and Charlotte C. Walden had married at the Prentis residence on July 24, 1841 (*Richmond Daily Whig*, July 24, 1841), but I have uncovered no other clues regarding the nature of the Stebbins-Prentis association.

Given his lifelong protestations of family affection, one of the most striking aspects of Prentis's will is the severity of his determination to exclude all of his and Catharine's biological connections, whether "friend or foe," from the benefit of "any of the fruits of our labor." His obituary asserted that Prentis "has left an affectionate wife and a large circle of deeply attached relatives," but the will told a less conventional story. After decades of craving his brother's love and approval, forgiving injuries done to him, and attempting to prove his love by acts of generosity, John Prentis used his last act of writing to financially disinherit and emotionally disown every member of his white birth family and all of their descendants. His will began to lift a veil, allowing us to glimpse a subterranean tangle of emotional and sexual investments. The peculiar institution encouraged slaveholding men to imagine themselves as fathers of "my family, black

and white." "Family" was understood as a biblical form of kinship, a hierarchical microcosm headed by a patriarch constructed as a miniature
model of the universe ruled by Father God. Synonymous with mastery
and possession, fatherhood was deployed as a spiritual metaphor with
a biological referent that was simultaneously unspeakable and endlessly
spoken, publicly recognized and vehemently repressed. The presence of
mixed-race children highlights the violence of the metaphor. Prentis directed his wife to emancipate and give one hundred dollars to Margaret
Jackson, "the mulatto girl . . . now living with us, who I bought with her
mother Fanny from Mr. William Lambert." Like Andrew Stevenson, from
whom Prentis had purchased Edmond's mother, Mary, William Lambert
had been Prentis's friend at least since the War of 1812. Lambert also was
one of the witnesses to Prentis's will. Born into a Virginia family that had
settled in Henrico County in the early seventeenth century, Lambert had
begun rising to social prominence during the war and subsequently prospered as a lawyer. In 1840, he was elected mayor of Richmond, a position
he held until his death on March 24, 1852. As mayor he drew a lavish
annual salary of $1,800, and his taxable assets included three slaves, eigh-
teen horses, one gold watch, one metallic clock, one piano valued at $75,
and 40 pieces of gold or silver plate. If Margaret Jackson, the enslaved
woman whom Prentis purchased from Lambert, was "mulatto," she must
have had a white father, possibly either Prentis or Lambert. Trapped in a
brutal regime of desire that imagined them as fungible, interest-earning
currency, Margaret and her mother were circulated among slaveholding
men. Yet something in Prentis's imagination faltered within this fiction of
circulating value. What motivated a man as entrenched in the system of
slavery as the jailer and slave trader John Prentis to emancipate and leave
money to Margaret and several other slaves?

Sinister entendres suffuse Prentis's direction to Catharine to free and
provide fifty dollars to "my boy Edmond that was born at our house of
a female servant named Mary." In the phrase *my boy Edmond*, the vise
of sentimentality is indistinguishable from the vise of slavery. As Michel
Foucault observes, in many languages there is "a very pronounced ambi-
guity between the sexual meaning and the economic meaning of certain
terms. Thus, the [Greek] word *soma*, which designates the body, also
refers to riches and possessions; whence the possible equivalence between the 'possession' of a body and the possession of wealth." In slave
societies, "the slave was so taken for granted as a household sexual object

that it might seem impossible to forbid a married man to use her" (27). Foucault continues, "Here one is in the domain of direct possession. It is not by analogy that slaves signify wealth; they are an integral part of it" (172). In extracting sexual pleasure from slaves and profiting from their children, the master saw himself as exercising a right: "one reaps benefits from one's property" (19). The system's perversities were embedded in language that frustrates attempts to identify signifier with signified. Just as slavery's possessive relations rendered the pronoun *my* ambiguous, they also destabilized the denotation of *boy*. In his voluminous correspondence, John usually referred to black men as boys, following the social custom of racial disrespect. The name *Edmond* was another unstable linguistic marker. John first mentioned a slave named Edmond in 1812, when he entrusted Edmond to deliver some goods to Joseph Prentis Jr. in Suffolk. "I have waited very patiently my brother," John wrote, "to hear directly from you or family, on the arrival of my trunks under the care of Edmond" (April 14, 1812, WPFP). Later that same year, John wrote again to Joseph, "Edmond is very well indeed and send[s] his love to his mother and you all" ([illegible] 1812, WPFP). Names were repeated not only in generation after generation of the white Prentis family but also in multiple generations of black families enslaved by the Prentises. Thus, it appears that Prentis named "my boy Edmond, born at our house of a female servant named Mary" after a favorite family slave. John's description of Edmond as "my boy" could mean that he was the child's father and his master or solely his master. The younger Edmond might have been the son of John's older "boy" Edmond, who may well have been John's age or older and may have been John's great-uncle, uncle, half-brother, or nephew. After John's death, his namesake nephew described Edmond as a "Negro boy" who had been an invalid for several years (John B. Prentis II to Joseph Prentis Jr., September 23, 1848, WPFP). Whether this Edmond was a sickly child or a frail elderly man is indiscernible. As Emily Dickinson noted, "Infection in the sentence breeds" (553).

Whether driven by pride, jealousy, and anger to repudiate his siblings' claims on him or by guilt, compassion, or affection to reward a few favorite slaves, John Prentis had opened a space in his mind where he stopped imagining slaves as currency and started imagining them as human beings deserving of freedom and purchasing power. He expunged from his last will and testament all signs of affection for legally recognized blood relations. Either the bonds of kinship that he endorsed were nonbiological (forged through marriage, adoption, or slavery), or their biological nature was unacknowledged and extralegal. In the face of death, he distanced himself from the version of family values that dominated white southern discourse.

John Prentis was not the only antebellum slave trader to form paradoxical bonds of affection with one or more of his slaves. Robert Lumpkin, one of Prentis's chief rivals in Richmond, legally married one of his former slaves, Mary Jane, after the Civil War. "The couple had two daughters together, both of whom Lumpkin had previously sent north for their education and protection. . . . The Charleston dealer John S. Ryan did not formally marry his black mistress, but he did have several children with her, and after the war he donated $500 to the erection of a school for black youth" (Deyle 241). Elihu Cresswell, a wealthy New Orleans slave trader who died in 1851, freed all fifty-one of his slaves in his will and provided them with funds to relocate to free states (Deyle 241).

Bringing his will—and its meditations on life and death—full circle, Prentis recalled his sense of place ("I am now still as at the beginning sitting in the old chair in my office") before closing with a prayer that can be read simultaneously as a pious convention and a gasp of remorse ("May God have mercy upon my poor soul"). The moments of self-reflection necessitated by the act of writing may have flooded his consciousness with memories or images that compelled recognition of his blood-soaked hands. A flash of self-revelation may have sparked his imagination and enabled him to feel shame, to conjure a truer understanding of ethics, of decency, of value. At the very least, his will suggests that he registered at some level his indebtedness to the enslaved members of his household. In the interstices of what the will says and does not say, the stories of violence and coercion that it acknowledges and erases, Prentis began to gesture toward repentance. His final words testified to the paradox that one's property (wives, children, slaves) could become one's heir; the possessed could become the possessor. Human beings are inevitably in some sense possessed by what and whom we imagine ourselves to possess. Possessions resist confinement in mundane space; they tend to leach into dream space, where they inhabit and define the dreamer, disarranging boundaries between animate and inanimate, living and dead. Imagining Simon Legree's haunted, insomniac nights, Harriet Beecher Stowe noted the permeability of souls and the vexatious nature of possessions: "After all, let a man take what pains he may to hush it down, a human soul is an awful ghostly, unquiet possession, for a bad man to have" (357).

John's namesake nephew conveyed to Joseph the sense of shock with which Richmond society received his uncle's will:

Every thing around here looks deserted and dreary, occasioned by the melancholy event of which I informed you in my last [letter]. Aunt Catharine can scarcely reconcile it to herself, every thing around her she says looks so unnatural and desolate. . . . You would perhaps like to know what he has done with his estate. He has left a will penned by his own hand, and a most curious and eccentric document it is. I have obtained a copy of it, not that I expect to be benefitted in any way thereby, but on account of its singularity. It is just such an instrument as I expected and as I had anticipated years since. You and your family are entirely excluded and debarred from any benefit thereof. . . . He devises to his wife Catharine the whole of his estate, real + personal of what nature or kind 'soever to be at her disposal. He requests her to provide for Emily A. H. McCabe after his death and make her, her only idol on earth—upon the death of Aunt C. he requests her to devise the whole of the estate to Emily. In the event of Emily's dying before Aunt C. he requests her (if it meets her approbation,) to devise the same to the children of Chas. Stebbins, by his present wife Charlotte Walden. It is his request the neither *his connexions* nor *those of his wife* shall inherit any part or portion of his estate. It is also his request, that Jno. C. McCabe, shall not receive any benefit from his estate. He desired that his servant Margaret (who was married a short time since,) shall be emancipated at the death of Aunt C. and receive from her $100. Negro boy Edmond (who has been an invalid for several years,) he desires to be emancipated at the death of Aunt C provided good conduct towards her will entitle him to freedom, and receive from her $50. He desires his wife to purchase a lot in the City Burrying Ground for the interment of his remains and of those of his wife, and Emily McCabe. He appoints his wife whole + sole Executrix. . . . Uncle's Will seems to have created quite a theme for discussion here; it appears to be in the mouth of every body; and every one surprised and astonished at its contents—I have more than once been asked and questioned in regard to its singularity, but I have as often forborne to express any opinion in regard to the same, being fully convinced that what I might say would be of no avail and of little consequence.—

I wrote you that Uncle was to have been interred with Military honors, but such was not the case—it seems that the Company to which he belonged has been disbanded, and consequently none left to perform that service—but aside from that, I am happy to inform you that his funeral was largely attended, and his remains followed to their last resting place on earth by a numerous + mournful procession. The funeral ceremonies were conducted by the Rev.d Jas. B. Taylor a Baptist minister of this City. His remarks were based on the 4th verse of the 39th Psalm—Lord, make me to know mine end. (September 23, 1848, WPFP)

In a return letter, Joseph defended his brother's decision to leave his estate to Catharine and rebuked his son for implying that Joseph expected an inheritance. This reaction, which worked to reinterpret and normalize John's jarring disinheritance of the (white) Prentis clan, was in perfect keeping with Joseph's determination to whitewash any fissures in his cherished self-image as benign patriarch of a loving family. He coldly ignored the fact that his son, the namesake who had spent months at the dying man's bedside, had been the presumptive heir and might have felt keenly disappointed. The younger John might have felt as unjustly disinherited as the elder John had felt. His older brothers, Robert Riddick Prentis and Peter Bowdoin Prentis, had followed their father's legal profession and were comfortably established as attorneys in Nansemond County with independent households staffed by multiple slaves. Peter had grown as wealthy as his father, who was distinctly well-to-do, despite his tendency to live beyond his means. In 1848, Peter Bowdoin Prentis was taxed at a slightly higher rate than his father. He paid $14.06 in taxes on 2 slaves above age sixteen, one slave above age twelve, a horse, a four-wheel pleasure carriage, a gold watch, another watch, a metallic clock, a piano and a $5 attorney fee, whereas his father paid $13.38½ in taxes on five slaves above age sixteen, a horse, a silver watch, another watch, a metallic clock, $89 worth of plate, $222 in interest or profits from interest, bonds, or dividends; and $657.74 in income over $400, received as salaries or fees of office (Nansemond County Personal Property Tax Lists).

In any case, John B. Prentis II responded defensively to his father's criticism.

I am fully sensible that you did not expect any aid from the estate of your late Bro' in fact, I premised my remarks to that effect before I informed you what disposition Uncle had made of his estate, but as an item of news, and thinking perhaps, you would like to know the contents of his will. Upon that ground, and that only, I transmitted you the intelligence—As you very justly + truly remarked, he accumulated his estate aided in a great measure by his wife, I think it nothing but right, that she should be entitled to the whole of it, and I trust she may long live in the enjoyment of the same. . . .

The handsome + appropriate obituary upon the demise of Uncle published in the "Enquirer" of this City, is from the pen of one whom you little suspect. It is from the pen of one of our mutual respected friends, the Revd. Dr. Jas. D. McCabe, who left here on Wednesday last for home.

Aunt Catharine was desirous that Dr. McCabe should perform that melancholy duty, thinking that he was better acquainted with, and understood the character of Uncle more fully than Mr. Ritchie. Accordingly upon the Dr.'s return from Phila. (I think) wither he had gone as a Delegate to the Gr. Lodge, she mentioned it to him and he most cheerfully + willingly consented so to do she requested him not to give Uncle a character he did not deserve; no high-sounding words no character which did not comport with his life; but to give a plain, simple tribute to his memory; in which effort, I think the Dr has succeeded most happily, at any rate it meets the approbation of Aunt Catharine. Quite a handsome and appropriate tribute of respect was paid to the memory of Uncle by the firemen of the "Perseverance" hose Company of Philadelphia, a Compy of which it is said, he was the founder while he resided in that City—An authenticated Copy of the meetg which was held at the Engine house and of the resolutions adopted upon that occasion—they bespeak the high estimation in which he was held as the founder and patron of that company, and the high respect in which he was held as a private man—the usual insignia of mourning was adopted and a deathlike silence reigned on the deliberations of that body—the copy of these proceedings were signed by the Chairn. Secy. + forwarded here, and addressed to the family of the late Captn Jno. B. Prentis—Aunt C. prized them highly and designed to preserve them as another momento of his memory.—

I have met with several of your acquaintants since my sojourn here among the number, I mention Capt Clement White, Mr Byrd Page of the day police, Genl Lambert, Mayor of this City, + several others. (October 7, 1848, WPFP)

The list of people paying their last respects to John B. Prentis indicates how integral he was to the highest levels of Richmond society. The honors paid him by the Perseverance Hose Company of Philadelphia displayed the strength of his bonds with white working-class men. Thomas Ritchie, editor of the *Richmond Enquirer*, was one of the most powerful forces in shaping proslavery opinion in the South.

Catharine's approval of her husband's rejection of upper-class social airs was evident when she asked the writer of the obituary, Rev. Mc-Cabe, "not to give Uncle a character he did not deserve." Although he was the brother of the reviled John C. McCabe, James McCabe did not utter a word of censure or ambivalence about Prentis's behavior or legacy in his obituary. The younger John Prentis's casual mention of McCabe's prominence in the Masons raises the possibility that Prentis's uncle was a Mason. It was not uncommon for slave traders and brokers to belong to Masonic lodges, boards of trade, and other business associations that offered extensive possibilities for networking. In any case, McCabe situated Prentis squarely within honorific and sentimental conventions. Both of Richmond's leading newspapers published the obituary (the *Richmond Whig* on the front page on September 15, 1848, and the *Richmond Enquirer* on page 4 on October 6, 1848), which suggests that Prentis's death was considered noteworthy on both sides of Virginia's political aisle.

> Died, at his residence, in this city, on Wed. morning, Sept. 13th [1848], in the 60th year of his age, Capt. John B. Prentis, one of our oldest and most esteemed citizens. Capt. Prentis was the second son of the late Judge Joseph Prentis, of Williamsburg, Va. . . . After having qualified himself for his chosen vocation, by seven years preparation under the instruction of some of the most distinguished architects of Philadelphia, he returned, in 1810, to his native State, and commenced his business in this city, where his skill and industry promised him abundant success. When the war of 1812 was declared, he abandoned his flattering projects in business, and promptly entered the service of his country as an officer in the Richmond Light Artillery, commanded by the Hon. (then Capt.) A. Stevenson. . . . In 1819 he was by the authority of the city, elected to a highly important civil office. . . . He has left an affectionate wife and a large circle of deeply attached relatives. (*Richmond Enquirer*, October 6, 1848)

Catharine Prentis and the six Prentis slaves (Fanny and Margaret Jackson, Mary and Edmond, and two others whose names are lost to history) had long been defined as extensions of John B. Prentis's will. Upon his death, they were left to continue figuring out how to survive his bonds of domestic affection and deep attachment.

CHAPTER 7   Relic(t)s

> **relic:** 1. Something that has survived from a past culture or period.
> 2. A keepsake: souvenir. 3. An object of religious significance.
> 4. **relics.** A corpse.
> **relict:** 1. An organism or species of an earlier era surviving in a
> changed environment. 2. A widow.
> —*Webster's Dictionary*, 1996

"All knowledge is, of course, to some extent imaginary," writes Ian Baucom in *Specters of the Atlantic: Finance Capital, Slavery, and the Philosophy of History*. "The boast of evidence, however, is that it limits and constrains the promiscuity of the imagination, weds imagination to a liturgy of facts, records, documented events. If to know is always, in part, to imagine, then evidence demands that imagination bind itself to the empirically demonstrable" (15). As long as we bind our imaginations to what is demonstrable in written documents, however, those who were dispossessed in life will remain dispossessed after death. Imagination is not merely personal; it is also social. The way we imagine antebellum history continues to inform and shape public debates, public policy, and social identities. Women such as Catharine Prentis appear in historical archives only as remnants of the remnants of their husbands, but they are a stubborn species that persists in the ways we in the twenty-first century imagine or fail to imagine them. The slaves who lived with the Prentises and the thousands of people in whose lives John Prentis speculated also persist as meaningful relicts, even when invisible. Saidiya Hartman notes that historians who want to recover the stories of the subaltern must "struggle within and against the constraints and silences imposed by the nature of the archive—the system that governs the appearance of statements and generates social meaning" (*Scenes* 11). Searching for people who have vanished from history not as a consequence of the natural cycle of life and death but through social acts of denial, repression, and forced disappearance requires an active quest through lights and shadows, facts and imagination. We must search for meaning not only in what we can demonstrate but also in what we imagine between the lines. We need to search for ways to register the significance of the lives of people who did not own their own stories and were not able to bear witness to their erasure. Registering absences, gaps, and vanishings in the archive, our gaze oscillates between the visible and the invisible. Silences and blank spaces are crucial components of what Baucom calls a counterarchive that testifies to the significance of lives that might remain unnamable, unnarratable, and never fully lived.

When Catharine Dabney married John Prentis in 1814, the two young people became, as the English judge William Blackstone infamously put it, "one person in law, so that the very being and existence of the woman is suspended during the coverture, or entirely merged and incorporated in that of her husband" (433). Upon John's death in 1848, the year in which Marx and Engels called for the abolition of the family because the "bourgeois family" was founded on "capital, on private gain" through the exploitation of wives, prostitutes, and children (100), Catharine became a relict in the tradition of English law. "In the decades after the American Revolution, widowhood made most women socially marginal and even destitute. Some widows, however, retained considerable economic, social, and political privilege; they lost their husbands but not all of their husbands' reflected glory" (Kirsten Wood 1). Catharine Prentis was in the latter group. Court records suggest that she became the executor of John's estate without difficulty or contestation.

> City of Richmond
>
> At a court of Hustings held for the said city, at the
> Courthouse, the 16th day of September 1848—
> This last will and testament of John B. Prentis, late of this city, deceased, was this day proved by the oaths of William Lambert and Charles Howard, two of the subscribing witnesses thereto and was thereupon ordered to be recorded. And at a like Court, held on the 10th day of October 1848. On the motion of Catharine Prentis, the only executor named in the last will and testament of John B. Prentis, late of the city deceased, who made oath thereto as the law directs, and entered into and acknowledged a bond in the penalty of thirty thousand dollars, conditional according to law (but without security, the will directing that none should be required

of her,) certificate is granted her for obtaining a probate of the said will in
due form.
　Testa.,
　Chs. Howard, Clk.
(Richmond Hustings Wills)

　The year before he died, John B. Prentis had been taxed $5.52 for
seven slaves, one horse, a carriage worth $70.00, two gold watches, and a
clock. Although John had requested that Catharine bequeath her property to the children of Charles Stebbins at the time of her death and only
if young Emily McCabe had predeceased Catharine, she appears immediately to have divided most of his personal property between Charles
and herself. In 1850, she was taxed $2.41 for four slaves, one gold watch,
and one clock, while Charles Stebbins was taxed $1.90 for three slaves and
one gold watch. This was his first appearance in Richmond's tax books.
If he had been John's agent in the slave trade and was now taking over
the business, the slaves Catharine gave him may have included Jack and
Bowles, who had been John's longtime assistants in the trade.
　Catharine also inherited 66.25 acres of land in Richmond plus three
lots on Church Hill, all of which she retained for the rest of her life. The
1850 U.S. Census listed her as a head of household with Emily McCabe as
the only other resident in the house, so the four slaves—probably Fanny,
Margaret, Mary, and Edmond—must have resided elsewhere. Catharine
may have hired them out to factories or to other white employers, or
she may have kept them laboring for herself while housing them in slave
quarters on one of her many other pieces of property. In any case, the
labor of slaves enabled her to sustain moderate prosperity.
　In 1851, Swedish writer Fredrika Bremer observed that a dealer in
the Richmond slave market "kept a few mulatto women in a separate jail.
The slave keeper told her that the women were 'fancy girls for fancy purchasers'" (White 37). No matter how hard Catharine Prentis may have
tried to keep herself in a state of denial about the realities of the sexual
fancies, fantasies, and violence that had characterized her late husband's
work and personal habits, as a widow she was forced to make decisions
about how to deal with Fanny Jackson and Mary as well as their enslaved children, Margaret and Edmond, who may have been fathered by
her husband. The archive does not bear direct witness to the brutalizing
effects of this social environment on Catharine specifically, but the odds

are that the lion's share of any hostility she felt would have been directed toward the enslaved women and children, not toward her husband or other powerful men. Elite women—that is, women who are socially defined as belonging inside the bounds and bonds of the respectable community—typically play a central role in maintaining social boundaries.

In the late 1820s, English novelist Frances Trollope, mother of novelist Anthony Trollope, was appalled by the behavior of slaveholding widows and their children. While residing in a Virginia household, Trollope observed the icy indifference shown by a widow and her four daughters toward the suffering and terror of an eight-year-old enslaved girl who ate a biscuit laced with arsenic intended for rats. The young ladies of the household answered Trollope's "anxious enquiries" about the sickened girl "with ill-suppressed mirth" and "uncontrollable laughter" (248). Trollope observed that slaveholders' power exercised the "most injurious" effects on their "moral feelings and external manners" (247). In particular, she asserted, "among the poorer class of landholders, who are often as profoundly ignorant as the negroes they own, the effect of this plenary power over males and females is most demoralising; and the kind of coarse, not to say brutal, authority which is exercised, furnishes the most disgusting moral spectacle I ever witnessed. In all ranks, however, it appeared to me that the greatest and best feelings of the human heart were paralyzed by the relative positions of slave and owner. The characters, the hearts of children, are irretrievably injured by it" (247). Bremer voiced similar concerns. She responded to a graduation address at the University of Virginia by exclaiming to her sister, "It is amazing what an enslaving power the institution of slavery exercises over the minds of the young, and over intelligence in general" (299–300). She found in southern white men a general lack of "moral integrity, of courage and uprightness of mind" (300–301).

Slaveholding women were socially empowered to indulge in passions in the privacy of their own households that were unimaginable in relationships with respectable white adults. If Catharine Prentis felt frustrated, angry, depressed, or fearful, the safest way for her to vent her passions would have been by raging against the members of the household who held less power than she: the slaves and little Emily. Sarah Moore Grimké, a member of a prominent South Carolina slaveholding family who became a prominent antislavery and women's rights activist, spoke from personal experience when she described the circumscribed lives of southern white women and their complicity in the wretchedness of enslaved women.

> During the early part of my life, my lot was cast among the butterflies of the *fashionable* world; and of this class of women, I am constrained to say, both from experience and observation, that their education is miserably deficient; that they are taught to regard marriage as the one thing needful, the only avenue to distinction; hence to attract the notice and win the attentions of men, by their external charms, is the chief business of fashionable girls. They seldom think that men will be allured by intellectual acquirements, because they find, that where any mental superiority exists, a woman is generally shunned and regarded as stepping out of her "appropriate sphere." . . .
>
> There is another class of women in this country, to whom I cannot refer, without feelings of the deepest shame and sorrow. I allude to our female slaves. Our southern cities are wheeled beneath a tide of pollution; the virtue of female slaves is wholly at the mercy of irresponsible tyrants, and women are bought and sold in our slave markets, to gratify the brute lust of those who bear the name of Christian. In our slave States, if amid all her degradation and ignorance, a woman desires to preserve her virtue unsullied, she is either bribed or whipped into compliance, or if she dares resist her seducer, her life by the laws of some of the slave States may be, and has actually been sacrificed to the fury of disappointed passion. Where such laws do not exist, the power which is necessarily vested in the master over his property, leaves the defenseless slave entirely at his mercy, and the sufferings of some females on this account, both physical and mental, are intense. . . . In Christian America, the slave has no refuge from unbridled cruelty and lust. (46–47, 51–52)

Grimké cites several instances of beautiful slaves sold for sexual purposes, including an article copied from the *New Orleans Picayune*: "A very beautiful girl, belonging to the estate of John French, a deceased gambler at new Orleans, was sold a few days since for the round sum of $7,000. An ugly-looking bachelor named Gouch, a member of the Council of one of the Principalities, was the purchaser. The girl is a brunette; remarkable for her beauty and intelligence, and there was considerable contention, who should be the purchaser. She was, however, persuaded to accept Gouch, he having made her princely promises" (53). Grimké concludes with a description of the precise predicament in which Catharine Prentis lived.

Nor does the colored woman suffer alone: the moral purity of the white woman is deeply contaminated. In the daily habit of seeing the virtue of her enslaved sister sacrificed without hesitancy or remorse, she looks upon the crimes of seduction and illicit intercourse without horror, and although not personally involved in the guilt, she loses that value for innocence in her own, as well as the other sex, which is one of the strongest safeguards to virtue. She lives in habitual intercourse with men, whom she knows to be polluted by licentiousness, and often is she compelled to witness in her own domestic circle, those disgusting and heart-sickening jealousies and strifes which disgraced and distracted the family of Abraham. In addition to all this, the female slaves suffer every species of degradation and cruelty, which the most wanton barbarity can inflict; they are indecently divested of their clothing, sometimes tied up and severely whipped, sometimes prostrated on the earth, while their naked bodies are torn by the scorpion lash. (53–54)

While inhabiting a society that, as Grimké powerfully described, was saturated in physical and emotional violence against black women, Catharine Prentis also bore witness to the ravages patriarchal society exacted from white women. During John's lifetime, she would have made herself vulnerable to violence had she displeased him or taken a slave's side in a confrontation. In 1810, for example, the wife of Richmond's James Young attempted to stop her husband from beating a servant boy, whereupon James turned on her and beat her to death (Sidbury 228n26). As long as Catharine Prentis consented to the system of subjugation, she was legally entitled to view the slaves as possessions that existed for her pleasure and enjoyment. As Saidiya Hartman observes, "From the vantage point of everyday relations of slavery, enjoyment, broadly speaking, defined the parameters of racial relations. . . . *Black's Law Dictionary* defines the term 'enjoy' as 'to have, possess, and use with satisfaction; to occupy or have the benefit of.' While enjoyment encompasses these rudimentary features, it also denotes more extensive capacities. It entails 'the exercise of a right. . . . Comfort, consolation, contentment, ease, happiness, pleasure and satisfaction. Such includes the beneficial use, interest, and purpose to which property may be put, and implies rights to profits and incomes therefrom.' At the outset, [it is] clear that to take delight in, to use, and to possess are inextricably linked" (*Scenes* 23–24). The institution of slavery encouraged white men, women, and children to enjoy violence and domination, to take pleasure from possessing and abusing the bodies and minds of other human beings. Hartman notes that "the most invasive forms of slavery's violence lie not" in instances of extreme suffering but in the relentless quotidian routines of terror on which the social system was predicated (*Scenes* 24).

The 1852 Richmond City Directory located the widowed Catharine Prentis on Webster Street, near Tyler. She was still living there after the war, and the Richmond City Directories of 1870 and 1871–72 placed her adopted daughter, Emily McCabe Shield, and her husband, Alfred Shield, at the same address, so the young couple either shared Catharine's house or occupied a house on an adjoining lot that Catharine owned. Shield, a clerk at the Richmond Circuit Court, came from an old Virginia family, and his father had been a schoolmate of John Prentis. Until her death in 1872, Catharine retained possession of and paid taxes on the lands she had inherited from John, and Emily expected to inherit the entirety.

In her final autobiographical act—her last will and testament—Catharine Prentis dutifully followed the requests of her "dear deceased husband," which echoed, she claimed, "her own wish and desire." Aligning her will with his was a practice to which she had long been accustomed. Throughout their married life, her ability to exhibit displeasure or dissent had been limited to the domestic sphere, and since she was far more confined to that sphere than John was, she would have suffered more than he from fissures or violence within their relationship. Whether Catharine was a sadistic mistress or a genteel woman who kept her passions submerged, the systematic inequities of a patriarchal society placed the risks of a clash of wills between husband and wife on the wife's side. For her to articulate or even to imagine dissident passions and desires in her relationships with other white adults would have jeopardized her economic security, her place in a network of kinship, and her social recognizability. Because fear of loss sabotages curiosity, openness, and honesty, Catharine would have been ill equipped to imagine a defiant role for herself.

The brutal quotidian force of slavery often shattered enslaved women's ability to imagine that the social system was just, meritocratic, or worthy of their collusion. Unlike Catharine, the women enslaved in her household—Fanny Jackson, Margaret Jackson, and Mary, the mother of John's "boy Edmond"—may have struggled daily to maneuver against, subvert, or manipulate their master's and mistress's power. Elizabeth Fox-Genovese asserts that "resistance was woven into the fabric of slave women's lives and identities. . . . The ubiquity of their resistance ensured that its most common forms would be those that followed the patterns of everyday life: shirking, running off, 'taking,' sassing, defying" (328). Hartman, in contrast, cautions against celebrating slaves as heroic actors in romances of resistance and "arrogating to the enslaved the illusory privileges of the bourgeois subject or self-possessed individual" (*Scenes* 54). In any case, slavery as an institution of social death worked to render the lives of Fanny, Mary, Margaret, and Edmond invisible, illegible, and virtually unimaginable. We can read them only as specters whose disappearance is constitutive of American history.

To remain within the bonds of respectable kinship, white women such as Catharine Prentis embraced a type of civic death—the abnegation of their will to a social will made manifest in the person of their husband— that usually left them significant room to maneuver. Their civic death was romanticized by traditional discourses that celebrated marriage as the "sharing of a common life" characterized by "mutual kindness," "shared pleasures," and "reciprocal fidelity"; in short, a "perfect community and a oneness of souls in separate bodies" (Foucault 230, 204). For black women who were constituted as socially dead by the institution of slavery, commitment to family and (black) community could represent "potent forms of resistance" (Varon 7). In contrast, white southern ladies' commitment to family and community implicated them in collaboration and collusion with the forces of patriarchy and white supremacy. Conforming to the cults of true womanhood and male honor could deliver tangible benefits. For the wife to submerge herself in the identity of her husband was the mandate of law, religion, and sentimentality. Most white women aspired to this state because of its combination of imaginary and real empowerment. By choosing "love" in a social system that equated love with possession, white women wittingly or unwittingly consented to legal subjection. Nancy Isenberg observes that "antebellum politicians and constitutional theorists argued that at marriage, women agreed to give up their property—their rights—and then to retreat from politics. Somehow a woman's choice to exercise her legal consent in marriage erased her right to political consent" (27). In the South, "ladyhood constituted a social armor; it bolstered slaveholding women's authority within and beyond their households. As ladies, slaveholding women believed they were superior to most of their sex. They also considered themselves superior to many white men in manners, morals, gentility, and piety, qualities that popular opinion deemed white women's special province" (Kirsten Wood 10).

In those cases where widowhood did not impoverish women, it enhanced their social power. Widows regained legal personhood and assumed control of whatever property was left to them by their husbands' wills. Although they could not vote, widows, like single women, could assert wills of their own. They "earned and kept their own wages, made binding contracts, moved freely from state to state, and established their own place of residence. . . . They displayed their moral virtue through church and benevolent activities, and . . . equaled men in civic virtue through the payment of taxes" (Isenberg 24). If a widow remarried, she again lost her legal personhood and usually lost control of her property as well. Widows, then, had little incentive to remarry, and few did (Kirsten Wood 38).

During the decades when they had exchanged tokens of affection such as letters and gifts, Catharine and her sister-in-law, Susan, affirmed the value of familial connections while avoiding socially sensitive topics. They praised each other and the next generation of girls for their accomplishments in the feminine arts of cooking and sewing. In 1831, for example, Catharine praised Susan's eldest daughter for the artistry of her needle. "My Dear Margaret," Catharine wrote, "I received your letter by Captain Cohoon with the lace collar. I am very much pleased to receive such a present its being the work of your own hands. I have shown it to a good many that has done a great deal of the same kind of work they were surprised when I told them it was your first attempt on lace I think you deserve great creddit for it is very neatly done indeed" (Catharine Dabney Prentis to Margaret Prentis Webb, January 1, 1831, WPFP). Catharine herself did not sew merely for pleasure and beauty; she colluded in the slave trade by sewing clothes to help her husband display slaves advantageously on the market. But her letters never mentioned such work. It is hard to imagine what she thought when she measured particular bodies for such a purpose. In fact, the archives provide few clues about Catharine's inner life. If we can reconstruct mere fragments of most men's lives, most women's lives are no more than fragments of fragments, relicts of relics. I can document Catharine's existence, but her *story* remains absent. The handful of extant letters that she wrote make it difficult to imagine her story "as other than a kind of visible invisibility: *I see you are not there*" (Gordon 16). What did she know of desire—that unruly human capacity to want ardently, to crave, to dream, wish, hope, long, hanker, yearn; to ache in a way that unleashes control and propels

the self toward encounter, dialogue, interaction, permeation, and transformation? Desire for another's desire—desire for reciprocity, in other
words—cannot be satisfied by commands, orders, violence, or coercion.
It necessitates a process of call and response, request and agreement, in
an interaction that recognizes the other's right to choose. To what extent
did Catharine claim the right of consent or refusal? Did she indulge vehement pleasures or suffer unbearable abandonments? Did she yearn for
passionate expression beyond the possessive love that both bound and
empowered her? Witness to and collusive in the abuse of other women's
bodies, was she able to imagine sexuality apart from violence? Could she
find pleasure in touching her own body? Did she enjoy anyone else's
touch? Were her nights haunted by implacable, unmanageable desires
for conversation with another's body, another's soul, or had her body and
soul withered to the point that she could not imagine communion? Did
she feel injured by, enraged by, or curious about her husband's wander-
ings? Was she cruel and tightfisted, kind and generous, even-tempered
or volatile? Did the repressed humanity of the enslaved members of her
household haunt her imagination? When she gazed in the mirror, did she
see serene glass, or did specters return her gaze? What did the mirror
demand of her?

Little of Catharine's soul—its beauty or corruption—can be extracted
from the archive, but signs of her dis-ease do appear in one letter that
suggests the extent to which her body and soul were twisted by her collusion with slavery and patriarchy. The letter, written to her niece, Margaret, during one of John's slave-trading expeditions, illuminates reasons for
the prevalence of insanity and premature death among multiple generations of Prentis women.

> I was thinking all day of writing to you thinking you had not received my
> letter or that some of the family was sick was the cause of not hearing
> from you before this. While thinking Mr John Priddy stept in just from
> the office with a letter from you and one from your Uncle John the first
> time I have heard from him since he left home being eight weeks this day
> you may be sure I have suffered much on his account. It has revived me
> very much he is well and is in Montgomery Alabama he did not intend to
> have been absent more than fifteen or twenty days when he left me so you
> may imagine what my mind has undergone—he writes me word in ten or
> twelve days after the arrival of his letter I will see him or hear from him
> again *I trust I shall see him*

My Doctor came to see me last week and told me he was convinced
that it was my mind that was diseased instead of my Body and seriously
advised me to stay no longer at home to go and visit, eat a plenty of Bread
and meat and try to cheer my spirits or some slow disease would destroy
my constitution

I can cheer up now but never could until I heard from my Dear Husband—I have suffered a great deal with Erysipelas over my face and neck
for three weeks past and am at this time. We have all escaped the Cholera
it is more than I could expect having so many negroes—it has been mostly
confined to couloured people they are so imprudent—I hope it will soon
disappear for it has terrified some persons almost to death I have known
several persons so much fritened it was as much as the doctors could do
to save them from nothing but fear. There has been a case here of a young
man that Mr. Prentis got to stay in the house of a night as a protector for
me in his absence he suffered it to prey on his mind until it completely
overpowered him and it was as much as the Doctors could do to persuade
him there was nothing the matter with him. I wish I could see you to tell
you the whole story for it is really a laughable one although I was very
much frighten myself when it took place. We all ran him very hard about
it to raise his spirits but he stand to it that he never will feel right again.
(Catharine Dabney Prentis to Margaret Prentis Webb, October 15, 1832,
WPFP)

Blaming slaves' "imprudence" rather than overwork, malnutrition, foul
water, corrupted air, and depression for their susceptibility to disease is
a sign of Catharine's determination to remain blind to the realities of the
brutal world that she helped to create and sustain. At the same time,
she and her "protector" found themselves almost debilitated by mental
dis-ease, by hauntings, loneliness, anxiety, and fear that laughter could
not fix.

If Catharine ever consciously regretted her collusion with her husband,
no signs of her regret survived. In the end, she aligned her last will and
testament with John's, as if she were indeed not an independent being
but merely a remnant of a departed man, an object of others' narration
who was never in possession of her own story.

Will of Catharine Prentis
In the name of God Amen. I Catharine Prentis of the City of Richmond,
State of Virginia, being of sound and disposing mind and memory do
make this my last will and testament in manner and form following. First,

I direct that all of my just debts, which are few and small, shall first be paid. Second, In compliance with the request of my dear deceased husband, as well as my own wish and desire, I give devise and bequeath unto Mrs. Alfred Sheild my adopted daughter who before her intermarriage with Alfred Sheild was Emily A. H. McCabe, every species of property of every kind whatsoever of which I may die possessed or entitled to, to her and her heirs forever. Third, I hereby nominate and appoint my friend Alfred Sheild, executor of this my last will and testament and request the Court not to require any security of him upon his qualification as such executor. In testimony whereof I have hereunto set my hand and affirm my seal this twenty-third day of December 1872.

Catharine Prentis
(Richmond Chancery Court Wills)

In this minimalist document, Catharine Prentis's personality is carefully contained within the rhetoric of sentiment and duty. Self-erasure was her socially prescribed destiny, and she obliged. The will suggests that she took pride in the fact that her debts were "few and small," which reinforces John's suggestion that she was industrious, steadfast, and financially trustworthy, after the model of King Solomon's virtuous wife as well as Benjamin Franklin's Deborah, whom he describes as "a good and faithful helpmate, [who] assisted me much by attending the shop" (63). In reality, Catharine must have been smart and resourceful as a financial manager to survive the hazards of widowhood and the devastation wreaked on Richmond by the Civil War. The Confederacy had unleashed a tsunami of death. Amid the carnage, Catharine faced the personal losses of her husband's namesake nephew, John Brooke Prentis, who died in September 1862 as a bachelor at the age of forty; her sister-in-law, Susan, who died the following month at seventy-one; and her niece, Marianna, who died in April 1864 at fifty-two. Whether Catharine had sold or freed the people she inherited from her husband or found them freed by Lincoln's Emancipation Proclamation is unknown. In any case, all her property in the form of slaves or Confederate bonds became financially worthless at the war's end. The emancipated slaves gained at least the promise of self-possession.

On April 2–3, 1865, fires and pillaging destroyed nine hundred buildings in Richmond's business district, including the Henrico County Courthouse, the General Court Building, bridges, railroad depots, tobacco warehouses, banks, the state armory, and a church. In the heart of

THE FALL OF RICHMOND, Vᵃ ON THE NIGHT OF APRIL 2ᵗᵈ 1865.

Confederate troop withdrawal over a bridge across the James River, built in the 1810s when John B. Prentis was a young architect in the city. The caption reads, "The Fall of Richmond, Va. on the Night of April 2nd 1865. This strong hold and Capital City of the Davis Confederacy, was evacuated by the Rebels in consequence of the defeat at 'Five Forks' of the Army of Northern Virginia under Lee and capture of the Southside Rail Road by the brave heroes of the North commanded by Generals Grant, Sheridan, and others. Before abandoning the City the Rebels set fire to it, destroying a vast amount of property, and the conflagration continued until it was subdued by the Union troops on the following morning." Lithograph by Currier and Ives, 1865. Courtesy of the Virginia Historical Society.

downtown, the only surviving building was the granite customhouse that had served as headquarters for the Confederate government. In 1861, Richmond voters had split between Unionists and Secessionists, and both sides now had deep reason for bitter anger against the enemies in their midst as well as the invading army. General Godfrey Weitzel, the triumphant Union army commander, observed that the Capitol Square "was covered with women and children who had fled there to escape the fire. Some of them had saved a few articles of furniture, but most had only a few articles of bedding, such as a quilt, blanket or pillow, and were lying upon them. Their poor faces were perfect pictures of utter despair. It was a sight that would have melted a heart of stone" (qtd. in Dabney 195). Weitzel ordered the Union troops, thousands of whom were black, to protect the citizens and their property amid the chaos and devastation. They apparently obeyed his order.

Steven Deyle recounts the symbolic denouement of southern slave jails, as reported in Philadelphia's *Christian Record* on April 22, 1865:

> Within hours of the fall of Richmond, a large crowd of black soldiers and local residents had assembled on Broad Street, near Lumpkin's Jail, the largest boarding house for traders and their slaves. As they did so, both those locked inside the compound and those congregating outside began to sing:
>
> > Slavery chain done broke at last!
> > Broke at last! Broke at last!
> > Slavery chain done broke at last!
> > Gonna praise God till I die!
>
> According to one black soldier, when the prison's doors were opened, those inside poured out onto the street, "shouting and praising God and . . . master Abe" for their freedom. (276–77)

No letters survive to illuminate how Catharine Prentis felt when President Lincoln walked through the conquered Confederate capital on April 4, 1865, greeted by the exultant cheers of thousands of black residents and many poor whites. A few days later, General Robert E. Lee surrendered. On April 15, the gloom engulfing Richmond was intensified by news of Lincoln's assassination, for which southerners were widely blamed. From the perspective of most white residents, "The future seemed bleak indeed for devastated, bankrupt Richmond, its people hungry and disconsolate, its soldiers returning penniless from the front, and many of its . . . young men killed, or maimed for life" (Dabney 198). The hospitals were crammed with wounded soldiers, the cemeteries and battlefields were overwhelmed by the dead, and the survivors, whether rich or poor, were reduced to waiting in line for Union rations. Touring the fallen capital, poet John T. Trowbridge reflected in his *Picture of the Desolated States*: "Inconceivable was the slaughter. Here two red rivers met and spilled themselves into the ground" (140). Richmond struck him as "almost uninhabited," with "signs of human life so feeble and so few"

(143). Early in the morning, he noted, "few white citizens were astir, but I saw a thin, ceaseless stream of negroes . . . going cheerfully to their daily tasks. The most of them took their way toward the burnt district; some crossed Capitol Square to shorten their route; and the sounds I had heard were occasioned by the slamming of the iron gates of the Park" (146). The lives of black residents were beginning anew, with meager resources and solid reasons for anxiety but rays of hope about a future that they might call their own, whatever its struggles and triumphs.

A year after the war, Richmond's white women, like thousands of white women across the South, were enraged by the federal government's expenditure of four million dollars to bury the northern dead while Confederate soldiers were left to rot. Raising money through private donations, an association of Richmond women worked with farmers to gather cadavers scattered around the city's outskirts. "Hundreds of bodies" were transferred "to new graves in the Richmond cemetery during the summer and fall of 1866," but tens of thousands were left decaying in nearby battlefields (Faust 239). Windstorms aroused foul miasmas.

Whatever her emotions during the desperate postwar years, the Union victory forcibly released Catharine Prentis from any ambiguities or embarrassments she might have felt in response to her husband's provisions for their slaves. She no longer had any choice in the matter of manumissions. Like all residents of Richmond, she witnessed and endured ghastly sights, but she remained possessed and entitled by the claims of her husband's will. Located outside of Richmond's centers of government and business, the Prentis lots had been spared the war's worst ravages. Catharine died as an old woman at the same time that the newly born Reconstruction, with its hard-earned dreams of freedom, justice, and equality, also expired. Her estate, valued at more than eight thousand dollars, passed to the control of Alfred Shield (Richmond Chancery Court Wills, November 29, 1878). Catharine Dabney Prentis was buried next to her husband in Richmond's Shockoe Cemetery on November 23, 1873. Their graves, indistinguishable amid weeds, are next to an alley in range 17, section 12, quarter 2, row 1.

I have been unable to find any clues about the fates of Prentis's slaves. Mary and Edmond, who lacked surnames, are untraceable. Jackson was a common surname in Richmond; the 1870 City Directory listed seventy-one Jackson households, seventeen of which were "white" and fifty-four "colored," but none of them were headed by someone named Fanny or

AS WE FOUND THEM.

These children were owned by Thomas White, of Mathews Co., Va., until Feb. 20th, when Capt. Riley, 6th U. S. C. L., took them and gave them to the Society of Friends to educate at the Orphan's Shelter, Philadelphia.

Profits from sale, for the benefit of the children.

AS THEY ARE NOW

The Mother of these children was beaten, branded and sold at auction because she was kind to Union Soldiers. As she left for Richmond, Va., Feb. 13th, 1864, bound down in a cart, she prayed "O! God send the Yankees to take my children away."

Profits from sale, for the benefit of the children.

Photographs published as postcards in France in 1865 with the caption, "Virginia Slave Children Rescued by Colored Troops: As We Found Them & As They Are Now." Courtesy of the Virginia Historical Society.

Margaret. Nor do Fanny and Margaret Jackson appear in census, tax, or vital records. As Eva Sheppard Wolf succinctly observes, "It is the nature of slavery to obscure the facts of biography" (ix). The Prentis slaves simply vanish from the archive, ghosts of stories we can glimpse only through the suggestive interplay of light and shadow in John Prentis's will.

Lest *ghosts* be dismissed as a cliché, I will explain my use of the term. Like *relics*, *ghosts* evoke a nonlinear sense of time. Our experience of the present not only is disturbed but more fundamentally is created by emanations from other times. A ghost is a metaphor or linguistic sign or manifestation of aspects of human existence that exceed the boundaries of the body, the material world, and chronological time. In religious discourse, we might see ghosts as emanations of the human soul. In secular discourse, we might see them as products of human psychology. Emily Dickinson observed in the midst of the Civil War,

One need not be a Chamber to be Haunted
One need not be a House
The Brain has Corridors surpassing
Material Place (333)

In literary language, ghosts open doors between spaces that we usually want to imagine as closed and discrete: self and other; past, present, and future; life and death. Ghosts are uncanny because they are neither one thing nor another, neither present nor absent, neither living nor dead, neither visible nor invisible. They are unsettling because they are simultaneously inside and outside, real and imaginary, intimations of our past and of our future. Like the wind, they speak enigmatically in sighs, whispers, howls, and heartbeats. Like texts, they live at the site of their reception. They unhinge emotions, overwhelming reason with desire, fear, dread, and curiosity. They disconcert and confound. Ghosts emerge from the human need for and resistance to truth, our longing to know and our terror of knowing.

In 1869, Yankee journalist Russell Conwell toured the South. In Virginia, he talked with farmers whose plows incessantly unsettled cadavers. He observed waves of destitute scavengers scouring battlefields for relics of slain men and horses. Along the beaches surrounding the ruins of Fort Wagner, South Carolina, a tumultuous sea heaved out bones, haversacks, belts, bayonet scabbards, shoes, and grinning skulls (Blight 176–77).

So it goes. A culture that chooses property rights over human rights, the dream of wealth over the dream of justice, is destined for nightmares of infinite violence. Material objects engorge our archives, libraries, museums, estate sales, landfills, and oceans, but their raisons d'être—the dreams and narratives of life—flee. Possessions often function as metaphors or signs or manifestations or perversions of human desire for something that eludes us—a dream of a better life or a higher good or a meaning to our existence beyond suffering, alienation, and death. The things we imagine ourselves to possess return to possess, overcome, and haunt us. When we amputate and cauterize our ability to recognize human kinship and interconnection, ghosts appear to warn of compulsive repetitions of violence and trauma to come. Ghosts are disobedient, disorderly, and rebellious because they reflect and bear witness to repressions, oppressions, and disappearances. Testifying to the paradoxical transience and unity of time, they possess us with consciousness of human (im)mortality. Impotent to change or act on the past, present, or future except through the soul, they, like writers, live in and produce intangibles: ideas, words, sounds, images that exist only in conversation between self and other, body and world, this time and that.

NOTES

Introduction

1. For other illuminating analyses of slave trading, see Bancroft, Gudmestad, Wendell Holmes Stephenson, Tadman, and Walvin. See Drago for a valuable compilation of letters written by South Carolina slave trader A. J. McElveen to a Charleston slave broker, Z. B. Oakes, from 1852 to 1857.

Chapter 1. Possessive Relations

Epigraph transcribed by Julian Prentis from records at the London Guildhall Manuscript Library. http://www.prenticenet.com/news/2005/prentices_halton_buckingham_england.htm.

1. Prentis's partner, John Norton, was willing to risk British condemnation for treason to protect his American business interests. He wrote a public apology from London on January 16, 1775, in which he averred, "My avowed principles (which I now publish) are, that the Parliament of Great Britain have not the least shadow of right to tax America; that I never will, directly or indirectly, deviate from these principles, which I have always professed, and which ought to govern every person that has any regard for the liberty of America" (*Virginia Gazette,* May 6, 1775).

2. The will ran as follows:

August 19, 1773
I John Prentis of the City of Williamsburg Merchant . . .
Give bequeath and devise unto my brother Joseph Prentis and his Heirs forever, my Lands in Surry, James City and York County's as also my waiting Boy Alexander and [other slaves]
I give to my sister Waters my sett of Table China, and if she is Indebted to me at the time of my death I desire she may not be called upon to pay it as I Give it her.
I desire my Man Squire may Chuse his Master. . . .
After the Payment of my just Debts I desire the Remainder of my Estate be equally divided Between my Brothers Daniel and Joseph Prentis and my Cousin Robert Prentis who I appoint my Executors and desire they may not be held to give Security to the Court. . . .
John Prentis
(York County Records)

3. Order of the York County Court, December 12, 1776. Robert and Joseph continued to pay an annuity to support Elizabeth, who survived into the nineteenth century.

4. Robert attempted to continue overseeing management of the store from Trinidad. The removal of Virginia's capital from Williamsburg to Richmond was "fatal" to business, he asserted. Suffering from debts in Trinidad, he pleaded with Joseph for financial assistance: "All I have to request & repeat to you is, to use your utmost Endeavors to extricate me from Debt here, & if it cannot be effected by any other means endeavor to raise it by a Mortgage on the Store, observing to make Insurance on what you send to avoid the Loss by risk of the Sea" (Robert Prentis to Joseph Prentis, June 23, 1786, WPFP).

5. William Bowdoin died at the age of one and a half. Joseph Jr. was born at Green Hill in January 1783, baptized at the Bruton Parish Church, and eventually followed in his father's footsteps. The third son, also named William, died at the age of five; fourth, John Bowdoin, died at the age of two. The fifth child, John Brooke Prentis, was born in 1788. Margaret next gave birth to her first daughter, Eliza Bowdoin, in 1791. Another son, Robert Waters, was born and died in November 1794. In 1796, Margaret gave birth to Mary Anne.

6. For thorough analyses of Tucker's life and work, see Hamilton and Doyle.

7. The book, along with many other books from Judge Prentis's library, is preserved in the Rockefeller Library of the Colonial Williamsburg Foundation.

BIBLIOGRAPHY

Archival Sources

Brown-Tucker-Coalter Collection. Swem Library, College of William and Mary. Williamsburg, Virginia.

Henrico County Land Tax Books. Library of Virginia. Richmond.

McCabe, William Gordon, Papers, 1757–1920. Accession #10568. Special Collections. University of Virginia Library. Charlottesville.

Nansemond County, Personal Property Tax Lists, 1815–52. Rockefeller Library, Colonial Williamsburg Foundation, Virginia.

Poe, Edgar Allan, to John C. McCabe. March 3, 1836. http://etext.lib.virginia.edu/toc/modeng/public/PoeUvax.html.

Prentis Family Papers. Rockefeller Library. Colonial Williamsburg Foundation, Virginia.

Prentis Family Papers, 1807–30. Swem Library, College of William and Mary. Williamsburg, Virginia.

Richmond, City of, Chancery Court Wills. Library of Virginia. Richmond.

Richmond, City of, Directories. 1852, 1860, 1870, 1871–72. Library of Virginia. Richmond.

Richmond, City of, 1850 Census. Library of Virginia. Richmond.

Richmond, City of, Hustings Wills, Inventories, and Accounts. Library of Virginia. Richmond.

Richmond, City of, Land Tax Books. Library of Virginia. Richmond.

Richmond, City of, Personal Property Tax Books. Library of Virginia. Richmond.

Riddick Family Papers, 1817–60. Accession #2227. Special Collections. University of Virginia Library. Charlottesville.

Saunders, Robert, Letters, 1829–67. Swem Library, College of William and Mary. Williamsburg, Virginia.

U.S. Bureau of the Census. 1850 Slave Schedules. Facsimiles reproduced at http://content.ancestry.com.

[Virginia] General Assembly, Records. Library of Virginia. Richmond.

Webb-Prentis Family Papers, 1735–1942. Accession #4136. Special Collections. University of Virginia Library. Charlottesville.

Williamsburg, City of, Personal Property Tax Books. Library of Virginia. Richmond.

York County Records, Wills and Inventories. Rockefeller Library, Colonial Williamsburg Foundation.

Published Sources

Allen, Richard. *The Life, Experience, and Gospel Labors of the Rt. Rev. Richard Allen, Written by Himself.* Philadelphia, 1793.

Andrews, Charles M. *Colonial Folkways.* New Haven: Yale University Press, 1919.

Arch, Stephen Carl. *After Franklin: The Emergence of Autobiography in Post-Revolutionary America, 1780–1830.* Hanover, N.H.: University Press of New England, 2001.

Axelrad, Jacob. *Patrick Henry: The Voice of Freedom.* New York: Random House, 1947.

Ballaugh, James Curtis. *A History of Slavery in Virginia.* Baltimore: Johns Hopkins Press, 1902.

Bancroft, Frederic. *Slave-Trading in the Old South.* 1931. Columbia: University of South Carolina Press, 1996.

Barthes, Roland. *A Lover's Discourse: Fragments.* Trans. Richard Howard. New York: Hill and Wang, 1978.

Baucom, Ian. *Specters of the Atlantic: Finance Capital, Slavery, and the Philosophy of History.* Durham: Duke University Press, 2005.

Belsches, Elvatrice Parker. *Richmond, Virginia.* Charleston, S.C.: Arcadia, 2002.

Benjamin, Walter. "Theses on the Philosophy of History." *Illuminations.* Ed. Hannah Arendt. Trans. Harry Zohn. New York: Schocken, 1969. 253–64.

Berlin, Ira. *Many Thousands Gone: The First Two Centuries of Slavery in North America.* Cambridge: Harvard University Press, 1998.

Binney, Charles James Fox. *The History and Genealogy of the Prentice, or Prentiss Family, in New England, Etc., from 1631 to 1883.* 2nd ed. Boston: Binney, 1883.

Blackstone, William. *Commentaries on the Laws of England.* 4 vols. Oxford, 1769.

Blight, David W. "Healing and History: Battlefields and the Problem of Civil War Memory." *Beyond the Battlefield: Race, Memory, and the American War.* Amherst: University of Massachusetts Press, 2002. 170–90.

Brace, Jeffrey, as told to Benjamin F. Prentiss. *The Blind African Slave; or, Memoirs of Boyrereau Brinch, Nicknamed Jeffrey Brace.* 1810. Ed. and intro. Kari J. Winter. Madison: University of Wisconsin Press, 2005.

Bremer, Fredrika. *America of the Fifties: Letters of Fredrika Bremer*. Ed. Adolph B. Benson. New York: American-Scandinavian Foundation and Oxford University Press, 1924.

Brown, John Howard, ed. *Lamb's Biographical Dictionary of the United States*. Vol. 5. Boston: Federal Book, 1903.

Burton, June K. *Napoleon and the Woman Question: Discourses of the Other Sex in French Education, Medicine, and Medical Law, 1799–1815*. Lubbock: Texas Tech University Press, 2007.

Calendar of Virginia State Papers, Jan. 1, 1808–Dec. 31, 1835. Vol. 10. Richmond, 1892.

Callender, Guy S. "The Early Transportation and Banking Enterprises of the States in Relation to the Growth of Corporations." *Quarterly Journal of Economics* 17.1 (1902): 111–62.

Caruth, Cathy. "Introduction." *American Imago* 48 (1991): 417–24.

College of William and Mary. Special Collections Research Center. "Prentis Award." http://scrc.swem.wm.edu/wiki/index.php/Joseph_Prentis.

Dabney, Virginius. *Richmond: The Story of a City*. 1976. Rev. and exp. ed.. Charlottesville: University Press of Virginia, 1990.

Defoe, Daniel. *Moll Flanders*. 1722. New York: Penguin, 1978.

Derrida, Jacques. *Specters of Marx: The State of the Debt, the Work of Mourning, and the New International*. 1993. New York: Routledge, 2006.

Deyle, Steven. *Carry Me Back: The Domestic Slave Trade in American Life*. New York: Oxford University Press, 2005.

Dickens, Charles. *American Notes for General Circulation*. Vol. 2. London: Chapman and Hall, 1842.

Dickinson, Emily. *The Complete Poems of Emily Dickinson*. Ed. Thomas H. Johnson. Cambridge: Harvard University Press, 1951.

Doyle, Christopher. "Judge St. George Tucker and the Case of *Tom v. Roberts*: Blunting the Revolution's Radicalism from Virginia's District Courts." *Virginia Magazine of History and Biography* 106.4 (1998): 419–42.

Drago, Edmund L. *Broke by the War: Letters of a Slave Trader*. Columbia: University of South Carolina Press, 1991.

Eltis, David, Stephen D. Behrendt, David Richardson, and Herbert S. Klein, comps. *The Trans-Atlantic Slave Trade: A Database on CD-Rom*. Cambridge: Cambridge University Press, 1999.

Emerson, Ralph Waldo. "Life and Letters in New England." In *The Blithedale Romance*, by Nathaniel Hawthorne. Eds. Seymour Gross and Rosalie Murphy. New York: Norton, 1978. 258–65.

———. *Selections from Ralph Waldo Emerson*. Ed. Stephen E. Whicher. New York: Houghton Mifflin, 1960.

Faust, Drew Gilpin. *This Republic of Suffering: Death and the American Civil War*. New York: Knopf, 2008.

Fehrenbacher, Don E. *The Dred Scott Case: Its Significance in American Law and Politics*. New York: Oxford University Press, 1978.

Felman, Shoshana. *What Does a Woman Want? Reading and Sexual Difference*. Baltimore: Johns Hopkins University Press, 1993.

Finkelman, Paul. *Dred Scott v. Sandford: A Brief History with Documents*. Boston: Bedford, 1997.

Fisher, George. "Narrative of George Fisher." *William and Mary College Quarterly Historical Magazine* 17.3 (1909): 147–76.

Fisher, Philip. *The Vehement Passions*. Princeton: Princeton University Press, 2002.

Foner, Eric. *Tom Paine and Revolutionary America*. New York: Oxford University Press, 2005.

Foucault, Michel. *The Care of the Self. The History of Sexuality*, vol. 3. Trans. Robert Hurley. New York: Random House, 1986.

Fox-Genovese, Elizabeth. *Within the Plantation Household: Black and White Women of the Old South*. Chapel Hill: University of North Carolina Press, 1988.

Franklin, Benjamin. *The Autobiography and Other Writings*. New York: Bantam, 1982.

Freehling, William W. *The Road to Disunion*. Vol. 1, *Secessionists at Bay, 1776–1854*. New York: Oxford University Press, 1990.

Fuller, Margaret. *"These Sad but Glorious Days": Dispatches from Europe*. Eds. Larry Reynolds and Susan Belasco Smith. New Haven: Yale University Press, 1991.

Furgurson, Ernest B. *Ashes of Glory: Richmond at War*. New York: Knopf, 1996.

Gaskell, Elizabeth. *The Life of Charlotte Brontë*. 1857. New York: Penguin, 1975.

Gilje, Paul A., and Howard B. Rock, eds. *Keepers of the Revolution: New Yorkers at Work in the Early Republic*. Ithaca: Cornell University Press, 1992.

Gill, Harold B. "Apprentices from Christ's Hospital Make Good in America." *Colonial Williamsburg: The Journal of the Colonial Williamsburg Foundation*, Autumn 1998, 15–18.

Gordon, Avery F. *Ghostly Matters: Haunting and the Sociological Imagination*. Minneapolis: University of Minnesota Press, 1997.

Gordon-Reed, Annette. *The Hemingses of Monticello: An American Family*. New York: Norton, 2008.

"Greenhow, Robert." American National Biography Online. http://www.anb.org/articles/16/16-03523-article.html.

Grimes, William. *Life of William Grimes, the Runaway Slave, Written by Himself*. 1825. Eds. William L. Andrews and Regina E. Mason. New York: Oxford University Press, 2008.

Grimké, Sarah Moore. *Letters on the Equality of the Sexes, Addressed to Mary S. Parker, President of the Boston Female Anti-Slavery Society*. Boston: Knapp, 1838.

Gudmestad, Robert H. *A Troublesome Commerce: The Transformation of the Interstate Slave Trade*. Baton Rouge: Louisiana State University Press, 2003.

Hamilton, Philip. *The Making and Unmaking of a Revolutionary Family: The Tuckers of Virginia, 1752–1830*. Charlottesville: University of Virginia Press, 2003.

———. "Revolutionary Principles and Family Loyalties: Slavery's Transformation in the St. George Tucker Household of Early National Virginia." *William and Mary Quarterly* 55.4 (1998): 531–56.

Harris, Leslie M. *In the Shadow of Slavery: African Americans in New York City, 1626–1863*. Chicago: University of Chicago Press, 2003.

Harrold, Stanley. *The Abolitionists and the South, 1831–1861*. Louisville: University Press of Kentucky, 2009.

Hartman, Saidiya V. *Lose Your Mother: A Journey along the Atlantic Slave Route*. New York: Farrar, Straus, 2007.

———. *Scenes of Subjection: Terror, Slavery, and Self-Making in Nineteenth-Century America*. New York: Oxford University Press, 1997.

Hodges, Graham Russell. *Root and Branch: African Americans in New York and East Jersey, 1613–1863*. Chapel Hill: University of North Carolina Press, 1999.

Howe, Daniel Walker. *What Hath God Wrought: The Transformation of America, 1815–1848*. New York: Oxford University Press, 2007.

Isaac, Rhys. *The Transformation of Virginia, 1740–1790*. New York: Norton, 1982.

Isaacson, Walter. *Benjamin Franklin, an American Life*. New York: Simon and Schuster, 2003.

Isenberg, Nancy. *Sex and Citizenship in Antebellum America*. Chapel Hill: University of North Carolina Press, 1998.

Jea, John. *The Life, History, and Unparalleled Sufferings of John Jea, the African Preacher. Compiled and Written by Himself*. Portsea, Eng.: Jea, 1811.

Jefferson, Thomas. *Notes on the State of Virginia*. Chapel Hill: University of North Carolina Press, 1955.

Johnson, Walter. *Soul by Soul: Life inside the Antebellum Slave Market*. Cambridge: Harvard University Press, 1999.

Keener, William G. "Blair-Prentis-Cary Partnership: The Store and Its Operation." Colonial Williamsburg Foundation Report, April 1957.

Kennedy, John P. *Memoirs of the Life of William Wirt VI: Attorney General of the United States.* 1849. Whitefish, Mont.: Kessenger, 2006.

Kete, Mary Louise. *Sentimental Collaborations: Mourning and Middle-Class Identity in Nineteenth-Century America.* Durham: Duke University Press, 1999.

Kimball, Gregg D. *American City, Southern Place: A Cultural History of Antebellum Richmond.* Athens: University of Georgia Press, 2000.

Klages, Mary. *Woeful Afflictions: Disability and Sentimentality in Victorian America.* Philadelphia: University of Pennsylvania Press, 1999.

Kramnick, Isaac. *Republicanism and Bourgeois Radicalism: Political Ideology in Late Eighteenth-Century England and America.* Ithaca: Cornell University Press, 1990.

LaCapra, Dominick. *History and Memory after Auschwitz.* Ithaca: Cornell University Press, 1998.

———. *Writing History, Writing Trauma.* Baltimore: Johns Hopkins University Press, 2001.

Levy, Andrew. *The First Emancipator: The Forgotten Story of Robert Carter, the Founding Father Who Freed His Slaves.* New York: Random House, 2005.

Lewis, Jan. *The Pursuit of Happiness: Family and Values in Jefferson's Virginia.* New York: Cambridge University Press, 1983.

Linder, Bruce. *Tidewater's Navy: An Illustrated History.* Annapolis, Md.: Naval Institute Press, 2005.

Lott, Eric. *Love and Theft: Blackface Minstrelsy and the American Working Class.* New York: Oxford University Press, 1995.

Ludlum, David M. *Social Ferment in Vermont, 1791–1850.* New York: AMS Press, 1966.

Madison, James. *Letters and Other Writings of James Madison.* Vol. 1, 1769–93. Philadelphia: Lippincott, 1865.

Marriage Notices from Richmond, Virginia, Newspapers, 1841–1853. Richmond: Virginia Genealogical Society, 1997.

Martin, Peter. *The Pleasure Gardens of Virginia: From Jamestown to Jefferson.* Charlottesville: University Press of Virginia, 2001.

Marx, Karl. *Economic and Philosophic Manuscripts of 1844.* Trans. Martin Mulligan. Moscow: Progress, 1959.

Marx, Karl, and Friedrich Engels. *The Communist Manifesto.* 1848. New York: Penguin, 1985.

Mason, Matthew. *Slavery and Politics in the Early American Republic.* Chapel Hill: University of North Carolina Press, 2006.

McCabe, John C. *Scraps.* Richmond: Walker, 1835.

McWilliams, James E. *A Revolution in Eating: How the Quest for Food Shaped America.* New York: Columbia University Press, 2005.

McWilliams, Mary E. *John Greenhow House Historical Report, Block* 13-2, *Building 23E, Lot* 159–60. Library Research Report Series 1264. 1942. Williamsburg, Va.: Colonial Williamsburg Foundation, 1990.

———. *Robert Carter House Historical Report, Block* 30-2, *Building* 13, *Lot* 333–36. Library Research Report Series 1605. 1945. Williamsburg, Va.: Colonial Williamsburg Foundation, 1990.

Morrison, Michael. "American Reaction to European Revolutions, 1848–1852: Sectionalism, Memory, and the Revolutionary Heritage." *Civil War History* 49.2 (June 2003): 111–32.

Morrison, Toni. *Beloved*. New York: Knopf, 1987.

National Cyclopaedia of American Biography. Vol. 8. New York: White, 1924.

North, Lee E. *The 55 West Virginias: A Guide to the State's Counties*. Morgantown: West Virginia University Press, 1985.

"North American Slave Narratives, Beginnings to 1920." http://docsouth.unc.edu/neh/.

Noyes, John Humphrey. *Bible Communism*. 1848. *Socialism in America: From the Shakers to the Third International, a Documentary History*. Ed. Alfred Fried. New York: Columbia University Press, 1992. 54–62.

Oakes, James. *The Ruling Race: A History of American Slaveholders*. New York: Vintage, 1983.

Painter, Nell Irvin. *Southern History across the Color Line*. Chapel Hill: University of North Carolina Press, 2002.

Patterson, Orlando. *Slavery and Social Death: A Comparative Study*. Cambridge: Harvard University Press, 1982.

Pell, John. *Ethan Allen*. Boston: Houghton Mifflin, 1929.

Pippenger, Wesley E., comp. *Death Notices from Richmond, Virginia, Newspapers, 1841–1853*. Richmond: Virginia Genealogical Society, 2002.

Poe, Edgar Allan. *The Fall of the House of Usher and Other Writings: Poems, Tales, Essays, and Reviews*. New York: Penguin, 2003.

Powers, Frank. *The Urban South and the Coming of the Civil War*. Charlottesville: University of Virginia Press, 2008.

Prentis, Joseph. *Monthly Kalender and Garden Book*. Intro. Rollin Woolley. Chillicothe, Ill.: American Botanist, 1992.

Preston, Daniel. *A Comprehensive Catalogue of the Correspondence and Papers of James Monroe*. Vol. 1. Toronto: Greenwood, 2000.

Randolph, Mary. *The Virginia Housewife; or, Methodical Cook*. Baltimore: Plaskitt and Cugle, 1838.

Richter, Caroline Julia. "The Prentis Family and Their Library." Master's thesis, College of William and Mary, 1985.

Ricoeur, Paul. *Memory, History, Forgetting*. Trans. Kathleen Blamey and David Pellaver. Chicago: University of Chicago Press, 2004.

Riley, Edward M. "William Prentis & Co.: Business Success in Eighteenth-Century Williamsburg." *Financial Executive*, April 1968, 35–41.

Rives, John C. *Abridgement of the Debates of Congress, from 1789 to 1856*. Vol. 6. New York: Appleton, 1858.

Rothman, Adam. *Slave Country: American Expansion and the Origins of the Deep South*. Cambridge: Harvard University Press, 2005.

Rowden, Terry. *The Songs of Black Folk: African American Musicians and the Cultures of Blindness*. Ann Arbor: University of Michigan Press, 2009.

Sarat, Austin. "Toward Something New or Maybe Something Not so New." *Yale Journal of Law and Humanities* 12.1 (2000): 133–35.

Sarudy, Barbara Wells. *Gardens and Gardening in the Chesapeake, 1700–1805*. Baltimore: Johns Hopkins University Press, 1998.

"Saunders, Robert." http://scrc.swem.wm.edu/wiki/index.php/Robert_Saunders.

Seed, David. "Exemplary Selves: Jonathan Edwards and Benjamin Franklin." *First Person Singular: Studies in American Autobiography*. Ed. A. Robert Lee. New York: St. Martin's, 1988. 37–56.

Sheldon, Marianne Buroff. "Black-White Relations in Richmond, Virginia, 1782–1820." *Journal of Southern History* 45.1 (1979): 27–44.

Sidbury, James. *Ploughshares into Swords: Race, Rebellion, and Identity in Gabriel's Virginia, 1730–1810*. New York: Cambridge University Press, 1997.

Stanton, Elizabeth Cady. *Eight Years and More: Reminiscences, 1815–1897*. New York: Fisher Unwin, 1898.

St. Clair, William. *The Door of No Return: The History of Cape Coast Castle and the Atlantic Slave Trade*. New York: BlueBridge, 2006.

Stephenson, Mary A. *Archibald Blair Storehouse (NB) Historical Report, Block 18-1, Building 6A, Lot 46*. Library Research Report Series 1397. 1954 Williamsburg, Va.: Colonial Williamsburg Foundation, 1990.

———. *Lots 319–28 (Green Hill) Historical Report*. Library Research Report Series 1603. 1958. Williamsburg, Va.: Colonial Williamsburg Foundation, 1990.

———. *Prentis House Historical Report, Block 17 Building 11A Lot 51*. Library Research Report Series 1365. 1958. Williamsburg, Va.: Colonial Williamsburg Foundation, 1990.

Stephenson, Wendell Holmes. *Isaac Franklin: Slave Trader and Planter of the Old South with Plantation Records*. Baton Rouge: Louisiana State University Press, 1938.

Stringfellow, Benjamin F. "Slavery a Positive Good." 1854. *American History Told by Contemporaries*. Vol. 4. Ed. Albert Bushnell Hart. New York: Macmillan, 1918. 68–71.

Stowe, Harriet Beecher. *Uncle Tom's Cabin*. 1852. New York: Dover, 2005.

Tadman, Michael. *Speculators and Slaves: Masters, Traders, and Slaves in the Old South*. Madison: University of Wisconsin Press, 1989.

Tate, Thad W. *The Negro in Eighteenth-Century Williamsburg*. Williamsburg, Va.: Colonial Williamsburg Foundation, 1965.

Taylor, A. J. P. Introduction. *The Communist Manifesto*, by Karl Marx and Friedrich Engels. New York: Penguin, 1985. 7–47.

Taylor, Amy Murrell. *The Divided Family in Civil War America*. Chapel Hill: University of North Carolina Press, 2005.

Thoreau, Henry David. *Walden and "Civil Disobedience."* Ed. Owen Thomas. New York: Norton, 1966.

Todorov, Tzvetan. *Mikhail Bakhtin: The Dialogical Principle*. Trans. Wlad Godzich. Minneapolis: University of Minnesota Press, 1984.

Trollope, Frances. *Domestic Manners of the Americans*. 1832. Ed. Donald Smalley. New York: Knopf, 1949.

Trowbridge, John T. *A Picture of the Desolated States, and the Work of Restoration, 1865–1868*. Hartford, Conn.: Stebbins, 1868.

Tucker, St. George. *A Dissertation on Slavery: With a Proposal for the Gradual Abolition of It in the State of Virginia*. 1796. Philadelphia: Carey, 1796.

Tyler, Lyon Gardiner, ed. *Encyclopedia of Virginia Biography*. New York: Lewis Historical, 1915.

Varon, Elizabeth R. *We Mean to Be Counted: White Women and Politics in Antebellum Virginia*. Chapel Hill: University of North Carolina Press, 1998.

Walker, Clarence E. *Mongrel Nation: The America Begotten by Thomas Jefferson and Sally Hemings*. Charlottesville: University of Virginia Press, 2009.

Walker, David. *Appeal to the Colored Citizens of the World*. Ed. Peter P. Hinks. 1829. University Park: Penn State University Press, 2000.

Walvin, James. *The Trader, the Owner, the Slave: Parallel Lives in the Age of Slavery*. London: Random House, 2008.

Wayland, Francis Fry. *Andrew Stevenson, Democrat and Diplomat, 1785–1857*. Philadelphia: University of Pennsylvania Press, 1949.

Weld, Charles Richard. *A Vacation Tour in the United States and Canada*. London: Longman, Brown, Green, and Longmans, 1855.

White, Deborah Gray. *Ar'n't I a Woman? Female Slaves in the Plantation South*. New York: Norton, 1985.

Whitman, Walt. *Leaves of Grass*. New York: Norton, 1973.

Williamson, Samuel H. "Seven Ways to Compute the Relative Value of a U.S. Dollar Amount, 1790 to Present." 2010. http://www.measuringworth.com/uscompare/.

Winter, Kari J. *Subjects of Slavery, Agents of Change: Women and Power in Gothic Novels and Slave Narratives, 1790–1865*. Athens: University of Georgia Press, 1992.

Wolf, Eva Sheppard. *Race and Liberty in the New Nation*. Baton Rouge: Louisiana State University Press, 2006.

Wood, Gordon S. *The Americanization of Benjamin Franklin*. New York: Penguin, 2004.

Wood, Kirsten E. *Masterful Women: Slaveholding Widows from the American Revolution through the Civil War*. Chapel Hill: University of North Carolina Press, 2004.

Worters, Garance. *American Biographical Archive*. Microfiche. London: Saur, n.d.

INDEX

RACE IN THE ATLANTIC WORLD, 1700–1900

The Hanging of Angélique: The Untold Story of Canadian Slavery and the Burning of Old Montréal
by Afua Cooper

Christian Ritual and the Creation of British Slave Societies, 1650–1780
by Nicholas M. Beasley

African American Life in the Georgia Lowcountry: The Atlantic World and the Gullah Geechee
edited by Philip Morgan

The Horrible Gift of Freedom: Atlantic Slavery and the Representation of Emancipation
by Marcus Wood

The Life and Letters of Philip Quaque, the First African Anglican Missionary
edited by Vincent Carretta and Ty M. Reese

In Search of Brightest Africa: Reimagining the Dark Continent in American Culture, 1884–1936
by Jeannette Eileen Jones

Contentious Liberties: American Abolitionists in Post-emancipation Jamaica, 1834–1866
by Gale L. Kenny

We Are the Revolutionists: German-Speaking Immigrants and American Abolitionists after 1848
by Mischa Honeck

The American Dreams of John B. Prentis, Slave Trader
by Kari J. Winter